INFORMATION PROCESSING
for
BTEC

INFORMATION PROCESSING
For
BTEC

GEOFFREY KNOTT

NICK WAITES

PAUL CALLAGHAN

ILLUSTRATIONS AND GRAPHICS BY
TREVOR MOORE AND B. D. WRIGHT

BUSINESS EDUCATION PUBLISHERS LIMITED

1990

Published In Great Britain by Business Education Publishers Limited
Leighton House 10 Grange Crescent Stockton Road Sunderland
Tyne and Wear SR2 7BN

Tel. 091 567 4963

ISBN 0 907679 35 8

First published in 1987

Reprinted 1988 (twice)

Reprinted 1989 (twice)

Second Edition 1990

Printed in Great Britain by M & A Thomson Litho Limited East Kilbride Glasgow

PREFACE

This book has been written to specifically cover the option modules, Information Processing 1 and Information Processing 2, of BTEC National courses. It is also useful to anyone doing a course with Information Processing input.

The book demonstrates the importance of Information Processing in modern organizations and the content of each chapter is developed through a series of realistic work-based assignments which form the basis of an active student centred learning programme. The text is designed to complement *Core Studies for BTEC National* and *The Abbotsfield File - a business in action* and provides a sound basis for integration between this option unit and the core of the course.

THE AUTHORS

Geoffrey Knott is Lecturer in Computing at Monkwearmouth College in Sunderland. He has had wide experience of teaching and developing BTEC courses and extensive practical experience in Computing and Information Technology before entering teaching. He is also a co-author of *Computer Studies for BTEC* and author of *Small Business Computer Systems*.

Nick Waites is Senior Lecturer in Computing at New College Durham. He has taught for many years on Computing and Information Technology and is currently responsible for staff development in computing and IT. His present research interests are in developments in artificial intelligence. He is a co-author of *Computer Studies for BTEC*.

Paul Callaghan is Principal Lecturer and Director of Studies for BTEC courses at New College Durham. He is the author of *The Business Environment, The Organisation in its Environment, The Abbotsfield File - a business in action* and *Core Studies for BTEC National*. He has played a major role in developing relevant and practical teaching materials for BTEC courses.

ACKNOWLEDGEMENTS

This book has been produced with the help of a number of people who deserve particular mention. Special thanks go to Jim Morton and Jim Cox of New College Durham who patiently read and commented upon much of the material. Thanks also to the computer staff at Monkwearmouth College, Sunderland for their encouragement and support and to Carolyn Knott who spent many hours proof reading. Julie Bransby, Kathryn Martin, Moira Page and Caroline White ably ensured that the publishing of the book ran smoothly and Sheila Callaghan and Lilias Smith managed as always to maintain calm control. Trevor Moore and B. D. Wright interpreted our rough sketches to produce the excellent graphics and Gerard Callaghan spent many long hours correcting proofs.

All errors and omissions should have been spotted. If they were not then they remain the responsibility of the authors.

Durham
January 1990

GK
NW
PC

Contents

Chapter 7   Control of Information Processing

Chapter 8   Management Information Services

Chapter 12   Financial Systems and Packages

Chapter 13   Programming

Chapter 14 Systems Development and Implementation

Chapter 15 Social and Organizational Effects of Computerization

Chapter 1

☐ BUSINESS APPLICATIONS OF INFORMATION PROCESSING

An Organization's Need for Information

The term 'business' is used to describe an extremely wide range of diverse organizations. It includes all types and sizes of enterprise from the self employed sole trader, perhaps operating as a greengrocer or a plumber, to the multi-national corporation producing oil or motor cars with subsidiaries in most countries of the world. Such extreme examples may appear to have little in common and yet one characteristic which all businesses share is their need to control and process information which is vital to their successful operation.

Such information includes that involving customers and clients, for example orders for goods or invoices and statements requesting payment. Most organisations will also deal with suppliers and inform them of their supply requirements using purchase orders and then acknowledge receipt when goods are delivered. Within the organization, information must be maintained and processed on the level of stocks held, the number of employees on the payroll and the amount of wages or salaries they are due. Perhaps most importantly, all organizations must keep accurate and up-to-date accounting records to allow effective management decisions to be made and to provide the appropriate financial information demanded by a company's shareholders, the Inland Revenue or the VAT authorities.

The preceding paragraphs have mentioned business organizations which operate in the private sector of the economy, in other words, organizations which are owned by private individuals and have as one of their objectives, the achievement of profit. The private sector, however, is but one aspect of society. Many of the most significant organizations in this society are owned and controlled by the state. The public sector encompasses central government departments, local authorities, and health service, educational institutions and public corporations such as British Rail, British Coal and British Steel. While some of these organizations have objectives which are significantly different from those in the private sector, they all process various forms of information in much the same way. They require records, generate documents and must produce financial statements. In this respect the information needs of all organizations, whether they are in the private or public sector, are very similar. Traditionally the processing of information has involved the use of clerical staff who would manually produce documents, update records, calculate figures, provide financial statements and perform a variety of other tasks. One factor that these tasks have in common is that they are all repetitive and routine. The same process is followed each time an item is issued from stock or a demand for payment is made. Usually the only variation involved is a change in the details of the transaction. A further common characteristic in the tasks mentioned earlier is that all require a high degree of accuracy. A zero negligently omitted from a bill may be welcomed by the organization's customer but could well lead to a loss of money for the suppliers. Similarly an underpayment of an employee's wages will not help to maintain the employer's popularity. Therefore such tasks require a continued degree of attention and concentration on the part of the clerical staff if errors are to be avoided.

It has been said that there is nothing as worthless as yesterday's news. This implies that information becomes less valuable if it is not presented or available at the time at which it is required. This is equally true of business information. A stock clerk who fails to notify the purchasing department that an item is out of stock until it is asked for by production may cause considerable problems for the organization. The stock may take time to order and unless delivered during this period, production may be halted. Similarly the salesperson who fails to advise production that an order has been placed may find that the order is consequently lost as a result of the delay in meeting it.

This does not mean all information must be processed immediately. Some types of information are required at once, such as the response to a telephone enquiry concerning the availability of a particular product. Other forms of information may be provided with a little less urgency. For example, the Inland Revenue may be willing to wait some months for an organization's annual accounts - but the taxman will not wait forever.

Business Information, therefore, should be:

> (i) accurate;
>
> (ii) up-to-date.

Furthermore, the processing of such information:

> (iii) is often routine and repetitive;
>
> (iv) must be organized in a prompt and efficient manner.

The need for accurate, up-to-date information is therefore a requirement of all organizations and this can only be achieved by an effective and efficient information processing system. For a small organization a manual system may well prove adequate if it is successfully managed, administered and operated. However technological developments have meant that even the smallest business now has a cost effective alternative in meeting its information processing needs. The introduction of a vast range of computerized systems, which can be selected to match specific requirements, allows an organisation to improve the effectiveness of all or some of its information systems.

Information Processing Applications

The following chapters will introduce many of these processes, explaining the computer equipment and the programs which are capable of performing these functions. The consequences of introducing such computerized systems will be analysed and the costs and benefits evaluated. First it is necessary to introduce a basic classification of the applications of computerized information processing. While it is not possible to comprehensively examine every feasible use of the computer to an organisation, a number of widely employed applications can be identified. These are

> (i) Word Processing;
>
> (ii) Financial Control Systems;
>
> (iii) Resource Management;
>
> (iv) Communications.

Each of these applications will be examined in detail in later chapters but first it is proposed to explain what is meant by each of them and examine how they may be applied in a typical business organization.

Word Processing

All organizations must produce a variety of documents including letters, reports, memos and invoices. Traditionally these have been typed using a conventional typewriter. However there now exist many software packages which allow a computer to be used for such tasks. Once text has been keyed in it can be edited and corrected, moved to different parts of the document, stored and retrieved or held as a 'template' so that the same document can be reproduced time and time again but with different details, such as names, addresses and quantities, substituted in each copy. More sophisticated word processing packages permit the paging of documents with appropriate 'headers' and 'footers' on each page. They may have an indexing facility, a spell checker and even a thesaurus which can suggest alternatives to chosen words in the document.

The benefits of word processing are that it allows 'professional' looking documents to be produced by an organization, it minimizes the likelihood of errors during typing and reduces the time involved in retyping a document which requires only certain changes or amendments. Wordprocessing and the wider applications of 'the electronic office' are examined in Chapter 9.

Financial Control Systems

The control of an organization's finances is often one of management's most crucial tasks. If it is handled efficiently it should ensure that the organization performs more profitably and is less likely to suffer financial loss. Computers have many characteristics which make them ideally suited for such applications. They can quickly and accurately handle arithmetic operations and provide checks and controls on the data entered. They can handle vast amounts of data which would otherwise require an army of clerical workers. They are also able to perform highly complex operations requiring involved mathematical formulae to produce statistical analysis.

Computerized information processing is used in a wide variety of financial control applications such as:

> (i) order processing and invoice control;
>
> (ii) purchase accounting;
>
> (iii) payroll calculations;
>
> (iv) stock control;
>
> (v) sales analysis;
>
> (vi) cost and management accounting;
>
> (vii) VAT accounting;
>
> (viii) budgetary control.

Most such applications use a combination of a database in which financial records relating to individuals or specific items can be stored and a spreadsheet which allows figures to be displayed and manipulated and financial changes to be reflected within the organization's financial statements. Examples of financial control systems are used throughout this book and particularly in Chapters 7, 12 and 15.

Resource Management and Planning

An organization must effectively plan and manage its resources. These are not only financial but also include its workforce, its plant and machinery and its output and stock. A computer model can be devised which predicts likely trends in an organization's demand and indicates what resources are required, at what times and in what order to meet such anticipated demand. Some systems are relatively simple such as stock control. Here the computer merely records stock as it is received and adds it to the total held. As stock is withdrawn, the computer reduces the total by the requisite amount. It should also note when stock falls to a certain critical level, when reordering should take place, either manually or by the computer generating an appropriate purchase order itself.

A more sophisticated application of a resource management application is Network Planning or Critical Path Analysis. This may be introduced if the production of major products, such as a power station or the Channel Tunnel, requires the successful combination of the efforts of many workers and involves a multitude of individual processes or procedures. Each must be performed in the right order or else the project as a whole may be delayed or valuable resources left idle. An overall planning schedule, produced using the computer, specifies the order and time at which each individual operation must take place. It will monitor progress, readjusting the schedule if the work is being delayed or proceeding quicker than expected. In this way the computer helps to most effectively manage the organization's resources.

A stock control system is used as a major example in Chapter 13 on programming.

Communications

One of the most exciting aspects of the information technology revolution is the combining of telecommunications and computing. This allows information to be processed by computer and then transferred down telephone lines to recipient computers. The speed at which this can be done far surpasses more conventional communication techniques. The process is no longer limited to text. Image transfer is becoming increasingly common and satellite technology means that data can be transferred worldwide almost instantaneously. The implications for business are enormous. Business transactions buying and selling stocks and shares or currency can be undertaken almost simultaneously between cities at opposite sides of the globe. Money can be transferred or offers made and accepted, without the need for tedious business trips by jet lagged executives, or reliance on the postal system.

The techniques involved in such communications are discussed in Chapters 9 and 10 and the implications and likely effects in Chapter 14.

Information Processing Systems in Practice

To illustrate the application of a number of information processing systems in a typical organization let us examine some traditional methods and suggest means by which they can be improved.

We shall take as our example, Wingrove Electrical Ltd., a small electrical company based on the outskirts of London. It employs 38 people and produces electrical components for use in central heating equipment. Let us trace some of their procedures to try and isolate the company's information processing problems.

An Enquiry from a Potential Buyer

A telephone enquiry from a potential customer is received by the company's telephonist who attempts to connect the caller with the company sales manager, who is unfortunately out of the office. She therefore makes a note of the caller's name and nature of his enquiry and promises to pass these on to the sales manager on his return to the office. The inevitable occurs and the paper with the message is lost - and so is the potential order.

The system would clearly have been improved if the company had installed a local area network. With such a system the telephonist could possibly have accessed sufficient information about the company's products to meet the initial enquiry of the potential buyer, or alternatively she could have logged the message onto the internal electronic mail system, so that the sales manager would have been alerted to the call as soon as he accessed his own terminal.

The Receipt of an Order

Let us suppose that the Wingrove organization is not so incompetent that they fail to receive any orders and that in fact a substantial order has been received by post. The manual procedures involve copying the order and sending a copy to finance and a copy attached to a 'job sheet' to production. When the order is completed and despatched, finance will invoice the customer and await payment. Unfortunately when the customer eventually pays he submits a cheque for an incorrect amount. The clerk in finance fails to notice that the amount on the invoice and that on the cheque do not tally and processes the invoice as paid; another fall in Wingrove's profitability.

The company could improve its financial control by installing a computerized order processing and invoice verification system. As each order is received into the company, the appropriate details such as customer, item, quantity, price and so on, are entered into its computer which automatically generates an invoice, statements and increasingly harshly worded reminders until the customer pays up. When the cheque arrives its value is also entered and the program automatically checks to ensure that the amount matches both the original price quoted and the invoice value. As a protection against the mis-keying of the cheque amount, a further check involves the computer totalling the outstanding invoices each month and also those which have been paid and reconciling the amounts. This is an application of a financial control system.

The Production of a Quotation

Wingrove's managing director is informed that Birmingham City Council is intending to replace the central heating systems in all its public buildings over the next three years and is seeking tenders for the component parts of the system. Wingrove would very much like to gain the contract and so decide to submit a detailed quotation document.

The quotation is 28 pages long and contains an extensive amount of technical detail as well as prices and delivery dates. Much of the technical data has been taken from the specifications of the company's product and is retyped into the new tender document. This involves a considerable effort by the Wingrove typist and requires a number of corrections to be made.

Alternatively the company could have produced the document using a word processing system. It could have been typed and then simply corrected. Much of the detail may already have been held on 'floppy disk' and simply incorporated into the new document. Alternatively if it was not already on disk the company may have used an Optical Character Reader to scan existing typewritten documents into the computer, where the information could then be edited, reformatted and incorporated. Such a word processing system would improve both the efficiency and the public image of the company.

Planning for Training

Like any far seeing employer Wingrove wishes to develop the skill and expertise of its workforce. The managing director decides to undertake a 'manpower audit' to determine what level and diversity of skill and training is held by the workforce. He asks the Personnel Department for the relevant details. Unfortunately the personnel records are held on cards and much of the information is now out of date, as it is not updated after a person's initial appointment. By means of a questionnaire, the personnel department obtains information about the skills and experience of the staff. The questionnaire is poorly drafted and a rumour quickly spreads that the real purpose is to identify poorly skilled staff for redundancy. This does little to enhance employer/employee relationships.

If the company had used a computerized personnel record system this may not have happened. A database would have allowed the managing director to quickly access the required information - providing of course that the information had been kept up to date.

All these examples seek to illustrate how the organization could benefit from computerizing some or all of its information processing requirements. Decisions on the selection of appropriate systems for any given organization have to take a number of factors into account. The procedures towards making such decisions are described in detail in Chapter 14.

Chapter 2

☐ THE NEED FOR INFORMATION IN ORGANIZATIONS

The Role of Information

In business, making decisions or taking actions without relevant information can be risky. Nevertheless, many decisions are made based on partial, inaccurate or irrelevant information. A gambler who bets on horse races may study 'form' but how reliable is that information? Generally, commercial organizations or governments will attempt to control the QUALITY of their information to provide the best possible basis for their decision-making.

If it is to act with any purpose an organisation needs information about itself, its customers (or clients) and suppliers (if any) and the environment in which it operates. By environment is meant influential factors which are external to the organisation, such as government legislation or bank lending rates. Without such information, an organisation cannot decide what to do next, what it is doing at present or how well it is doing it.

The following example illustrates how a commercial organisation uses information for these purposes.

Surf's Up Limited is a manufacturing company producing windsurfers and related equipment.

a. The Planning Position

The company's planned production of windsurfers for the next three months is based on information obtained from:

        (i) its past sales figures;

        (ii) market research results.

Such PLANNING or STRATEGIC information allows management to decide what to do next.

b. The Dynamic or Active Position

The company monitors its production figures, its stocks of raw materials and finished products, to obtain information on what the production side of the company is doing at present. The other functional areas of the company are similarly monitored.

c. The Snapshot Position

The production of financial statements such as the Profit and Loss Account provide information necessary to assess how well the company is or was doing, up to a particular point in time (the time when the statements were produced).

Of course, not all information generated within or used by an organization can be categorized in this way. Instead, information may well be used for more than one purpose at a time, or at different times.

Systems for the Production and Flow of Information

The production of information needs to be a controlled process and control can be exercised through the use of SYSTEMS; hence the term INFORMATION SYSTEM.

Organisations are divided into functional areas such as Sales, Marketing, Production and Accounts and each will require its own information system or sub-system. Although the term 'information system' will continue to be used in this chapter, it should be clearly recognised that the information requirements of one functional area within an organisation cannot be considered in isolation as they will only be part of a global information system for the whole organisation. Information systems within an organisation interact with and affect one another. The organisation also interacts with and is influenced by individuals and organisations in the surrounding 'environment' and the organisation's information systems should be co-ordinated if common aims are to be achieved.

These interactions can be illustrated diagrammatically with the use of Information Interface or Flow Diagrams. The figure on the next page is one such example and illustrates the information flows for Surf's Up a manufacturer of windsurfers and other sporting equipment. The diagram makes a number of assumptions concerning Surf's Up:

<ul style="list-style:none">
<li>(i) It obtains raw materials from a number of suppliers;</li>
<li>(ii) It stores raw materials and finished goods from the factory in its warehouse;</li>
<li>(iii) Orders from retail outlets are received and processed by the Sales section;</li>
<li>(iv) The company only supplies its own manufactured goods.</li>
</ul>

An examination of the diagram illustrates the ways in which each department, or functional area, is dependent on one or more of the other departments for information, to allow it to perform its function.

For example, in order to charge the retail outlets (the company's customers) for the windsurfers supplied, the Accounting department requires information from Sales on the details of goods sold to each retailer, to allow preparation of the appropriate invoices.

Similarly, Purchasing needs to be kept informed by Stock Control of raw materials which require reordering from suppliers to replenish stocks.

These examples of OPERATIONAL information allow day-to-day decisions to be made on the operation of the company. To keep the diagram relatively simple, certain vital functions such as Production Control and Marketing are not shown. Obviously, their inclusion would increase the information flows. The information flows shown in the Surf's Up diagram will be related to activities taking place within the various functional areas of the organization. The table following the diagram summarizes the likely activities within Sales Order Processing, Purchasing, Stock Control and Accounting which can be related to the information flows in the information interface diagram.

An Information Interface Diagram to illustrate the flows of information within a typical manufacturing/wholesaling, organization Surf's Up.

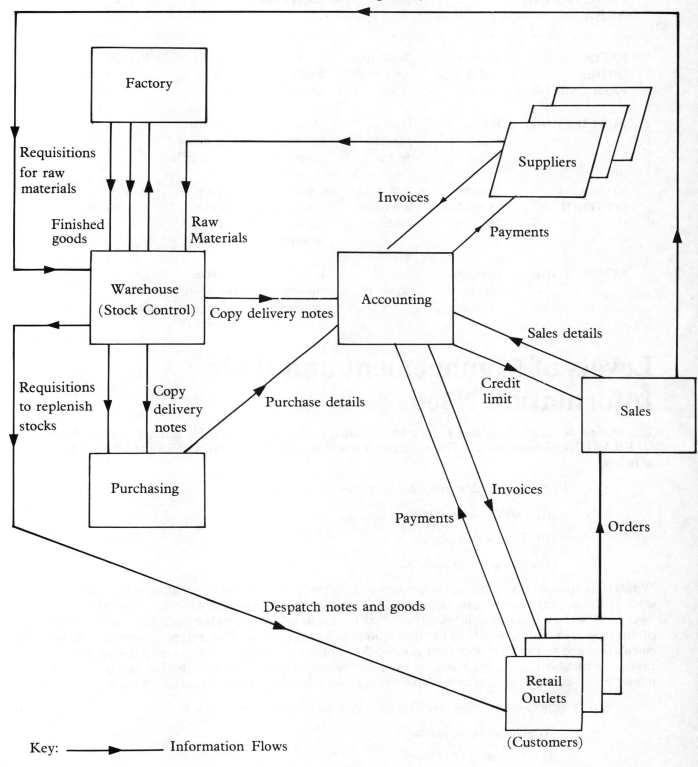

Activity Table - Surf's Up

FUNCTIONAL AREA	ACTIVITIES				
SALES ORDER PROCESSING	Receive and check orders	Requisition stock to fill orders	Check credit limits	Produce picking lists	Produce delivery notes & sales details
PURCHASING	Raise purchase orders	Provide purchase details	Decide on suppliers	Negotiate cost prices with suppliers	
STOCK CONTROL	Receive, inspect and bin stock	Pick, load and deliver goods	Check stock levels for re-ordering	Report current stock levels	Report deficiencies
ACCOUNTING	Receive suppliers' invoices	Pay suppliers	Issue customer invoices	Receive payments from customers	Set credit limits

Levels of Management and their Information Needs

The routine activities described earlier and detailed in the Activities Table require and produce OPERATIONAL information. There are other levels of management tasks which can be described as follow:

(a) Highly systematic management operations such as:

　　(i) Selecting suppliers;

　　(ii) Production planning;

　　(iii) Setting cash budgets.

Without computers, these tasks usually involve considerable work by middle management and their staff. With the use of computers, the routine information gathering needed for such operations can be carried out by the machine, leaving the overall decisions to be made by the managers. An example of this type of operation would be the preparation of a cash budget. Without the computer tedious calculation and re-calculation of formulae would be necessary whereas with a computer an appropriate 'spreadsheet' program could be used for its preparation. The information needs of such management operations tend to be departmental and relate to particular functional areas.

(b) Corporate Planning and Decision Making relate to areas such as:

　　(i) Deciding on prices;

　　(ii) Targeting of markets;

　　(iii) Decisions on production of new products;

　　(iv) Overall financial target setting;

　　(v) Advertising campaign decisions.

These tasks will be largely retained by individual managers because such information needs tend to be on demand, unsystematic and unpredictable. This is not to say that computers cannot help. Database systems with flexible 'on demand query facilities' can be designed, but the complexity of decision making at this level is likely, at least for the foreseeable future, to ensure a largely human control.

The Quality of Information

The quality of information will depend on several factors, but generally, the larger and more complex the organization, the more difficult it is to maintain high quality information without highly systematic procedures. Having said this, a larger organization will tend to have more specialized staff to aid the efficient running of the organization. Smaller organizations often have to employ staff, some of whom are 'Jacks of all trades' and 'masters of none'. The proprietor of a one-man business with only a few products and a few customers may be able to control the whole business without assistance. However, this may not necessarily be in the most efficient manner. The owner may, for example, take a customer order, check the stocks, reorder if necessary, supply the customer, update the customer's account and produce the necessary invoice. In this way, the sole trader is able to maintain an overall view of the business. As the business grows it may become necessary to employ others to carry out the bookkeeping tasks. At a later stage, the activities of sales, stock control and accounts may have to be carried out by different people. Even at this stage it may be possible for the proprietor to retain an overview of the business and have sufficient 'management' information to make well informed decisions.

As the volume of data to be processed increases, it becomes necessary to employ more staff, to introduce some mechanization and at this stage computerization may be necessary.

However, to use a computer merely to process and produce OPERATIONAL information would be an under-use of the computer's power. In fact, the power of the computer has evolved so that the traditional Data Processing (DP) department is now generally referred to as Management Information Services. Computerization can lead to an improvement in the QUANTITY and QUALITY of MANAGEMENT information as well as the accuracy and control of operational information. When quality of information is considered, the following characteristics are important.

Accuracy

This is of primary importance because good decisions can only be made on the basis of accurate information. For example, the decision to increase production in a factory based on last year's sales figures (which prove to be inaccurate) and market research (which proves to be unreliable) may result in disaster for a business, leaving it with large stocks of unsold goods. Inaccurate information from a computerized system may be the result of hardware, software or transmission errors. Such errors can, of course, be controlled. More seriously, inaccurate information may result from inaccurate input data. Chapter 7 deals with the techniques for preventing such inaccuracies.

Tailored Information

The presentation, layout and detail of information presented to a user can affect its usefulness. For example, a three page report on a customer's credit history will be too detailed for the sales order clerk who wishes to check the customer's credit limit before processing an order. Similarly, if a report is required for the shareholders of a holding company, a bar graph showing comparative trading profit for two subsidiaries may be of more use than a tabular presentation of the figures. The figure below illustrates this using Daybreak Ltd and Sunrise Ltd as two subsidiaries of Sunshine Holidays. The important fact to remember is that information should be tailored to the needs of the user.

Comparison of Annual Trading Profits of Daybreak Ltd and Sunrise Ltd from 1983 to 1987

(a)   in tabular form

	Daybreak Ltd	Sunrise Ltd
1983	140000	90000
1984	230000	180000
1985	250000	200000
1986	340000	270000
1987	350000	220000

(b)   as a bar grapn

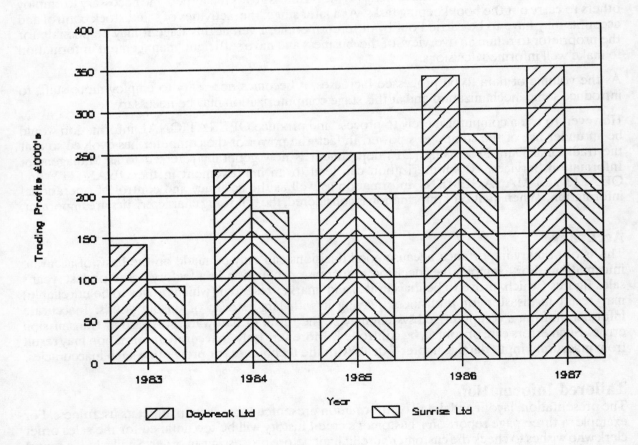

Relevance

Information should be relevant to the purpose for which it is provided. For example, it would not be relevant to produce outstanding debit balances for all customers' accounts if management merely required information on customers who live within a specific geographical area such as the West Midlands.

Timeliness

Information must be as up-to-date as necessary. However this does not mean that all information must relate to a precise moment. In one situation, information several weeks old may be appropriate. In another, the information may be useless to the recipient if it is more than 24 hours old.

Legibility

The user must be able to read and understand the information.

Significance

The significance of the information must be apparent to the recipient. Usually, proper presentation, format and a suitable report heading will ensure this quality.

Completeness

The recipient should be satisfied that he or she has received ALL the information needed. If information is missing and the recipient is unaware of this fact, any decision based on the information may be ill-founded. Even if the recipient is aware that it is incomplete, pressure of time may force him or her to act before the rest can be obtained.

Brevity

The presentation of information will be enhanced if relevant facts are not obscured by irrelevant facts and so the presentation should be kept as brief as possible.

Justifying an Information System

In the early days of computing, the justification for a computer system was based on the likely speeding up of data processing and the consequent reduction in staffing. We now refer to them as Information Systems rather than Data Processing Systems because the justification of 'taking over the donkey work' is insufficient. An information system can only be justified on the value of information it provides. The value of the information must exceed the cost of producing it.

Cost Effectiveness

It is a fairly straightforward process to quantify the benefits of computerizing Operational information systems. For example, computerizing the Sales Order Processing function may allow a considerable growth in business without the need to recruit more staff.

It is more difficult, however, to quantify the benefits of Management information. For example, the percentage growth in sales of different ranges of products in different geographical areas may be very useful to a company but the costs of obtaining the information with a manual system may well exceed the benefits. The information could be obtained from a manual system but the time taken would probably render it out of date and of little use to management.

To assess the value of such information one would need to know to what use, if any, it was put by management.

Fortunately, certain types of management information are readily available as by-products of operational information systems and the standard computer software for common business applications will usually incorporate options to produce reports on, for example, annual sales figures, percentage of customer accounts overdue, etc.

On-demand Enquiries

Other management report requirements are not standard and cannot be readily anticipated. To design such a flexible system requires the use of sophisticated database techniques. These are examined more closely in Chapter 6. In any case, such flexible information systems can only be judged by their current users within the specific organization for which they were designed, and cannot be judged necessarily as being of value to others.

Assignment   The Property File

McManus, Lorimar and Barnes is a firm of Estate Agents based in Portsmouth. The firm's junior partner, Peter Jones believes that the service to clients could be improved by computerization or, at the very least by some modification of the existing manual procedures. The firm's share of the Portsmouth area property market has been reduced by the increased competitiveness of other estate agencies in the area and Peter Jones suspects that the loss of business results from certain problems in the matching of prospective purchasers with properties for sale. A brief outline of the procedures involved in the process of property sales can be described as follows:

1. The initial request from a client wishing to sell a property is dealt with by one of the four partners. The partner then makes an appointment to visit the property and record the details of location, type, price range, number of rooms etc.

2. The property details are transcribed onto one of two standard forms, depending on whether the property is residential or used for business purposes. This task is carried out by staff in the Property Registration Section.

3. A copy of the property registration form is passed to Property Sales Section, where staff categorize the property according to basic criteria, including property location, type, size, quality, number of rooms and price range. These basic details are transcribed onto record cards which are then used as the initial point of reference when a prospective purchaser makes an enquiry.

4. In order to match prospective purchasers with properties for sale, a Purchase Clients File is maintained. Details of suitable properties are sent on a mailing list basis to each client.

Mr. Jones is preparing a report on the existing procedures to present to the senior partners. The firm will be approaching a Computer Software Consultancy with a view to the possible computerization of the property and client recording procedures. The report will be used as a basis for the detailed analysis of the procedures, by the software consultancy.

Task

You are employed as a trainee office manager/ess by the estate agency. Mr. Jones has asked you to outline the procedures described above with the use of diagrammatic representations. He has suggested that these take the form of an Activity Table and Information Interface Diagram. The latter diagram should include both the firm's internal information flows and those between clients and the firm.

Developmental Task

Examine some of the estate agents' property advertisements in your local newspaper, in order to discover the criteria on which properties may be selected. Use the data collected to produce a simulation of the procedures and activities you described in your main task.

Chapter 3

☐ COMPUTER SYSTEMS

The Computer

a. The Computer as a System

Any SYSTEM consists of a number of separate elements working together to achieve a common aim. A car, for example, is a form of transport system comprising such elements as an engine, wheels and a gear box. Its aim is to transport people from one place to another. The system will only operate successfully if all these major components work. An essential additional element is the driver, without whom the car is simply a motionless piece of metal.

In the same way a COMPUTER SYSTEM consists of a number of individual elements working together with the common aim of processing DATA to produce INFORMATION.

Data ⟶ Process ⟶ Information

As computer processing is carried out electronically, a computer system may also be called an Electronic Data Processing System.

Data and Information
The difference between data and information can be illustrated by a simple example. If a company wishes to provide the information necessary to produce a customer invoice (which notifies a customer of the amount owed in respect of an order), several separate items of data need to be processed, including the prices and quantities of items ordered by the customer. To be described as information, the computer's output must be relevant and useful to the user receiving it.

b. The Elements of a Computer System

The elements which make up a computer system are called HARDWARE and SOFTWARE. The system requires both, as neither can perform any useful function without the other.

Hardware
The term 'hardware' is used to describe all the physical electronic and mechanical elements forming part of a computer system.

Software

The term 'software' describes the instructions or programs which the hardware needs in order to function.

Another term, FIRMWARE, is used to describe programs which are 'hardwired' into the computer using integrated circuit 'chips'. Such storage is termed Read Only Memory (ROM). ROM is 'non-volatile', in other words the programs are not lost when the machine is switched off. Also, the contents cannot be overwritten by other programs or data.

Hardware

a. The Elements of Hardware

The hardware of a computer system comprises the following elements:

Input

To allow the computer to process data it must be in a form which the machine can handle. Before processing, data is normally in a 'human readable' form, for example, as it appears on an employee's time sheet or a customer's order form. Such alphabetic and numeric (decimal) data cannot be handled directly by the internal circuitry of the computer. Firstly, it has to be translated into the binary format which makes the data 'machine-sensible'. There are a wide variety of input devices which carry out this function but the most common are keyboard devices.

The function of an input device, therefore, is to translate human readable data into a machine-sensible form which the computer can then handle.

Data is transferred from the input device to Main Memory.

Main Memory

The main memory has two main functions:

(a)   to temporarily store programs currently in use for processing data;

(b)   to temporarily store data:

(i)   entered via an input device and awaiting processing;

(ii)   currently being processed;

(iii)   which results from processing and is waiting to be output.

Central Processing Unit (CPU) or 'Processor'

The CPU carries out instructions and consists of two elements:

The Arithmetic-Logic Unit(ALU). The ALU carries out arithmetic operations such as addition, multiplication, subtraction and division. It can also make 'logical' comparisons between items of data, for example, it can determine whether one value is greater than another. Such logical operations can also be performed on non-numeric data.

The Control Unit. The control unit controls the operation of all hardware, including input and output devices and the CPU.

It does this by fetching, interpreting and executing each instruction in turn. The 'Fetch-Execute' cycle is described in detail in Chapter 11.

When an instruction (such as an input instruction to accept data via a keyboard) is to be executed, the control unit sends the appropriate signals to the keyboard device. Similarly, an instruction involving an arithmetic computation will be signalled to the ALU which carries out such functions.

Output

Output devices perform the opposite function of input devices by translating machine-sensible data into a human-readable form, for example, onto a printer or the screen of a visual display unit (VDU). Sometimes, the results of computer processing may be needed for further processing, in which case, they are output to a storage medium which retains it in machine-sensible form for subsequent input. Usually, the storage medium will be magnetic disk or tape.

Backing Store

Backing store performs a filing function within the computer system. In this context it is important to consider a couple of important concepts.

Memory Volatility. It is not practical to store data files and programs in main memory because of its VOLATILITY. This means that the contents of the main memory can be destroyed, either by being overwritten as new data is entered for processing and new programs used, or when the machine is switched off. Such volatile memory is termed Random Access Memory (RAM).

Retrievable Data. Backing storage media provide a more permanent store for programs (which may be used many times on different occasions) and data files (which are used for future reference or processing).

When the results of processing are output to a printer or VDU screen, the user is provided with visual information which is not normally retrievable by the computer unless it is also recorded on a backing storage medium such as magnetic tape or disk. The following example illustrates some aspects of file storage.

Example

In a payroll operation, data on hours worked by employees, together with other relevant data for the current pay period, needs to be processed against the payroll details held on the payroll master file in order to produce the necessary payslips. The payroll master file is stored on backing store and is placed 'on-line' when needed for processing. Any such files can be stored indefinitely on backing storage media. Magnetic disk and magnetic tape are re-useable. When a file is no longer required, it can be overwritten by new data.

b. Peripherals

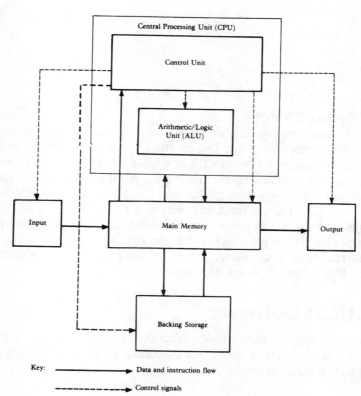

Those hardware devices which are external to the CPU and main memory, namely those devices used for input, output and backing storage are called PERIPHERALS.

The previous diagram illustrates the relationships between the various hardware elements. It illustrates the data flow through the system and the flow of control signals from the control unit. The diagram illustrates what is usually called the Logical Structure of the computer.

Software

Software is examined in great detail in Chapter 11. Introduced here, are some basic concepts which allow a simple understanding of computer systems. The role of software is to run the hardware. Software can be broadly divided into two types:

    (a)   Systems Software;

    (b)   Applications Software.

a. Systems Software

Systems software is 'dedicated' to the general organization and running of the computer system, in other words such software is written specifically for that purpose. Standard tasks, such as handling files on disk and tape systems, are common to most computer applications and are controlled by a particular group of systems programs called the OPERATING SYSTEM.

The following diagram illustrates the relationship between the hardware and the operating system:

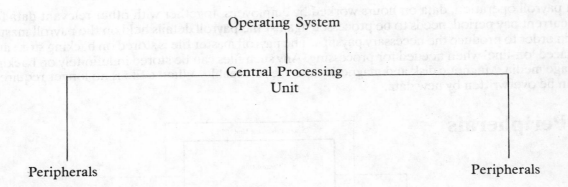

Types of Operating System

Different types of operating system are necessary to handle the range of different computer configurations which are available and the variety of processing modes in which they can operate. For example, a microcomputer system with keyboard, monitor, disk drive and printer, requires a much less sophisticated operating system than a mainframe computer system with a large number and variety of input, output and storage devices. Computer systems which allow multi-user operation, that is, the serving of more than one user at a time, require a multi-user operating system. Conversely, single-user microcomputer systems require only single-user operating systems. There are a variety of operating systems which serve the requirements of different computer processing methods such as real-time processing, batch processing and time-share processing. Computer processing methods are described in Chapter 6.

b. Applications Software

Applications programs make the computer function in a specific way for a particular user requirement, for example, for use in stock control or invoicing. Increasingly, many applications are catered for by pre-written Applications Packages.

A Classification of Computer Systems

Computer systems can be classified according to the following characteristics:

> (a)   Purpose;
>
> (b)   Size and Complexity;
>
> (c)   Generation (Place in Historical Development).

a. Purpose

There are two categories under this heading:

General Purpose Computers

As the term suggests, general purpose machines can carry out processing tasks for a wide variety of applications and most organizations will make use of this type of machine.

Dedicated or Special Purpose Computers

In their logical structure, these machines are fundamentally the same as the general purpose machine except that they have been programmed for a specific application. Dedicated word processors provide one example. The advent of cheap, microprocessor-based systems has led to an expansion of their use in controlling machines and many household products such as washing machines and microwave ovens are controlled by such systems.

b. Size and Complexity of Computer Systems

It should be emphasized that the following categories are only broad guidelines and changes in technology are continually blurring the differences between them. However, the generally accepted categories of computer system are as follow:

Mainframe Computers

Mainframe computer systems are the largest and most powerful type of computer and are used by large organizations such as banks, airlines and government departments.

They usually support a large number and variety of peripherals and can process a number of applications concurrently. This is called MULTIPROGRAMMING. The mainframe's power stems from the phenomenal speeds of the processor and the large size of the main memory.

Mainframes may also be used for Wide Area Networks (these are examined in detail in Chapter 10). For example, in the case of an international airline with offices throughout the world, incoming and outgoing communications traffic will probably be controlled by minicomputers (this is referred to as Front End Processing or simply FEP), leaving the mainframe free to carry out the main processing tasks. It may be necessary to employ two mainframes working 'back to back', either to share the processing load or to provide a backup in the event of the breakdown of one processor. In this case also, a minicomputer will be employed to control the flow of data between the processors. The use of two processors working in tandem is known as MULTIPROCESSING.

Mainframe computers are generally accommodated in special-purpose, air-conditioned rooms to ensure trouble free operation.

Minicomputers

Minicomputers are scaled-down versions of mainframe computers. The division between the two types becomes rather blurred when referring to small mainframes and large 'minis'. Costing less and being robust enough to operate without a special environment, they can be used in 'real-time' applications such as controlling manufacturing processes in an engineering factory. They are also used by medium sized organizations for all their processing needs or by larger organizations as part of a network system.

Minicomputers can support a number of applications concurrently and are often used with 'time-share' operating systems (this is discussed in some detail in Chapter 6) and intelligent terminals to provide organizations with decentralized processing facilities. Used in this way, many applications such as word processing, invoicing and customer enquiry can be carried out by users in their own departments. Generally, the volumes of input will be relatively small. This contrasts with the multiprogramming mode of operation often used in mainframe systems where large volume, batch processing jobs are processed centrally and users are not directly involved.

Microcomputers

Microcomputers were originally unique in their use of single 'chip' processors. The Central Processing Unit (the control unit and arithmetic-logic unit) are stored on a single 'chip' to form a microprocessor. A whole series of such processor chips are currently in use, including, for example, those manufactured by Motorola and Intel.

Originally, microcomputers were only capable of supporting a single user and a single application at any one time. The increase in processor speed and memory capacity and the facility for networking (for multi-user operation) now permits their use for MULTI-TASKING (the running of several tasks concurrently by one user). It is now extremely popular to link microcomputers into a Local Area Network, to allow sharing of disk and printer facilities, as well as electronic communications between users (Electronic Mail). They can now support applications packages previously restricted to mini and mainframe systems, including, for example, those used for database and computer aided design (CAD) work.

The low cost of microcomputers and the increase in the range of software available, makes their use possible in almost any size and type of organization. In the small firm, a microcomputer may be used for word processing, stock control, costing, and general accounting. In the larger organization they may be used as 'intelligent' terminals in a distributed processing system (Chapter 6). Such systems provide the user with the processing facilities of a central mini or mainframe computer and at the same time, a degree of independent processing power through the use of the microcomputer's own processor and memory store.

c. Generations of Computers

Since the first electronic computers were built in the 1940s, a number of developments in electronics have led to computer hardware being categorized by 'generation', that is, its place in the history of the computer. These generations can be simply defined as follows:

First Generation

During the 1940s, this first generation of computers used electronic components including vacuum tubes. The first computer to allow a program to be stored in memory (a stored-program computer) was EDSAC, developed at the University of Manchester. The vacuum tubes were fragile, subject to overheating and caused frequent breakdowns.

Second Generation

The introduction of low-cost and reliable transistors allowed the computer industry to develop at a tremendous rate during the late 1950s. The cost and size of the machines was radically reduced so it became possible for large commercial organizations to make use of computers. Examples of such machines include LEO III, UNIVAC and ATLAS.

Third Generation

The development of integrated circuit (IC) technology in the mid-1960s heralded the development of more powerful, reliable and compact computers, such as those of the IBM 360 series.

Fourth Generation

This generation is typified by large scale integration (LSI) of circuits which allowed the development of the microprocessor, which in turn allowed the production of the microcomputer. All computers used today make use of such silicon 'chip' technology.

Fifth Generation

At present, most computers are still of the fourth generation variety. Developments are continuing towards expanding memory size, using very large scale integration (VLSI) techniques and increasing the speed of processors. This increasing power is allowing the pursuit of new lines of development in computer systems:

(i)   More human orientated input/output devices using voice recognition and speech synthesis should allow communication between computers and humans to be more flexible and 'natural'. In the future, the aim is to allow computers to be addressed in languages natural to the users. Current techniques on some microcomputers allow acceptance of some spoken commands. Others allow the selection of user options displayed as graphics on the screen via a hand-held 'mouse'.

(ii) Parallel processing techniques. Mainframe computers with several internal processors are moving computer processing away from the sequential (one instruction after another) operation of earlier generations. The transputer, which was developed by INMOS as a computer on a 'chip', can be used as the basic building block for a number of new computer architectures including parallel processor computers. Parallel processing radically increases the power of the computer to handle the complex programming needed for 'expert' systems and artificial intelligence (AI). Expert systems already exist for medical diagnosis, and legal advice. The main applications to benefit from parallel processing are likely to be those which make extensive use of graphics, for example, computer-aided design (CAD).

Existing sequential programming languages (such as BASIC, COBOL, Fortran and Pascal) will be inappropriate to make proper use of parallel processing machines. A new group of languages based on Prolog (PROgramming in LOGic) should allow logic programming techniques to maximize use of parallel processing computers.

Assignment   Taking Stock

Perkins Ltd. is a private limited company which runs a discount warehouse in Leeds. The warehouse sells a wide range of DIY, gardening and car maintenance goods. The profitability of the company depends on a rapid stock turnover and minimum levels of stock. At the same time, customers expect to be able to buy any of the items advertised in the company catalogue on demand.

To help achieve these objectives, the company uses a minicomputer system for stock control and most of its other applications. At present, the stock control system is run on a batch processing basis, transactions for stock issues and receipts being posted to the master file, at the end of each day. This delay means that the stock master file does not always reflect the up-to-date position and it has been decided that a new system is to be introduced to enable transactions to be posted to the master file as soon as stock is sold or received. The new system uses VDU terminals which are linked to the minicomputer and data entry is to be carried out interactively. This means that data is entered in response to message prompts on the screen. Errors are indicated on the screen as they occur and the data entry operator has to correct them immediately.

The new system will require more highly trained operators than are necessary for a batch data entry system and a staff training programme is to be introduced.

Task

You have previous experience of an interactive stock control system and, in your present role as data entry supervisor, are to be involved in the staff training programme. The Management Information Services Manager believes some basic understanding of the role of the computer helps staff in their work and has asked you to give an introductory talk or other form of presentation to the data entry staff, concerning the new system and the role of the computer in it. Your talk should cover the following points:

1. a description of the information flows from data collection to the updating of the master files and the production of stock reports.

2. a diagram, appropriately simplified, which illustrates the logical structure of a computer system and the functions of each component in the structure.

3. a description of the relationships between each stage of processing in the stock control system and the functional components described in 2.

You may use any form of presentation you wish and it may include, for example, the use of flip charts, OHP slides, wall displays, video, handouts, etc. It may also be appropriate to develop the presentation as part of a group project.

Development Task

Use a stock control package and for one processing routine, for example, the entry of transactions for goods issued, produce a simple user manual describing the prompts which appear on the screen and the necessary responses.

Assignment

A New System For Milford

Milford Communications Limited is a small company based in Cirencester specializing in the manufacture of telephone equipment for the United Kingdom market. Its business has grown dramatically in the last few years, since the removal of British Telecom's monopoly on the supply of telephone equipment. The business has taken advantage of the popular demand for sophisticated telephone handsets which'remember' a range of regularly used telephone numbers specified by the user.

There are twenty five staff at the Cirencester Head Office and all the office administration systems are computerized, using a number of 'stand-alone' microcomputer systems and software packages. The financial director, Arthur Danish, is confident that the business can be further expanded by improving the efficiency of the information processing systems. At present, the separate microcomputer systems do not facilitate management in obtaining a 'global' view of the organisation's operation. You are employed as a systems development assistant, responsible to Mr. Danish and he has asked you to produce a report on the alternative computer systems which may be of use in this situation.

Task

1. Prepare an informal report for Mr. Danish, in which you consider the various alternative types of computer system which may be used in the organization. Also present any arguments for and against each alternative.

2. As an appendix to your report, explain the significance of systems software and the purchases which may be needed, in addition to the computer hardware.

Developmental Task

Research from computing magazines, or journals, a range of computer systems which could be used in this situation and produce a table detailing the approximate costs, general features and limitations of each system. Make argued recommendations as to the type of system which is likely to be most appropriate.

Chapter 4

☐ FILING INFORMATION

This chapter deals with the ways in which information is stored, organized and processed by computer.

Files, Records and Data Items

In data processing, it is necessary to store information on particular subjects, for example, customers, suppliers or personnel and such information needs to be structured so that it is readily controllable and accessible to the user.

In traditional data processing systems, each of these 'topics' of information is allocated a FILE.

The figure below illustrates the structure of a typical Personnel FILE

Works Number	Surname	Initial	Depart-ment	Grade	D.O.B.	Salary
357638	Watkins	P.	Sales	3	100755	9500
367462	Groves	L.	Marketing	4	170748	12800
388864	Harrison	F.	Sales	2	121066	6500
344772	Williams	J.L.	Production	4	010837	14700

A file consists of a collection of related RECORDS. The Personnel file which is shown above has a record for each employee. For example, the row containing information on P. Watkins is one individual RECORD. The complete file would be made up of a number of such records, each one relating to a different employee.

Each record contains specific items of information relating to each employee. In the example, SURNAME is a DATA ITEM TYPE and listed in this column are DATA ITEM VALUES for each record shown. It is important to distinguish between data item type and data item value. The data item type refers to the category of information, in this case Works Number, Surname, Initial and so on. The data item value is the specific value that each individual record has for that type. Thus, the data item value of record 388864 for Department is 'Sales'. In other words F. Harrison works in the Sales department.

a. Fixed and Variable Length Records

The extent to which the information in a particular file can be standardized and categorized will determine whether each record in the file can be FIXED or VARIABLE in LENGTH. The 'length' of the record is the number of 'character positions' allocated to it within the file. In the example shown above the file would probably contain FIXED LENGTH records because:

(i)   the number and types of data items required in this case are likely to be the same for each employee;

(ii) the number of character positions for each data item can be fixed or at least set to a maximum. For example, the Works Number is fixed at 6 character positions and Surname could be set to a maximum of 20, provided that no surnames exceeded this length.

VARIABLE LENGTH records may be used in files which have storage requirements markedly different from those referred to above, for instance:

(i)   Some records could have more data items than others. In a personnel file, for example, each record may contain details of previous jobs held. As the number of previous jobs may vary considerably from employee to employee, so the number of data items would be similarly varied;

OR

(ii) the number of character positions used for data item values within a data item type or types is variable. For example, in a library system each record may contain a data item which describes the subject of the book. The amount of text needed to adequately describe this may vary from book to book.

Listed below are some of the advantages of fixed length records:

(i)   Fixed length records are simpler to process, in that the start and end point of each record can be readily identified by the number of character positions. For instance, if a record has a fixed length of 80 character positions, a program reading the file from the start will assume that the second record starts at the 81st character position, the third at the 161st character position and so on. Thus, programming for file handling operations is made easier;

(ii) Fixed length records allow an accurate estimation of file storage requirements. Therefore a file containing 1000 records, each of fixed 80 characters length, will take approximately 80000 characters of storage;

(iii) Where direct access files are being used, fixed length records can be readily updated 'in situ' (in other words the updated record overwrites the old version in the same position on the storage medium). As the new version will have the same number of characters as the old, any changes to a record will not change its physical length.

There are some instances when variable length records are more appropriate. For example:

(i)   Where records in a file contain highly variable quantities of information, variable length records may be more economical of storage space;

(ii) When the saving in storage space makes the introduction of more complex file handling techniques worthwhile.

b. The Identification of Records – Primary and Secondary Keys

In most organisations, when an information system is operational it will be necessary to identify each record uniquely. In the Personnel File example given above, it might be thought that it is possible to identify each individual record simply by the employee's Surname. This would be satisfactory as long as no two had the same surname. In reality most organisations will of course have several employees with the same surnames. To ensure uniqueness therefore, each employee is assigned a unique Works Number. This is then used as the PRIMARY KEY in the file system. Each individual will have his or her unique Works Number and so a unique primary key.

There are certain circumstances when the primary key may be a COMPOSITE KEY, that is made up of more than one data item. The example below shows how a pair of data items, which individually may not be unique, can be combined to provide a unique identifier.

The figure below shows an extract from a file which details suppliers' quotations for a number of different products. There is a need for a composite key because there may be a number of quotations from one supplier (in this case, supplier 41192) and a number of quotations for the same part (in this instance, part number A112).

Quotation File (extract)

Supplier-No	Part-No	Price	Delivery-Date
23783	A361	2.59	31/01/86
37643	B452	1.50	29/01/86
40923	A112	3.29	30/01/86
41192	A112	3.29	28/01/86
41192	C345	2.15	30/01/86

It is necessary, therefore to use both Supplier-No and Part-No to identify one quotation record uniquely.

Sometimes uniqueness is not always necessary. For example, if it is required to retrieve records which fulfil a criterion, or several criteria, SECONDARY keys may be used. Thus, for example, in an information retrieval system on Personnel, the secondary key Department may be used to retrieve the records of all employees who work in, say, the Sales Department.

File Storage Media

There are basically two types of file storage media:

    (a)   Serial Access Media;

    (b)   Direct Access Media.

a. Serial Access Media

Serial access means that in order to identify and retrieve a particular record it is necessary to 'read' all the records which precede it in the relevant file. An example of such a storage medium is a normal cassette tape. One of the difficulties with such a storage medium is that there are no readily identifiable physical areas on the medium which can be ADDRESSED . In other words, it is not possible to give a name or code and refer this to a particular location. It is said to be NON-ADDRESSABLE. To look for an individual record stored on such a medium requires the software to examine each RECORD KEY in sequence from the beginning of the file until the required record is found.

b. Direct Access Media

Storage media such as floppy or hard disks allow DIRECT access to individual records without reference to the rest of the relevant file. They have physical divisions which can be identified by computer software (and sometimes hardware) and are ADDRESSABLE so that particular locations can be referred to by a name or code to retrieve a record which is stored at that location. Looking for an individual record stored on such a medium is possible (depending on the way the file is organized) by specifying the relevant RECORD KEY, thus providing the software with a means of finding and retrieving the specific individual record directly.

File Organization Methods

Another function of the primary key is to provide a value which can be used by computer software to assign a record to a particular position within a file. The file organization method chosen will dictate how individual records are assigned to particular LOGICAL positions within a file.

File Storage Media and File Organization Methods

Serial access media are limited in the file organization methods they permit because they are NON-ADDRESSABLE. Direct access media are more versatile in that they allow a variety of file organization methods in addition to those allowed by serial access media. The different types of file storage media are discussed in some detail in the next section.

Magnetic Tape - a Serial Access Medium

a. Physical and Logical Records

Because of the physical characteristics of magnetic tape it is necessary, when processing a file, that the tape unit (the device onto which a tape is loaded for processing) starts to read the tape at the beginning of the reel. The 'takeup' spool receives the tape from the 'feed' spool via a 'read-write' head in the unit which can either record information onto or read information from the tape as it passes. As there are no specific physical locations on the tape which can be identified and referred to by the computer (except of course the beginning and end), the only way it can find a particular record is by 'reading' the whole file. Unless the whole tape is to be processed, it may only be necessary to read up to the point where the specific record it is seeking is found. There may well be more than one logical file on a tape but these will have to be read in the sequence that they appear on the tape. As the tape is read, the computer will compare the record key of each record which it comes to, with the specified key, until the required record is found. The diagram on the following page illustrates the way in which a file is arranged on tape both LOGICALLY and PHYSICALLY.

You should note from the diagram that records R1,R2,R3 etc. are LOGICAL records. For example, if this were a stock file, each logical record would relate to one commodity held in stock. On the other hand each BLOCK or PHYSICAL record consists, in this illustration, of 4 logical records. The reason for making the distinction between logical and physical records stems from the fact that data is transferred between the computer's internal memory and the tape storage medium in 'manageable chunks'. The optimum size of each 'chunk' (or to give it its proper name, BLOCK), will depend on factors such as the size of the computer's internal memory.

Each block of data is referred to as a physical record. Between each block transfer, the tape has to stop while the previous block is processed by the computer. In order to give the tape time to stop and then restart for the next block, there is an Inter Block Gap (IBG), a blank area of tape between each block. It is unlikely that the optimum block size will coincide with the actual length of a single logical record, so it is necessary to transfer a number of logical records between tape and internal memory at one time. Thus, a PHYSICAL record or BLOCK will often consist of a number of LOGICAL records.

Illustration of how a file is stored on tape

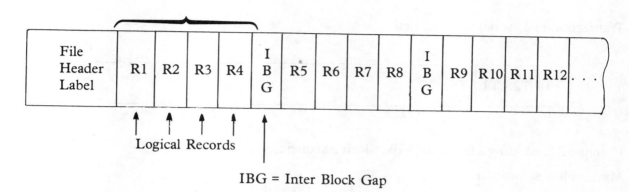

IBG = Inter Block Gap

The example of a stock file is used again to illustrate this point further. Assume that each block contains 3 logical stock records (in other words three individual commodities). If the first record to be processed is stored in the fifth block, then the first four blocks have to be read in sequence into memory and each logical stock record examined for its record key, without any records actually being used. When the fifth block is eventually read into memory each of the three logical stock records is then examined for its record key until the required key is identified.

b. File Organization Methods Using Magnetic Tape

There are two ways in which a file can be organized on tape:

(i) Serially;

(ii) Sequentially.

This restriction stems from the fact that magnetic tape is a serial access medium. As is noted earlier, this means that it has no addressable locations and so records have to be traced by reading the file from beginning to end.

The processing of tape files can only be carried out satisfactorily if they are organized in the sequence of their record keys. This point is illustrated on the next page. This restriction applies to both master and transaction files. Serial files, which are out of sequence, are only useful as an interim measure, prior to processing.

Generally, when a transaction file is being created on tape, for example, when customer orders are received, they are written to tape in the order in which they are received. This creates a serial file. Before the master file can be updated, the transaction file has to be sorted by the computer to become a sequential file.

Serial and Sequential Files

Example 1 illustrating a transaction file which is serial and unsorted

Master File - sequential

| R1 | R2 | R3 | R4 | R5 | R6 | R7 . . . . . |

Transaction File - serial and unsorted

| T3 | T2 | T1 | T5 | T7 . . . . . |

Example 2 illustrating a transaction file which is sequential

Master File - sequential

| R1 | R2 | R3 | R4 | R5 | R6 | R7 . . . . . |

Transaction file - sequential

| T1 | T2 | T3 | T5 | T6 . . . . . |

Updating the Master File

When a tape file is updated, a new master file must be created on a new reel of tape. This is because the tape drive unit cannot guarantee to write an updated record to the exact position from which it was read. There is a danger, therefore, of adjacent records being corrupted or completely overwritten.

The following procedures are followed during the update (assuming that no new records are to be inserted).

  (i)   A transaction is read into memory.

  (ii) A master record is read into memory. If the record keys do not match, the master record is written, unchanged, to the new reel. Master records continue to be read, examined and written in the original sequence to the new reel until a match for the transaction is found.

  (iii) Once the match is found, the master record is updated in main memory and then written to the new reel.

These steps are repeated until all transactions have been processed and the complete updated master file has been written to the new reel.

Unless the transaction files are sorted into the same sequence as the master file, it is necessary to rewind the master file whenever a transaction requires a master record which has already passed through the system. Such rewinding would clearly be both inefficient and impractical.

The following Systems Flowchart illustrates the updating procedure:

Systems Flowchart - Magnetic Tape File Update

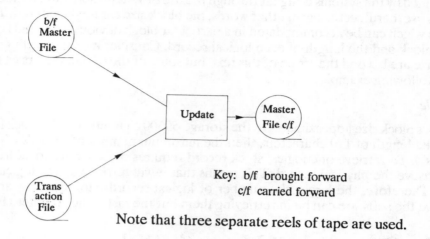

Key: b/f brought forward
      c/f carried forward

Note that three separate reels of tape are used.

Magnetic Disk - a Direct Access Medium

a. The Means of Addressing Magnetic Disk.

Magnetic disk provides file storage facilities which are more flexible and powerful than those provided by magnetic tape. As an addressable medium, the surface of the disk is divided into physical locations which are illustrated in the figure below.

The Addressing Structure of a Magnetic Disk

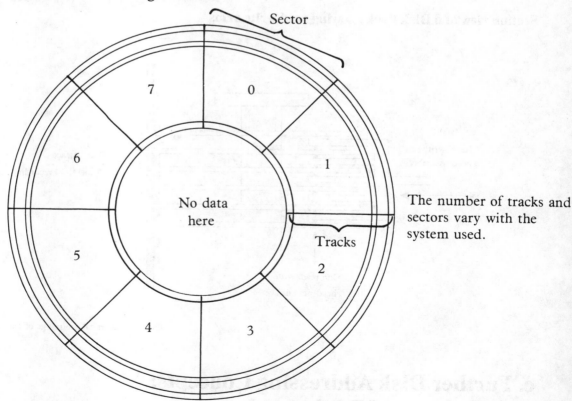

The number of tracks and sectors vary with the system used.

The 'address' of any one physical location on a single disk incorporates a track number, and within that track, a sector number. Addressing in this way is rather like providing a street name (the track) and a house number (the sector). This addressable unit is the smallest physical area on the disk which can be addressed. Each of these addressable units is referred to as a 'block' or 'physical record'. (The meaning of this type of record is described earlier in the chapter). The size of the blocks is normally determined by the systems designer through the use of systems software, although some disk storage systems use 'hard' sectoring; in other words, the block size cannot be altered. The number of logical records which can be accommodated in a particular block obviously depends upon the physical size of the block and the length of each logical record. Considerations regarding the determination of block size are beyond the scope of this text, but some of the design factors can be readily explained by the following example:

Example

If a disk's block size approximates to the storage of 500 characters and a stock file has logical records of a fixed length of 110 characters, then the maximum number of records which can be stored in a block is 4. To retrieve one logical stock record requires the software to address the relevant block and retrieve the physical record. This means that it will retrieve all the logical stock records in the block. Therefore, the larger the number of logical records stored in any specific block, the less selective the software can be in retrieving them but the faster the complete file is processed.

b. The Operation of Magnetic Disk

Although there are many variations in the capacities and sizes of disk that are available, there are certain physical characteristics which are common to all.

On smaller computer systems disks tend to be handled singly on individual disk drive units. On larger systems a number of disks may be mounted on a central spindle. This is shown in the figure below. To transfer data to or from the disk pack it is necessary to mount it on a disk drive unit which rotates the pack at high speed. Data is recorded magnetically on disk in a similar fashion to the recording on magnetic tape. Special 'read-write' heads are mounted on moveable arms within the disk drive unit in such a way that they move in synchronization across the disk surface. The software positions the heads for the writing or retrieval of records.

Section view of a Disk Pack showing read/write arms

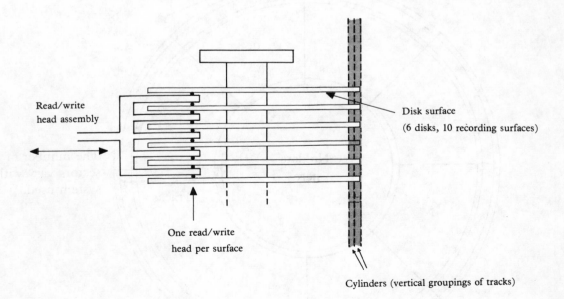

Read/write head assembly

Disk surface
(6 disks, 10 recording surfaces)

One read/write head per surface

Cylinders (vertical groupings of tracks)

c. Further Disk Addressing Concepts: Cylinders and Buckets

Cylinders

If the two previous figures are considered together it can be seen that in a disk pack a specified

Track on one disk (Track 0) is vertically above other tracks on lower disks which are also specified as Track 0. In other words, all the Track 0s are in the same vertical plane. Such a grouping is known as a 'cylinder' or 'seek area'. Similarly, all track 1s form another cylinder, as do track 2s and so on. It can be seen therefore, that there are as many cylinders as there are tracks on each disk surface.

The fastest way of reading or writing records on disks is by minimizing the movement of the read/write arms. This is achieved by positioning associated records, which are likely to needed as a group (they may form a complete file), into sequence (as a sequential file) on tracks in the same cylinder. Records are written to the disk pack, such that track 1 on surface 1 is filled first, followed by track 1 on surface 2 and so on, until all number 1 tracks are filled (the first cylinder). Then, if the file requires more than one cylinder, adjacent tracks are filled to form further cylinders, until the file is complete.

When access is required to the file it is quickest, in terms of keeping read/write head movement to a minimum, to deal with a cylinder of records at a time. Thus, a complete cylinder of records is processed before any head movement is required. A cylinder is also known as a 'seek area', because all records in a cylinder can be accessed by the read/write heads while they are positioned in that cylinder.

Buckets

The minimum amount of data which can be transferred between the backing store of the computer and its internal store is the 'Block'. However, there are occasions when a larger unit of transfer is required. On such occasions the concept of the 'Bucket' is used. Thus a number of blocks (up to the maximum of one track) may be given the same disk address (this is usually the address of the first block in the bucket) and any logical records held within such a bucket are retrieved when that disk address is used.

d. File Organization Methods using Magnetic Disk

Magnetic disk supports the following file organization methods:

Serial

As is the case for a serial tape file, records are placed onto disk one after the other in no particular sequence;

Sequential

As for a sequential tape file, records are stored on disk ordered by record key;

Indexed Sequential

Records are stored in sequence according to their record keys and an index is produced when the file is created. This allows the direct retrieval of individual records. The retrieval of records involves the software searching different levels of the index - the cylinder index, track index and the bucket or block index- before positioning the read/write heads to retrieve the block containing the required record. This method allows the efficient sequential processing of the file as well as direct retrieval of records using the indexes. Indexes can become quite large and the file may need to be reorganized periodically so that new records can be inserted in the correct sequence. Records which are marked for deletion need to be removed from the file and the indexes then have to be reconstructed. The frequency with which such reorganisation is necessary depends on the level of file activity and the number of inserts and deletions. File reorganisation is a 'house-keeping' activity;

Random

This is a method which is impractical in any non-computerized situation. However, in a computerized system it is feasible to place records onto disk at random. The procedure for placing specific records in a particular position on disk uses a mathematical formula called an 'algorithm', which generates a disk address from the record key. The same mathematical formula is used to subsequently retrieve records. This is ideal in situations where random enquiries are the norm and there is little need for sequential processing. Randomly organized files can be processed sequentially but with less efficiency than sequentially organized files. An advantage of this method is the lack of large indexes which tend to take up considerable storage space on the disk.

e. Accessing Disk Files

Serial Files
As with magnetic tape, the only way to retrieve records is serially, in other words, one after the other.

Sequential Files
The addressing features of disk are not used and the method is the same as that for sequential tape files.

Sequential Files
There are 3 methods of retrieving such records:

Sequentially. Transactions are sorted in to the same sequence as the master file. This is suitable when a large proportion of the records in the file are to be processed in one run, that is, when the 'hit rate' is high. (The term 'hit rate' is explained in Chapter 14 Systems Development and Implementation). Minimal use is made of the index. The cylinder index and track index may be searched, then the whole track is read into memory, block by block, without reference to the block index;

Selective or Skip Sequentially. The transactions are sorted into master file sequence and the indexes are used, so that only those blocks containing master records for which there is a transaction are read into memory. This is suitable when the hit rate is low;

Randomly. Transactions are not sorted. They are processed in the order in which they occur. The indexes are used to find the relevant master records as they are required. The read/write heads have to move back and forth through the file and so head movement is greater than with sequential methods of processing. This method is appropriate when records are updated immediately after the transaction occurs or, for example, when there is a need for random enquiries of a stock file.

Random Files
Records need not be in any logical sequence. Records are retrieved by generating the physical address from the record key. The software uses the same algorithm it used to assign the record to its address in the first place.

Assignment

Sally's Wholefoods

Sally's Wholefoods is a small, one woman business, with three shops in York. They each stock a wide range of vegetarian foods, some of which is ready-cooked and pre-packed. However, most of the food is sold loose and constitutes ingredients for home cooking. The business is extremely successful and attracts large numbers of academics and students from the university and colleges in York. The proprietor, Sally Henderson, employs two full-time assistants at each shop and occasionally employs one or two students during the summer vacation.

Although much of the stock consists of dried food items, freshness is important, so Ms. Henderson has to keep careful track of stocks held, outstanding orders from suppliers and orders made by her customers. She operates a home delivery service, which adds to the problem of control, since she keeps some stocks at home for this purpose. There are hundreds of different food items, some of which are seasonal, so the range of goods is not always the same. To keep tighter control of stock, orders from suppliers and customer orders, she has decided that a computer will be of service.

Task

You are employed by Ms. Henderson in a general accounting and clerical role and she has asked you to produce an informal report suggesting how best to structure the data files for a computerized system. The report should consider the following:

1. The design of suitable file structures for the stock, supplier and customer order files, with identification of the file, record and data item levels. Suggest appropriate data items for the unique identification of records in each file. Explain why uniqueness is necessary. It may also be useful to identify any secondary keys which may be helpful in the production of summary reports; explain the role of secondary keys.

2. The alternatives available for file storage. Give a reasoned recommendation as to which is needed for the applications in question.

Developmental Task

Research some of the operational characteristics of storage systems for micro-computers and draw up a table of comparisons. Include it as an appendix in your report to Ms. Henderson.

Assignment   Building a System

Home Extensions Ltd is a building firm operating in the Swindon area. The two directors, Jim Atkinson and Arthur Haines, have bought a microcomputer system, primarily for job costing and control. It is envisaged that other applications will benefit from computerization in the future. The microcomputer system only has cassette tape storage. Generally, the firm has about thirty to forty jobs 'on the go' at one time and for each job, a record needs to be kept of the basic details, such as site location and the initial costings. Another record needs to be maintained to monitor spending on each job, as it progresses; this includes materials, labour and overheads. Jim Atkinson has attended a BASIC programming course and intends to write his own job costing package.

Task

Mr. Atkinson employs you as a trainee Site Manager and is aware that you have gained some computing knowledge during your studies. His knowledge of BASIC does not extend to the use of computer files and he does not seem to realise that the cassette tape system will be wholly inadequate for the application he has in mind. He does not want to spend any money consulting a specialist and has asked you to advise him of the need for a disk-based system. He would like to know the reasons behind any advice you give. To this end, Mr. Atkinson wishes you to provide him with some explanatory notes on the way files can be organized on magnetic tape and magnetic disk. Hopefully, by the time you have finished, he will see the sense of consulting a dealer and buying some packaged software, instead of writing his own programs.

Prepare some notes for Mr. Atkinson, explaining:

1. The file organization methods possible on magnetic tape and the reasons for its unsuitability for the above application;

2. The file organization and access methods possible on magnetic disk which make it appropriate for the above application.

Illustrate your notes with some sample data from building jobs.

Chapter 5

☐ PERIPHERALS

Overview of Peripherals

As the name suggests, peripheral devices are the external elements of the computer system described in Chapter 3. They provide a means of communication between the central processor and its human operators. Peripheral devices can be categorized according to their general function. These functions are identified at the beginning of Chapter 3 as part of the logical computer configuration. The functions are:

      (i) Backing Storage;

     (ii) Input and Output.

There are two sections in this chapter. The first deals with Backing Storage devices and media and the second with Input and Output peripheral devices.

Backing Storage

All backing storage systems consist of two main elements, a DEVICE and a MEDIUM. For example, a disk drive is a device and a magnetic disk is a storage medium. Under program control, data files are generally read from and written to via the storage device which is connected on-line to the CPU. The most important kinds of backing storage devices in use today are those using magnetic tape and magnetic disk.

a. Magnetic Tape

Despite the continued evolution of disk storage, magnetic tape continues to be used in most large scale computer installations as a cheap and secure method of storing large volumes of data which are normally processed in a serial fashion. It is also useful for the storage of historic files where rapid access to individual records is not essential. An example of the former use is in the processing of an organisation's payroll. An example of storing historic data on tape is provided by the Police National Computer system in Hendon. Here, millions of records of current criminal activity are kept 'on-line' and are directly accessible from magnetic disk. Records which are not currently 'active' are held off-line on magnetic tape. When a record needs to be retrieved, the relevant tape has to be placed on-line and searched until the required record is found. It would be inefficient and expensive to keep all records, no matter how old, on-line all the time.

General Features of Magnetic Tape

The tapes used on mainframe and minicomputer systems are stored on detachable reels up to 26.7cm in diameter. A tape is usually between 0.38cm and 2.54cm wide. It is made of plastic and is covered with a coating which can be magnetized. The most commonly used tapes are 1.27cm wide. In larger systems, tapes may be 730m in length and able to record 15000 bytes of information per cm.

A particular type of cartridge tape, which looks like a cassette tape but is slightly larger, is often used as a backup for 'hard' disk on microcomputer systems. These tapes have huge capacity (up to 60mb - million bytes) and can copy the contents of a hard disk in a few minutes. This type of tape is called a STREAMER tape.

The rest of this section concentrates on the large reel-to-reel systems.

Processing Tapes

A tape must be mounted on an on-line TAPE UNIT when it is to be used by a computer system. The figure below illustrates the main features of a large tape unit for reel-to-reel tapes.

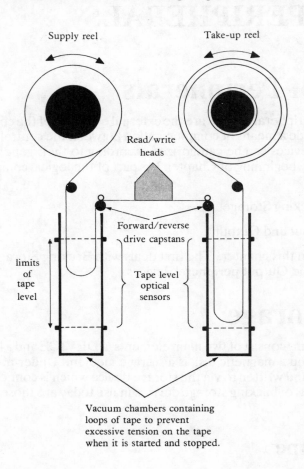

Supply reel   Take-up reel

Read/write heads

Forward/reverse drive capstans

limits of tape level

Tape level optical sensors

Vacuum chambers containing loops of tape to prevent excessive tension on the tape when it is started and stopped.

Large Magnetic Tape Unit

It can be seen from the figure that there are two reels. The supply reel contains the tape that is to be read from or written to by the computer system. The takeup reel collects the tape as it is unwound from the supply reel. During processing, the tape is propelled past separate 'read' and 'write' heads at high speed. As is explained in Chapter 4, data is transferred between tape and main memory in physical blocks. A small gap called the INTER BLOCK GAP is left between each block of data, to allow the tape to decelerate and stop and accelerate again to the correct speed for data transfer. To keep the tape at the proper tension, even during acceleration and deceleration, vacuum chambers are used to allow some slack in the tape beneath each reel. The optical level sensors in each vacuum chamber detect the level of 'droop' and when necessary, signal the supply reel to release more tape or the takeup reel to takeup more tape.

When processing is finished, the tape is rewound onto the supply reel, which is then removed from the tape unit. The takeup reel remains in the unit.

Data Storage on Magnetic Tape

The figure below shows how data is stored on magnetic tape. The coding system used is either ASCII or EBCDIC (which is used for IBM equipment),

Data Storage on Magnetic Tape (Nine-Track, Even Parity)

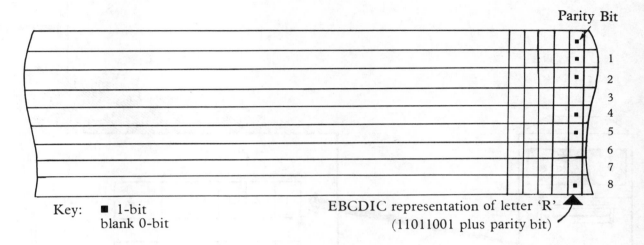

Key: ■ 1-bit
       blank 0-bit

EBCDIC representation of letter 'R'
(11011001 plus parity bit)

The coding systems are binary and in the case of EBCDIC, each character is represented by a group of 8 binary digits (bits), either 0 or 1, plus a parity bit (for checking transmission errors), across the width of the tape. As the figure shows, each 0 or 1 bit is accommodated in a single track and each group of bits representing one character occupies one frame across the tape.

The method of representing a 0 or 1 bit depends on the recording system in use but simplified examples are as follow:

    (a)   the presence of a magnetic field to represent 1 and the lack of a magnetic field to represent 0;

    (b)   the 0 and 1 bits are represented by magnetic fields of opposite polarity, say north for 1 and south for 0.

The tape unit reads across the nine tracks in a frame to identify the character represented.

Blocking Data on Magnetic Tape

The organization of files on magnetic tape is described in Chapter 4, so this section deals with the operational characteristics of storing data on tape.

In order to transfer data to or from tape, the tape has to pass the read/write heads at a particular speed. Data transfer takes place in BLOCKS because, for example, it is not generally possible to read a complete logical file into memory at one time. Instead, suitably sized blocks are transferred to be processed in turn, requiring the tape to stop and start repeatedly. The inter-block gap allows for such stops and starts.

As is explained in Chapter 4, a file is made up of a number of LOGICAL records. For example, a stock file contains a logical record for each commodity in stock. Generally, a logical record will not be large enough to constitute a physical record or block, so a number of logical records are grouped for transfer at one read or write instruction. The number of logical records in each physical record indicates the BLOCKING FACTOR. Large blocks save space (fewer inter-block gaps) and speed processing. Memory size is a limiting factor on the size of blocks.

To speed processing, many computer systems contain special high-speed memory areas called BUFFERS. A buffer acts as a waiting area for a transferred block from where it can be quickly accessed and processed by the CPU. DOUBLE buffering makes use of two buffers which work 'in tandem' to speed processing. The following diagram illustrates the buffering process.

Buffering of Blocks of Data in Main Memory

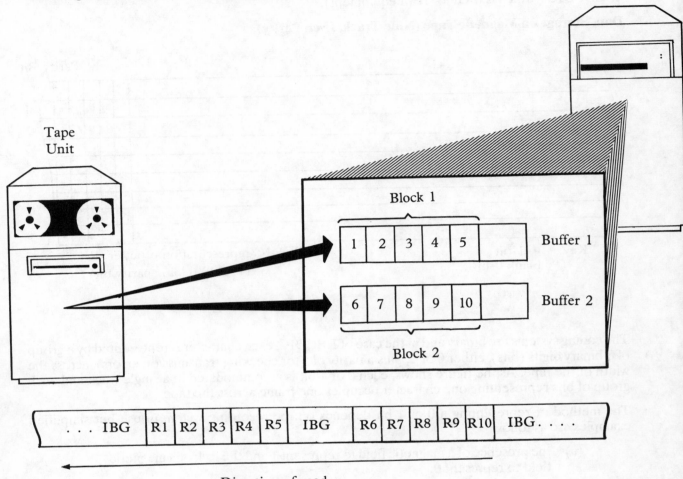

IBG   = Inter-block Gap
Rn   = Logical record number

If the records are blocked as shown above, the systems software initially places the first block into buffer 1 and the second into buffer 2. READ instructions from the applications program retrieve the data from these buffers. The CPU can retrieve logical records faster from the buffer than from tape. As soon as all logical records from buffer 1 have been processed, the reading process transfers to the logical records in buffer 2. Meanwhile, the next block on tape can be transferred into buffer 1 and so on.

Security of Files on Magnetic Tape

There are two major areas of concern:

(i) It is important that the correct file is used in a file processing operation to ensure correct results. Thus, the subject of the file and the version must be identifiable. For example, it is no good producing monthly payslips using information from a payroll master file three months out of date.

(ii) A tape file must be protected against accidental erasure. This may occur because tapes are reusable and when a file is no longer required it can be overwritten by new information.

To ensure that the correct file is used for any particular job, a tape file usually has an INTERNAL HEADER LABEL. The label appears at the beginning of the tape and identifies it. The identifying information in the label is usually recorded under program control or by a data encoding device.

A tape header label usually contains the following items of information:

(a) File name e.g. PAYROLL, STOCK, SALES;

(b) Date created;

(c) Purge date - the date from which the tape is no longer required and may be re-used.

The label is checked by the program, before the file is processed, to ensure that the correct tape is being used.

A device called a FILE PROTECTION RING can be used to prevent accidental erasure. When tapes are stored off-line, the rings are not fitted. To write to a tape, the ring must first be fitted to the centre of the reel. A tape can be read by the computer whether or not a ring is fitted. The simple rule to remember is 'no ring, no write'.

b. Magnetic Disks

Many computer applications require fast, direct access to   individual records within a file and this facility is provided by magnetic disk. For this reason, magnetic disks are the most important backing storage media in use today.

Two popular types of magnetic disk are:

(i) Hard disks;

(ii) 'floppy' or flexible disks.

Hard Disks

General Features

The disk is usually made of aluminium with a coating of a magnetizable material on which data can be recorded. Records are stored in concentric rings or TRACKS. The method of encoding is fundamentally the same as that for tape, except that the magnetic states representing binary patterns are stored in single-file around the tracks. The diagram on the following page illustrates these features.

Each track is divided into a number of SECTORS and each sector has a given storage capacity. Each track and sector has a physical ADDRESS which can be used by software to locate a particular record or group of records. The central area of the disk is not used, because to do so would necessitate a higher packing density than can be read or recorded by the read/write head. The number of tracks and sectors is known as the disk's FORMAT. The sector size can either be fixed permanently or can be altered by software. The former is known as HARD sectoring and the latter as SOFT sectoring.

Hard Sectoring

The position of each sector can be indicated by a slot or reflective marker which can be detected by sensors in the drive unit. As the smallest unit of data transfer between disk and CPU is a sector (BLOCK), this means that any application is restricted to the disk's block size. Consider, for example, an application which uses logical records of 64 bytes, stored on a disk with 512 byte 'hard' sectors. A minimum of 8 logical records needs to be transferred to memory even if only one is required out of the sector.

Soft Sectoring

This method allows the sectors to be set by software. All microcomputer systems use soft sectoring.

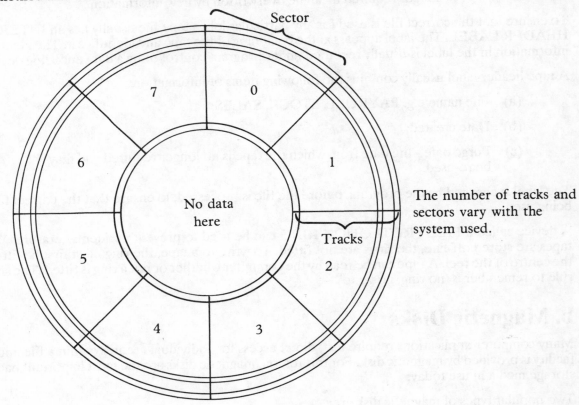

Operational Characteristics

During computer operation, the disk revolves continuously. The read-write head does not actually touch the disk surface as this would result in rapid wear of the disk surface and the head. Instead, the head 'floats' very close to the surface of the disk, so that information can be recorded on or read from the concentric tracks. The head is shaped so that as the disk revolves at high speed, a flow of air forces the head a minute distance above the surface. When the disk is not revolving, the air pressure beneath the head is reduced. This may result in a 'head crash' which causes damage to both the disk surface and the read-write head. Two main methods are available to prevent such an occurrence.

Firstly, the head can be automatically retracted away from the surface before the disk stops revolving. An alternative method, used on WINCHESTER drives, is to make the head 'take-off' and 'land' as necessary on the disk surface. To prevent disk damage, the surface is lubricated and the whole unit is hermetically sealed to prevent dust from entering. This second method allows the head to fly closer to the surface than on conventional drives, thus increasing the reading accuracy and enabling greater packing density.

The use of flying heads requires the disk drive environment to be completely free from dust and other impurities which may cause a 'head crash'. A human hair or even a smoke particle can be large enough to cause damage. The IBM 3360 disk heads, for example, glide 17 millionths of an inch above the recording surface. A human hair is approximately 2500 millionths of an inch. The following illustration shows these and similar comparisons.

There are two main approaches to the design of the access mechanization of the read-write head:

(i)   FIXED head;

(ii) MOVEABLE head.

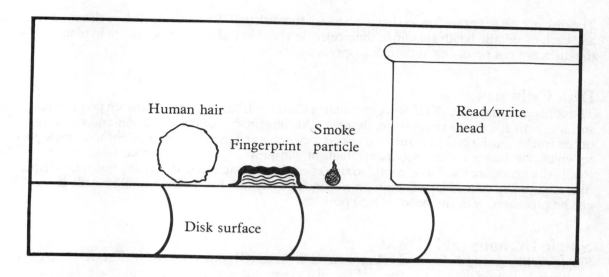

Fixed Head Disks

The access mechanism has a read-write head for each track. Each head is positioned permanently over its particular track so no lateral motion is necessary. However, a disk with 400 tracks on two surfaces would require 800 read/write heads mounted onto a fixed access arm. Access time is shorter than is possible for moveable head systems, but their high cost has restricted their use.

Moveable Head Disks

This mechanism only uses one read/write head per disk surface. The head is moved to the required track by a moveable arm.

In order to increase on-line storage capacity, a stack of disks can be formed into a DISK PACK.

Exchangeable Disk Packs

Disks are often assembled into groups of six, eight, ten or twelve and mounted on a central spindle which rotates all the disks at the same speed. There is sufficient gap between each surface to allow read/write heads to move in and out between the disks. Only one head may be actively reading or writing at any one time. The disk pack is enclosed in a plastic shell, to protect the disk surfaces from dust or other foreign objects.

The diagram below illustrates the disk pack and the access mechanism.

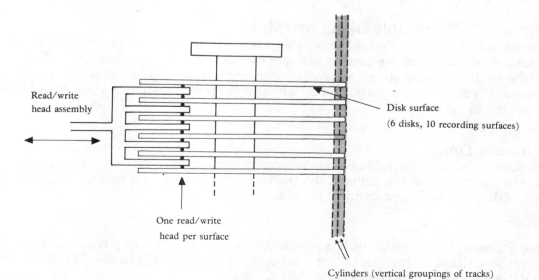

The disk pack is generally loaded from the top of the disk unit. Because the disk pack can be removed and exchanged, the heads remain in their retracted position when the pack is not in place and when the disks are not revolving at their full operating speed.

Disk Cylinders

The concept of the CYLINDER is explained in Chapter 4. Briefly, if there are ten possible recording surfaces with 200 tracks per surface, there are 200 imaginary, concentric 'cylinders', each consisting of ten tracks. Each vertical plane of tracks is a cylinder and as such is equivalent to a track position to which the heads on the access mechanism can move. With a moveable head system, all the read/write heads are fixed to a 'comb' so that each is in the same cylinder at any one time. Sequential files are applied to a disk pack on a on a cylinder-by-cylinder basis so that all records in a cylinder can be processed with the heads in one position.

Single Exchangeable Disks

Single exchangeable disks are also known as CARTRIDGE disks and can be inserted into the front of the disk unit, in which case, part of the disk cover automatically slides to one side to allow the read/write heads to move in, or it can be 'top loaded' and the plastic cover removed by the operator once the disk is in place. As is the case with the exchangeable disk pack, the moveable heads remain in the retracted position except when the disk is revolving at full speed.

Winchester Disks

When first introduced, Winchester disks were designed for large computer systems and are still popular on such systems. They are now used as an alternative to floppy disks on microcomputer systems. Winchester disks provide a much greater volume of on-line storage and faster access to programs and data than is possible with floppy disks.

Winchester disk systems consist of packs of hard disks, stacked in the same way as the exchangeable disk pack systems described earlier. The disks are not removable and are hermetically sealed in the storage units together with the read/write mechanism. The contamination-free environment in which the disks are stored allows very high speeds of rotation, typically, 3600 revolutions per minute. Storage capacities are increasing as technology advances, but commonly available systems for microcomputers provide up to 300 megabytes of storage.

Winchester disk units can be stored internally within the computer unit. For example, in the IBM PS/2 it is placed in the position normally occupied by one of the two floppy disk drives. Large volume storage presents problems in terms of security backup. A large number of floppy disks would need to be used to back up one Winchester disk, so many systems are stored externally and provide a built-in slot for a tape cartridge. The tape backup system is known as a 'tape streamer' and can be used with both internally and externally housed hard disk systems.

The Bernoulli Removable Disk Cartridge

An alternative technology is used in a removable disk cartridge called the Bernoulli Box. A floppy disk enclosed in a sealed casing uses air pressure caused by the disk's revolution to flex the disk around the read/write head, so that it never touches the surface. The manufacturers claim that if dirt lodges in a Winchester drive, a head crash is invariably the result, whereas a Bernoulli disk would simply flex out of the way.

Disk Access Time

'Access time' is the time interval between the moment the command is given to transfer data from disk to main memory and the moment the transfer is completed. In a moving head system the retrieval of data involves three identifiable tasks.

Seek Time

Suppose, for example, the read/write head unit is in cylinder 5 and that data is required from cylinder 24. To retrieve the data, the mechanism must move inwards to cylinder 24. The time taken to accomplish this movement is known as the 'SEEK TIME'.

Rotational Delay

When a read or write instruction is issued, the head is not usually positioned over the sector where the required data are stored, so there is some ROTATIONAL delay while the disk rotates into the proper position. On average, the time taken is half a revolution of the disk pack. This average time is known as the 'LATENCY' of the disk.

Data Transfer Time

This is the time taken to read the block of data into main memory.

Two strategies can be used to reduce disk access time. The first solution is to store related records in the same cylinder so that head movement is minimized. This strategy is usually adopted for sequential files when the records are to be accessed sequentially. Even with random files it is sometimes possible to group related records in the same cylinder. The second solution is to use the fixed head disks described earlier. As each track has its own read/write head, no seek time is involved. It has to be said, however, that this second option is no longer used in disk drive systems.

Floppy Disks or Diskettes

Floppy disks are physically and operationally different from hard disks. They are flexible and encased in a square plastic protective jacket. The diskette revolves inside the jacket at approximately 360 revolutions per minute, more slowly than a conventional disk. The jacket is lined with a soft material which helps to clean the diskette as it revolves. The read/write head makes contact with the diskette surface when data transfer is in progress and withdraws at other times to reduce wear. The diskette does not rotate continuously. A diskette will eventually wear out after about 500 to 600 hours of contact. Some systems offer a non-contact flying-head system which allows the diskette to revolve at 3000 rpm. This removes the problem of wear and speeds access time.

The following diagram shows the component parts of one type of floppy disk, the 5.25 inch, which is still extremely popular, despite increasing competition from its more robust 3.5 inch rival (described later).

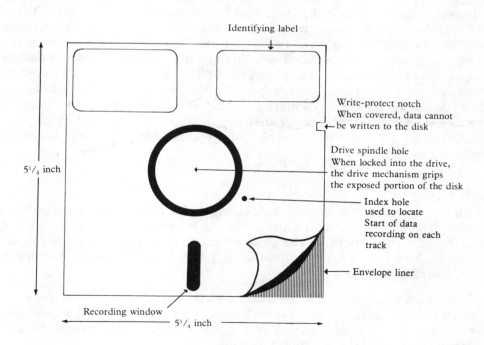

There is a slot in the jacket to allow the read/write head to access the diskette and a central hole for the drive shaft. The diskette has to be inserted into the disk drive and then locked into place by closing the drive door. The locking-in step locks the drive shaft into the central hole in the disk.

Types of Floppy Disk

Floppy disks are available in two sizes according to diameter - 5.25 inches and 3.5 inches. Diskettes can be either 40-track or 80 track and the number of sectors can be varied (soft-sectoring is used). Suppose, for example, that a diskette has 80 tracks and that a particular computer system formats the diskettes into 9 sectors. Formatting causes it to be divided up into nine sectors 0 to 8 as shown below. Thus with 80 tracks and 9 sectors, the diskette has 720 addressable locations. Soft sectoring is used because the operating systems of different computers use different addressing formats. Thus, in principle, standard diskettes can be sold which only require formatting to be used on a particular machine. The formatting procedure also sets up a DIRECTORY which is automatically maintained by the computer system to keep track of the contents of each location.

Formatted Floppy Disk

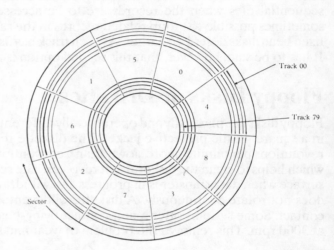

The floppy disk is addressed according
to Track number and Sector number.
In this illustration, the formatting allocates
9 (sectors) x 80 (tracks) = 720 addressable locations.
Each location can accommodate, say 256 bytes.

Double and Quad-Density Disks

Double-density disks are designed to store 48 tracks per inch (tpi) and are referred to as double density because they use double the track density available with earlier disks. The actual number of tracks available on a double density disk is 40 per side, as described in the previous section. Although the disks are designed to store data in a given number of tracks, it is the disk drive which dictates exactly how many are used. Thus, although quad-density disks are designed to support 96tpi, they can be used in drives which record at 48tpi. Quad-density disks used in quad-density disk drives can store 1.2mb compared with the 360kb possible with a double-density system. The quadrupled capacity is achieved by doubling the number of sectors per track as well as doubling the track density. It is important for users to ensure that good quality quad-density disks are used in high density drives, as inferior disks will not support the required recording densities, resulting in unreliable data storage.

3.5 inch Disks

The 3.5 inch disk is stored in a rigid plastic casing which makes it more robust than its 5.25 inch counterpart. A metal sliding shutter which covers the recording surface access slot slides open when the disk is placed in the drive unit. The greater protection provided by this casing allows data to be recorded more densely on a 3.5 inch disk than is generally practicable on a floppy disk. A storage capacity of 1.44mb is typical.

A small hole with a sliding shutter located in one corner of the casing acts as the 'write protect' slot. The drive unit uses an infra-red light source to determine whether or not the slot is open. An open slot indicates that the disk is 'read only'. This is opposite to the condition used with a 5.25 inch floppy disk drive when a covered slot indicates 'read only'.

Alternative Backing Storage Devices and Media

Magnetic tape and disk systems account for a very large proportion of all storage systems in use, but there are a number of alternative systems. These include:

(i) optical disks;

(ii) magnetic bubble memory.

Optical Disks

The optical disk uses laser beam technology to allow data to be recorded and read using bit-densities several times greater than a typical magnetic disk. Data is recorded as bit-patterns using high-intensity laser beams to burn tiny holes into the surface of the disk. The data can then be read from the disk using a laser beam of reduced intensity. A similar technology is used for Compact Disk (CD) digitized recordings of music and film. Its application in computing is still in the early stages of development but it is likely to have a profound impact on backing storage usage.

There are two main types of optical disk system presently available.

CD-ROM (Compact Disk-Read Only Memory) Systems

As the title suggests this type of disk only allows the computer to read data from the disk. The disk is pre-recorded by the manufacturer. It is of no use for the storage of data which requires updating. Its main application is for Interactive Video Disk systems. A video disk can store text, images and audio signals and is of use in advertising, training and education. Sequences of film and sound can be retrieved under computer control.

WORM (Write Once, Read Many)

The large storage capacity of optical disks means that the writing facility can be used for a considerable period before all space is used up. Storage capacities are measured in gigabytes (thousands of millions of characters), way beyond the capacity of any magnetic disk systems. Optical disk systems which provide an erase facility are available but are still too expensive for most users.

Apart from its vast storage capacity, the optical disk is less prone to environmental hazards such as dust. The main reason for this is that the read signal is more intense and the laser head can be fixed 2mm from the disk surface, allowing dust and other particles to pass underneath.

The large investment in conventional hard disk systems, both in terms of hardware and software, is likely to slow the widespread introduction of optical disk for backing storage.

Magnetic Bubble Memory

Unlike disks and tapes, which are electro-mechanical devices, magnetic bubble memory has no moving parts at all.

Bubbles are formed in thin plates of magnetic material as tiny cylindrical 'domains'. The presence of a bubble in a location represents a 1-bit and the absence of a bubble, a 0-bit. The bubbles can be moved within the magnetic layer by tiny electrical forces, thus altering the bit patterns. Bubbles can be created and destroyed by similar forces.

Because there are no moving parts, bubble memory is potentially more reliable than its electro-mechanical counterparts but as yet it has not been brought into general use for a variety of reasons. Firstly, storage capacities and access times for magnetic disks are continually being improved. Secondly, except for very small systems, magnetic bubble memory is more expensive per bit of storage, than magnetic disk. This is likely to remain so until increased volume of production brings down production costs. Its non-volatility makes it a possible alternative to the small disk memories used on some microcomputer systems. Currently, magnetic disk provides better access times than bubble memory.

The main applications of magnetic bubble memory are for memory units in terminals, microcomputers, robots and telecommunications equipment where the memory capacity required is not large. It appears that magnetic bubble memory has failed to make any real impact on storage systems.

Input and Output Devices

Overview of Input and Output Equipment

This section is concerned with equipment designed for input, output or both.

The most common methods of input involve the use of DISPLAY devices such as the Visual Display Unit (VDU) and the first part of this section deals with such equipment. Printers are the next devices to be considered in that they provide 'hard copy' output of the results of computer processing, sometimes at incredible speeds.

The next part examines equipment which automates input and removes the need for keyboard data entry. Equipment in this category includes, for example, OCR (Optical Character Recognition) devices and Bar Code Readers.

Finally, an examination is made of some special-purpose output devices involving output onto microfilm and speech synthesis.

a. Display Devices

Visual Display Unit

The most commonly used device for communicating with a computer is the Visual Display Unit (VDU). Input of text is via a full alphanumeric keyboard and output is displayed on a viewing screen similar to a television. The term VDU terminal is normally used to describe the screen and keyboard as a combined facility for input and output. On its own, the screen is called a MONITOR. In order that an operator can see what is being typed in via the keyboard, input is also displayed on the screen. A square of light called a CURSOR indicates where the next character to be typed by the operator will be placed.

Display Screen Characteristics
Text and Graphics

Most display screens provide both a TEXT and GRAPHICS facility. Text consists of letters (upper and lower case), numbers and special characters such as punctuation marks. Most applications require textual input and output. Graphics output includes picture images, such as maps, charts and drawings. In business applications, for example, a company's sales figures can be graphed on the screen if the screen provides graphical output. Most computer games rely on graphics.

Screen Resolution

A screen's resolution dictates the clarity or sharpness of the displayed text or graphics characters. The achievement of high quality graphics generally requires a higher resolution or sharper image than is required for textual display. Images are formed on the screen through the use of PIXELs. A pixel is a tiny dot of light on the screen and the resolution is determined by the number of pixels on the screen. The greater the density of pixels, the greater the resolution.

Resolution is measured by the number of columns and rows of pixels, for example, a resolution of 720 x 350 indicates 720 columns x 350 rows = 252,000 pixels.

Dot Matrix Characters

Textual characters are usually formed using a matrix of pixels as is shown in the following example. As with screen resolution, the clarity of individual characters is determined by the number of pixels used. Selected dots within the matrix are illuminated to display particular characters. A 10 x 14 matrix obviously gives greater clarity and definition than a 5 x 7 matrix and many display screens use even greater resolutions. Although both upper case and lower case can be accommodated in a particular size matrix, it is usual to add extra rows for the 'tails' of lower case letters such as g,p,y,j. Different character sets can be displayed using dot matrix representation.

A 5 x 7 Pixel Dot Matrix Forming The Letter 'F'

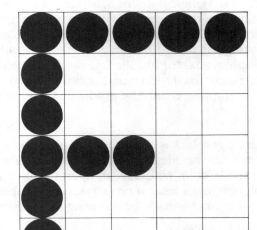

Graphics Display with Bit Mapping

To provide maximum control over the screen display, each pixel can be individually controlled by the programmer. This allows maximum flexibility in the design of individual images. Where image movement is required, in for example computer games, this is achieved in a similar manner to filmed cartoons. Smooth movement is simulated by making minute changes to the shape and location of the image. This requires the high degree of precision available at the individual pixel level. Apart from movement simulation, bit mapping allows the drawing of extremely complex and life-like pictures and is therefore used in the development of, for example, application packages for Computer Aided Design (CAD).

Graphics Standards

A number of graphics standards can be identified. Each is better known by its acronym, shown in brackets.

       (i) Monochrome Graphics Adaptor (MGA);

      (ii) Colour Graphics Adaptor (CGA);

     (iii) Enhanced Graphics Adaptor (EGA);

     (iv) Video Graphics Array (VGA).

The word 'adaptor', used with each standard (apart from VGA) relates to the plug-in card which allows a screen to be set or upgraded to a particular graphics standard.

Monochrome Graphics Adaptor (MGA)

As the name suggests, the MGA standard allows the screen to display monochrome graphics. This can mean white on black, green on black or amber on chocolate. Medium resolution may provide a pixel density of around 320 columns x 200 lines, compared with say, 720 columns x 350 lines for high resolution. Even for word processing, the higher resolution is advisable because the improved clarity of display reduces the likelihood of eye fatigue. Much graphical work, for example that involved with computer-aided design (CAD), benefits from the use of colour and this is made available with CGA, EGA and VGA in varying resolutions. It must be said, however, that what ranks as high resolution today will warrant only medium resolution status in the future.

Colour Graphics

Unlike a monochrome pixel, which is a single point of light, colour pixels consist of a tight group of three dots called a 'triad'. A dot may be red, green or blue and by varying the proportional intensity of each of these primary colours, the full spectrum of colours can be generated. The dots are so close together that they are indistinguishable with the naked eye. The quality of resolution depends on the monitor as well as the graphics adaptor installed. It is not possible, for example, to produce a high resolution colour display on a low resolution monitor, even if a high resolution colour graphics card is installed. Similarly, colour graphics cannot be produced on a monochrome monitor.

Colour Resolution

The sharpness and detail of colour graphics is continually improving, so resolution figures given here only provide comparison between the identified standards. CGA provides a resolution of 320 columns x 200 lines and a palette of 16 colours. EGA can operate with a resolution of 640 columns x 200 lines and a palette of 16 colours (lower resolutions modes are also available). There is no single standard for VGA but a comparison can be made by referring to the following example.

Example of VGA: the Artisan Graphics System.

The monitor is manufactured by Cambridge Computer Graphics and provides a 20 inch (across diagonal) screen with a resolution of 1,024 columns x 768 lines. Up to 256 colours chosen from a palette of over 16 million can be displayed at any one time.

Of course a palette of 16 million colours is probably unnecessary for most applications and is aimed at those involved in the creation of complex graphics and publishing layouts, but the example illustrates the advances made in computer graphics.

Choosing a Graphics Adaptor

If a user wishes to use software for business presentations, Computer Aided Design (CAD), Desk Top Publishing or other special applications, then high quality graphics are desirable. Before making a choice, the prospective purchaser must address several questions:

> (i) Will the graphics standard in use support the graphics capa-
> bilities of the chosen software?

> (ii) Any software which needs CGA, EGA or VGA capabilities will
> not work unless the relevant adaptor card is fitted.

Will the user's monitor support the graphics adaptor?

If the user has already invested in computer hardware for other applications, it is possible that the system's monitor will not support the required graphics adaptor. For example, Standard RGB (red, green, blue) monitors will not support VGA and certain modes of EGA; instead an enhanced RGB monitor is needed.

> (iii) Do any of the envisaged applications packages require differ-
> ent graphics modes?

If so, then the graphics standard should support all required modes and also automatically switch between them under the control of the software packages. The alternative is for the user to key in mode-switching commands.

Downward Compatibility

This refers to a graphics adaptor's facility to support earlier graphics standards. Thus, for example, VGA cards also support EGA and CGA modes. This is obviously important to users who wish to run VGA-supported software but also have older packages which only require EGA or CGA.

Dumb and Intelligent Terminals

A DUMB terminal is one which has no processing power of its own, possibly no storage, and is entirely dependent on a controlling computer. Where a terminal is connected via a telecommunications link, each character is transmitted to the central computer as soon as it is entered via the operator. This makes editing extremely difficult and slow and for this reason, they are not generally used for remote data entry.

An INTELLIGENT terminal has some memory and processing power and as such, allows the operator to store, edit and manipulate data without the support of the computer to which it is connected. The processing facility is provided by an internal processor, usually a microprocessor. Storage is normally in the form of 'buffer' memory in which several lines of text can be held and manipulated before transmission. The facility may also include local backing storage on floppy disk and a printer.

A number of tasks required for text editing involve the use of control codes and these can be built into ROM (Read Only Memory) or magnetic bubble memory, both of which are non-volatile. Typical control codes are those which, via single key-presses, execute functions such as clearing the screen, moving the cursor up or down, and homing the cursor to the top-left of the screen. Function keys for these and other functions are generally specifically marked.

It is also likely that the terminal is programmable, probably in BASIC, thus allowing specific routines to be developed for validation of data.

Microcomputer systems are often used as intelligent terminals.

b. Keyboards

The only standard feature common to all keyboards is the layout of the 26 keys for the letters of the alphabet. The standard stems from the layout of the earliest manual typewriter keyboards and is referred to as the QWERTY layout (the first six alphabetic keys on the top left of the keyboard). There are many other keys with special functions but their location will vary from one keyboard to another.

Function Keys
There are generally ten or twelve of these labelled F1, F2, F3 .... etc. They have no standard meaning, instead being programmable by whichever software package is being used. Thus, for example, pressing F5 in a particular word processing package may delete a complete line of text, whilst in a given spreadsheet package F5 may allow direct transfer to a referenced cell. As part of the user documentation, many packages provide a function key overlay which readily identifies the purpose of each key for that particular package.

Navigation Keys
There are four of these labelled with arrows indicating up, down, left and right; most packages make use of them. In addition, there are keys marked PgUp(page up), PgDn(page down), Home and End which are also used extensively in word processing and other packages where movement about the screen is necessary.

Editing Keys
Three keys are usually available for the deletion and insertion of characters on screen. The destructive backspace moves the cursor to the left rubbing out characters as it goes. The delete (Del) key is used to delete characters to the right of the cursor. Finally, the insert (Ins) key is generally used to allow characters to be inserted within text without overwriting existing characters to the right. This key is often programmed by software packages to fulfil different functions. For example, Framework uses it to allow selection from a menu of instructions from the top of the screen.

Numeric Keys
Apart from the numeric keys located above the alphabetic keys, a separate set is usually provided on the right of the keyboard for users who need to enter a large volume of numeric values. Sometimes, the navigation keys and one or two other special keys also act as numeric keys. This function can be set by pressing a key marked Num Lock.

Control and Alternate Keys

The Control (Ctrl) and Alternate (Alt) keys can each be held down while pressing another key to achieve some special function; the use will vary from one package to another. In combination with the delete (Del) key, IBM microcomputers and 'compatibles' can be re-booted, in other words, restarted as if the machine had been switched off and then on again. The three keys are used in combination to prevent accidental re-booting of the system.

Escape and Break

The Escape (Esc) and Break key are used to interrupt the execution of a process. Most software packages disable them from this purpose and often give the Esc key an alternative function, such as leaving a particular activity within the package.

Many keyboards are detachable, enabling the operator to position it to suit personal comfort. Usually the keyboard remains physically connected via a stretch-coil but a few systems use infra-red in a similar fashion to the remote control unit of a television set or video recorder.

Concept Keyboards

In specialist applications, the standard keyboard is not always the most convenient method of input. In a factory, for example, a limited number of functions may be necessary for the operation of a computerized lathe. These functions can be set out on a touch sensitive pad and clearly marked. This is possible because all inputs are anticipated and the range is small. The operator is saved the trouble of typing in the individual characters which form instructions.

Concept keyboards also have application in education, particularly for the mentally and physically handicapped. Instead of specific functions, interchangeable overlays, which indicate the functions of each area of the keyboard allow the user to design the keyboard to particular specifications. For example, if the responses required by a user are limited to 'yes' and 'no', the overlay is simply divided into two parts, one for each response. The keyboard is housed in a flat, wipe clean, touch sensitive aluminium box. The membrane on which overlays are placed is divided into a matrix of cells, for instance 128 on a 16 x 8 format. The cells have to be programmed to conform to the desired overlay.

c. Alternatives to Keyboards

Two methods of input make use of the screen display itself.

Touch Screen

Touch screen devices allow a screen to be activated by the user touching the screen with a finger. This is particularly useful where a menu of processing options is available on the screen for selection.

Light Pen

A light pen is shaped like a pen and contains a photo-electric or light-sensitive cell in its tip. When the pen is pointed at the screen the light from the screen is detected by the cell and the computer can identify the position of the pen. By 'mapping' the screen to allocate particular functions to particular locations on the screen, the position of the pen indicates a particular function. The light pen enables specific parts of a picture on display to be selected or altered in some way, making it particularly useful for applications such as computer aided design (CAD).

Devices to control cursor movement include the JOYSTICK, the MOUSE and the CROSSHAIR cursor.

Joystick

The joystick is similar to a car's gear lever, except that fine variations in the angle of movement can be achieved. The cursor movement is a reflection of the movement of the joystick in terms of both direction and speed. It is commonly used for computer games and for CAD.

Mouse

The mouse has a roller which dictates cursor movement. The user can move the cursor by moving the mouse across a flat surface. It is very popular with 'user friendly' software which requires the user to select from displayed screen options. A select button is fitted on the mouse to enable the user to choose a particular screen position or function.

Crosshair Cursor

The crosshair cursor has a perspex 'window' with 'cross hairs' rather like a telescopic rifle's sighting mechanism. It can be moved over hard-copy images of maps, or survey photographs and allows precise selection of positions through the crosshair 'window'. The images are digitized into the computer's memory and can then be displayed on the screen for modification. The keyboard or a keypad built into the device can be used to enter additional information, for example to identify rivers or roads on a digitized map.

d. Printers

Printers can be categorized according to SPEED of operation and the QUALITY of print. Printers are also identifiable as either IMPACT or NON-IMPACT devices.

Impact Printers

Impact printing uses a print head to strike an inked ribbon which is located between the print head and the paper. Individual characters can be printed by either a dot-matrix mechanism or by print heads which contain each character as a separate font (solid font type).

Dot Matrix Printers

Operation. Dot matrix printers form characters from a matrix of dots produced by a column of pins in the print head (sometimes the pins may occupy two columns). Each character printed involves incremental movements of the pin column, so that a head using seven columns per character requires seven movements of the pins. The number of pins in the column is one factor determining printing quality. Thus, for example, the most basic of printers provides a nine-pin head, which is insufficient density for high quality printing but is adequate for everyday office data processing. An 18-pin head offers reasonable quality (Near Letter Quality or NLQ) at high speed and the 24-pin (arranged in two columns of 12) provides both high print quality and high speed.

The user should examine the printer specification before making a choice and may need to look at the following elements in particular:

        (i) print quality;

        (ii) print speed;

        (iii) paper-handling facilities;

        (iv) ease of use;

        (v) software package compatibility;

        (vi) graphical output.

Print Quality. Nearly all dot-matrix printers offer two speeds, one for draft and one for Near Letter Quality (NLQ). In NLQ, the printer produces the higher quality by slowing the printing speed and by overtyping. The overtyping is achieved by shifting the location of the printer pins slightly and then reprinting the same character. In draft mode, the print head only makes one pass to print a complete line.

Print Speed. The speed at which the printer operates is measured in characters per second (cps), which varies from printer to printer and according to whether draft or NLQ mode is used. The NLQ mode usually prints at 25 to 30 per cent of the printer's draft speed. Thus, for example, a dot-matrix printer which prints draft quality at 160 cps will usually slow to 30 or 40 cps in NLQ mode. Some dot-matrix printers offer a range of speeds and modes. For example, draft mode which produces legible but rough print at the highest speed, correspondence mode which is suitable for internal office communications and NLQ mode, which is the slowest but produces the highest quality print.

Paper-Handling. Most dot-matrix printers can handle a wide variety of paper media such as multi-part forms and labels, as well as different paper sizes, which can range from A4 to about 18 inches on wide carriage machines. Paper can be fed through, either by a tractor mechanism which is used for continuous stationery, or by friction for single sheets. A single sheet feeder bin can often be purchased to allow automatic paper-feed for multiple-sheet documents. Some printers have a 'paper-park' function which allows single sheet operation without first removing the continuous stationery.

Ease of Use. All dot-matrix printers have small 'dip' switches inside the casing (sometimes accessible through a slot at the back of the printer) for the selection of different printing configurations such as the character set and automatic line feed or suppression. Alteration of print settings can be difficult for the inexperienced user and many machines now offer a front control panel with a small range of alternative print styles. In addition, some printers provide a 'font slot' for the insertion of different 'font cards'. This extends the range of type styles available via the front selection panel.

Software Package Compatibility. Most software packages support a limited number of printers. In addition, some printers have emulation capabilities to 'mimic' the operation of more well-known brands such as Epson. Before purchasing a printer, the user must check that the chosen software supports it.

Graphical Output. Printers which support bit-mapping (software control over individual pins in the matrix head) can produce graphical output. Without colour, pictorial effects can be achieved by double-striking to emphasize some areas of print and by moving the paper in very small increments rather than a line at a time. With a bit mapping facility and a 3-colour ribbon, a variety of colours can be produced by a printer. Colours beyond those directly available can be mixed by using slight paper shifts and double striking to mix new colours. This method makes use of software control to achieve colour output comparable with more expensive multi-colour printers.

Solid Font Printing

A solid font head uses a separate font for each character and character sets have to altered by changing the head.

Because they form a solid image, they have until recently, provided a better quality of print than the dot-matrix type. There are a number of types, three of which are described below.

Daisy-wheel Head

As the name suggests, character fonts are attached to 'petals' on a central wheel which has to revolve to place a particular character in the print position. Inevitably, the considerable movement required between each character print means that daisy-wheel printers operate relatively slowly, about 30 to 60 characters per second. The quality of print is very high which makes it a popular device for the production of, for example, legal documents and other output where image is vital. Amongst impact printers, the daisy wheel is the noisiest and to be tolerable in an office environment, should be fitted with an acoustic hood to help deaden some of the sound. Recently, a heavier daisy wheel has been produced which is much quieter.

The daisy wheel's inherent disadvantages and the improvements in other printing technologies are likely to hasten its demise.

Cylinder Print Head

This type is only used on teletypewriter or teleprinter terminals and is consequently becoming uncommon. A teletypewriter has a keyboard and printer only and although largely replaced by the VDU, is still used for telex communications. The cylinder print head has 64 symbols embossed on a cylinder. Lower-case characters are not provided. An individual character is selected through a clockwise or anti-clockwise turn and an appropriate vertical movement of the head. Impact with the ribbon is achieved by a hammer which strikes the back of the print head whenever a character is to be printed.

Golf-ball Head

The golf-ball head also has characters embossed on its surface but it differs from the cylinder print head in three main ways. Firstly, the spherical shape accommodates a wider range of characters than the cylinder shape. Secondly, different character sets can be obtained by changing the print head. Thirdly, the head is made to strike the ribbon by a cam mechanism. No hammer strikes the head. Individual characters are obtained by the rotation and tilting of the head.

Dot-matrix printers are much faster than solid-font printers. Speeds of 100 to 300 characters per second are common for low-speed, impact dot matrix printers.

All the printers described above are CHARACTER printers in that they print a single character at a time. Faster printing can be achieved by LINE and PAGE printers

Line Printers

A line printer prints a complete line of characters, rather than in the serial fashion used by character printers.

Two types of line printer are described here, the BARREL or DRUM printer and the CHAIN printer.

Barrel Printer

The barrel printer has a band with a complete set of characters at each print position. Each print position has a hammer to impact the print ribbon against the paper. There are usually 132 print positions on the barrel. The mechanism is illustrated below.

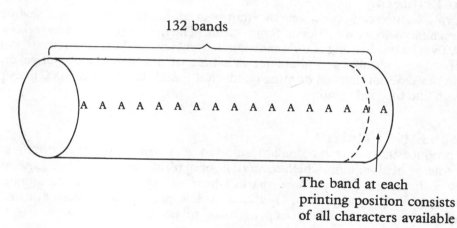

132 bands

The band at each
printing position consists
of all characters available

One complete revolution of the barrel exposes all the characters to each print position. Therefore a complete line can be printed in one revolution. The characters on the barrel are arranged so that all characters of the same type are in the same horizontal position. Thus, in a line of print, any required As can be printed, then Bs and so on, until the complete line is printed. The barrel revolves continuously during printing, the paper being fed through and the process repeated for each line of print. Typical printing speeds are 100 to 400 lines per minute.

Chain Printer

The chain printer mechanism is illustrated on the following page.

Several complete sets of characters are held on a continuous chain which moves horizontally across the paper. The ribbon is situated between the chain and the paper and an individual hammer is located at each of the 132 print positions. A complete line can be printed as one complete set of characters passes across the paper. Thus, in one pass as many lines can be printed as there are sets of characters in the chain. Printing speeds are higher than is possible for barrel printers.

Chain Printer

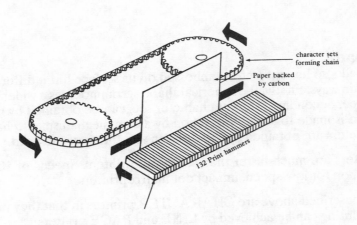

Line printers are expensive compared with character printers but may well be necessary where large volume output is required. Printing speeds of up to 3000 lines per minute are achieved with impact line printers. Even higher speeds are possible with non-impact printers.

Non-Impact Printers

Most non-impact printers use dot-matrix heads. They do not require mechanical hammers and print heads do not strike the paper. A variety of printers are available using a wide range of technologies. The most popular are as follow.

Thermal Printers

Characters are burned onto heat-sensitive thermographic paper. The paper is white and develops colour when heated above a particular temperature. The heat is generated by rods in the dot-matrix print head. By selective heating of rods, individual characters can be formed from the matrix. Printing can be carried out serially, one character at a time or, through the use of several heads, on a line-by-line basis. Serial thermal printing is slow but speeds in excess of 1000 lines per minute are possible with line thermal printing.

Electrosensitive Printers

This type produce characters in a similar fashion to the thermal printer except that the paper used has a thin coating of aluminium which covers a layer of black, blue or red dye. Low voltage electrical discharges in the matrix rods produce sparks which selectively remove the aluminium coating to reveal the layer of dye underneath. Operated as line printers with heads at each print position, printing speeds in excess of 3000 lines per minute are achieved.

Laser Printers

Laser printers use a combination of two technologies, electro-photographic printing used in photo-copying and high intensity lasers. A photoconductive drum is initially charged and then a high intensity laser beam selectively discharges areas on the drum. As with photocopiers, toner material is spread over the surface to form an ink image. This is then transferred to the paper and made permanent through heating. Achieving print speeds of 21,000 lines per minute, the laser printer is used in very large systems requiring exceptionally high speed output.

Effectively, complete pages are printed at one time so they come under the heading of PAGE printers.

Laser Printers and Microcomputers

Laser printers used to be too costly for use in a microcomputer environment, but with rapidly falling prices, they are providing some competition for the dot matrix printers. Although still more costly than dot matrix printers, laser printers offer greater speed and quality.

Printing Quality. The quality is determined largely by the resolution or dot density forming each character. A commonly used resolution is 300 dots per inch (dpi), which provides a printing quality superior to most dot matrix printers, but still not quite up to daisywheel standards. Machines offering 600 dpi are coming onto the market and these will produce printing quality to match the daisywheel.

Printing Speed. The printing speeds of laser printers are far beyond anything possible with any dot matrix printer and for this reason are referred to as page printers. Printing speeds range from 6 pages per minute (ppm) to 26 ppm. Its high speed makes the laser printer highly suitable as a printer server to be shared by a number of microcomputers in a network.

Ink Jet Printers

Ink jet printers spray high-speed streams of electrically charged ink droplets from individual nozzles in the matrix head onto the paper to form characters. Many will hold colour cartridges to produce excellent colour output.

Ink jet printers provide a possible alternative to the laser printer.

Case Study: The Hewlett Packard (HP) Deskjet

The HP Deskjet offers three possible print resolutions, 75, 150 and 300 dots per inch (dpi). At 300 dpi, which matches the resolution of laser printers, the Deskjet can produce near-typeset quality fonts. The noise level is extremely low but its operational speed is about 2 pages per minute (ppm) in draft mode and 1ppm in letter-quality mode. The slowest laser printer operates at about 6ppm.

The ink jet printer cannot match the laser printer for speed but it provides a possible alternative for users whose printing requirements are not satisfied by any printer in the dot matrix impact range.

Summary of Printers

Generally speaking, the smaller, low speed, character printers are of use with microcomputer systems, but the increasing popularity of such systems has demanded increased sophistication in small printers. Features which have improved printing speeds include BI-DIRECTIONAL printing (printing in two directions) and LOGIC-SEEKING which allows the printer to cut short a traverse across the paper if only a few characters are required on a line.

The most popular printers for microcomputers are, impact dot-matrix, daisy-wheel, electro-sensitive, ink jet and laser.

e. Data Capture Devices

Source data is normally collected in human-readable form. For example, customer orders are recorded on order forms and weekly pay details may be recorded on time sheets. Prior to processing, such data has to be translated into machine-sensible form and this usually involves a keying operation. There are a number of DATA CAPTURE devices available which allow data to be collected in a printed or hand-written form directly readable by a computer input device.

Optical Character Readers (OCR)

OCRs are designed to read stylized characters which are also readable by humans. There are a number of designs for such characters but any individual design is known as the character FONT. There are a number of industry standard fonts and an example selection from an optical character set is shown on the next page.

The OCR reflects light off the characters and converts them into digital patterns for comparison with the stored character set. Originally, a highly stylized appearance was preferred to aid machine recognition but some OCRs can read the character sets of popular makes of office typewriter. Ideally, OCRs should be able to read any characters but the wider the range of styles that need to be read, the more difficult becomes the recognition process. In some applications, a restricted character set of, perhaps numerals and certain alphabetic characters may suffice and the reading process becomes quicker and more accurate. Nevertheless, large OCRs are capable of reading several character sets comprising more than 300 characters.

```
ABCDEFGHIJKLMN
OPQRSTUVWXYZ
1234567890.
```

The reading of hand-printed characters presents particular problems because of the almost infinite variation of printing styles. Recognition is possible provided that the person preparing the data has a visual guide of the preferred style. The character set will usually be limited to numerals and a few alphabetic characters.

Artificial intelligence techniques are being applied to OCRs to allow the 'learning' of new character sets.

Applications of OCR

OCR is often used to capture sales data at the point-of-sale (POS). A POS terminal is essentially an electronic cash register linked to a computer or with storage of its own. Data captured at the terminal can, for example, be sent to update computer files. Sometimes POS registers have direct-access memory to hold product prices and descriptions, so that the details can be printed on the customer receipt. An OCR-character-coded price label, attached to each product, can be scanned with a wand (light pen) or laser 'gun'.

Optical Mark Readers (OMR)

An OMR is designed to read marks placed in preset positions on a document. The document is preprinted and the values which can be entered are limited as each value is represented by, for example, a box in a certain position. Thus, a suitable application for OMR is a multi-choice exam paper, where the answer to each question has to be indicated by a pencil mark in one of several boxes after the question. The figure on the next page illustrates such a form:

The OMR scans the document for boxes containing pencil marks and thus identifies the values selected.

Optical mark readers can read up to 10,000 A4 documents per hour.

Bar Code Readers

The bar code is also an optical code which is normally read by a light pen. The code makes use of a series of black bars of varying thickness. The gaps between each bar also vary. These bars and gaps are used to represent numeric data. The values represented are often printed underneath in decimal form.

Bar codes are commonly used to store a variety of data such as price and stock code concerning products in shops and supermarkets. A sticker with the relevant bar code (itself produced by computer) is attached to each product. Sometimes, the check-out will have a built-in scanner station over which the goods pass. This is convenient if packages are of regular shape but soft packages with creases may cause problems for the scanner. In such cases, the light pen or wand provides a more practical solution. By using the data from the code, the cash register can identify the item, look up its latest price and print the information on the customer's receipt.

Another useful application is for the recording of library issues. A bar code sticker is placed inside the book cover and at the time of issue or return it can be scanned and the library stock record updated. By providing each library user with a bar coded library card, the information regarding an individual who is borrowing a book can be linked with the book's details at the time of borrowing.

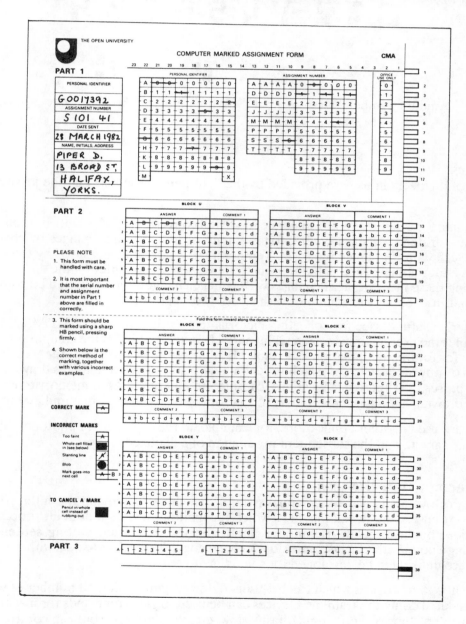

Magnetic Ink Character Reader (MICR)

This particular device is employed almost exclusively by the banking industry, where it is used for sorting and processing cheques in large volumes. The millions of cheques which pass through the London Clearing System could not possibly be sorted and processed without the use of MICRs.

Highly stylized characters, usually of the E13B font illustrated below, are printed along the bottom of the cheques by a special printer, using ink containing iron oxide. The MICR first magnetizes the characters as the cheque passes through and then decodes them by induced voltage signals. A high degree of reliability and accuracy is possible, partly because of the stylized font, but more importantly, because the characters are not affected by dirty marks. This is obviously important when cheques may pass through several hands before reaching their destination. Such marks may cause problems for an optical character reader.

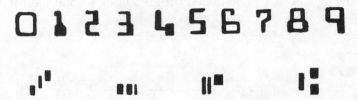

Amount symbol   Dash symbol   "On-us" symbol   Sorting Code Symbol

Digitizers

Examples of digitizers in use are provided by the light pen, the mouse and the joystick, described earlier.

Another name for a digitizer is an Analogue to Digital converter (ADC). Data is often not in digital format but is instead a measurement, for example, of temperature changes or changes in light intensity. Such data is in analogue form. Temperature is normally measured by the movement of mercury in a thermometer and light intensity by movement of a pointer on the dial of a light meter. By reflecting these measurement changes with voltage changes, they can then be converted to the digital signals useable by the computer with an ADC or digitizer.

A particularly useful device for collecting pictorial data is the GRAPHICS TABLET. A pen-like stylus enables the user to 'draw' on the tablet and reflect the results on the computer screen or store the results for future manipulation. The tablet is addressable by the computer through a matrix of thousands of tiny 'dots', each of which reflect a binary 1 or 0. When a line is drawn on the tablet, the stylus passes over these dot locations, causing the binary values in memory to change. Thus a particular drawing has a particular binary format which can be stored, manipulated or displayed.

Digitizers are used in other applications, for example, in the capturing of photographic images, via a 'digitizing' camera and the subsequent production of a digitized image.

Voice Recognition Devices

Human speech varies in accent, personal style of speech and pitch and the interpretation of the spoken word makes the development of voice recognition devices a difficult process. In normal conversation, humans make assumptions about the listener, often cutting sentences short or emphasizing a point with a facial expression. Voice recognition devices to deal with complete human language are unlikely to be developed for some time to come.

There are however, devices which can be 'trained' to recognize a limited number of words spoken by the individual doing the training. Devices can be used to give commands for machinery control, for example, 'up', 'down', 'left', 'right', 'fast', 'slow' etc. Paralysed persons can control a wheelchair or lighting and heating through a voice recognition device controlled by a microprocessor.

f. Special-Purpose Output Devices

Computer Output Microform (COM) Recorders

COM recorders record information from computer storage onto microfilm or microfiche. Microfilm is a continuous reel, whereas, microfiche is a sheet of film with a matrix of squares or pages. Either form can be viewed with a magnifying viewer. COM can result in large savings in paper costs, storage space and handling. For example, a 4 inch x 6 inch microfiche sheet can store the equivalent of 270 printed pages.

COM is particularly useful for the storage of large amounts of information which do not need to be updated frequently.

Graph Plotters
A plotter is a device designed to produce charts, drawings, maps and other forms of graphical information on paper. There are a variety of methods for producing the image.

Pen Plotters
Pen plotters use an ink pen or pens to create images on paper. There are two types:

      (i) Flatbed plotters;

      (ii) Drum Plotters.

A FLATBED plotter is illustrated below.

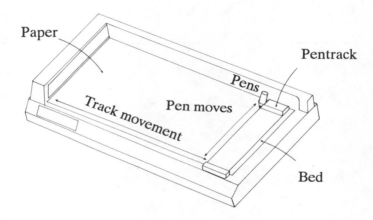

It looks like a drafting board with pens mounted on a carriage which moves along guide tracks. The paper is placed on the 'bed'. The pens can be raised or lowered as the image being created requires and different coloured pens can be brought into use at various stages of the process. Drawing movements are executed by movement of the carriage along the tracks and by the pens along the carriage. The size of paper which can be accommodated is limited by the size of the plotter 'bed', but this can be extremely large.

A DRUM plotter has a different drawing mechanism. Instead of the paper remaining still, it moves to produce one of the lateral movements whilst the pens move to execute the other movements. In order to control the paper, the drum plotter uses sprocket wheels to interlock with the paper. The main advantage of the drum plotter is its ability to handle large sheets of paper. The operation of a drum plotter is illustrated on the following page.

Electrostatic Plotters
The electrostatic plotter is relatively fast, but the output is of poorer quality than that produced by pen plotters.

Voice Output Devices
Voice synthesis is still in its infancy, in that the complexities of human speech have yet to be mastered satisfactorily. There is a tendency for such devices to become confused between the pronunciation of words such as 'though' and 'plough'. Speech ROM 'chips' are available for many microcomputer systems. Educational applications include 'speak and spell' and arithmetic. Large scale application

is possible where the range of output can be anticipated, for example, stocks and share prices, railway timetables, speaking clock etc. Such services may be provided via an answerphone service.

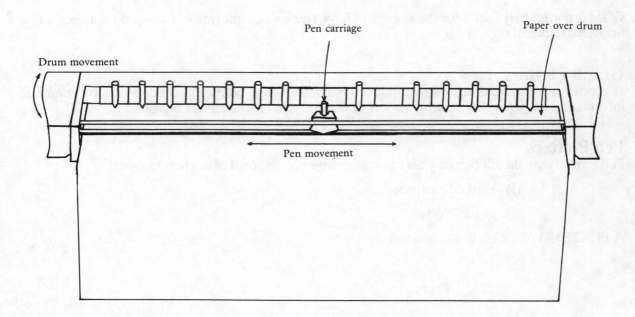

Assignment

Gotta Lot of Bottle

Fine Wines Limited is a medium sized company with a chain of off-licence shops in the Somerset area. Its Registered Office and central warehouse are in Bath. A minicomputer is used for most of the company's accounting and administrative applications. A telecommunications link between warehouse and main office allows the updating of stock files via VDU terminals at the warehouse. In addition, a printer at the warehouse is used to print details of orders from the various shops in the off-licence chain. Each week, the company's delivery lorries deliver the goods ordered by each shop manager a week previously. At the same time, the driver collects the completed order forms for the following week's delivery. The drivers return the order forms to the Bath office where they are keyed in and processed.

You are employed by Compudata, a software house based in Bristol as a trainee systems analyst. Fine Wines Ltd. have approached Compudata regarding the improvement of the order collection procedures. It is apparent that the data collection procedure could be automated because the Fine Wines order forms are designed with pre-printed item lists and choices of quantities which can be ordered. In other words, all the shop manager has to do is tick chosen quantity boxes next to selected items in the list. Your team leader, Ken Barlow, has given you the task of preparing a preliminary report for presentation to Fine Wines Limited, outlining the use of Optical Mark Reading (OMR) techniques to automate order collection.

Tasks

1. Prepare a preliminary report for Fine Wines Ltd., outlining the OMR proposals and briefly explaining the principles of the technique. In addition explain how the present design of forms may be utilized and how they must be completed by the shop managers. Identify any extra equipment which needs to be purchased.

2. In order to give Fine Wines Limited some element of choice, briefly outline any possible alternatives they may adopt for their order collection procedures.

Assignment   A Mountain of Paper

Everest Equipment Limited is a medium-sized company, based in Swansea and specializing in the manufacture of clothing and accessories for walking and climbing enthusiasts. The company has a factory on the outskirts of the town, where most of the goods are manufactured. The clothing and accessories produced are sold to specialist retail shops located throughout the United Kingdom and about half of their production is for export. The company employs 20 office staff and 105 factory staff and the working atmosphere is very relaxed and friendly. The IBM mini-computer system is used for all the main information processing applications, including production control. Large volume hard copy is required on a number of occasions and the present line printer is considered to be too slow; in any case it is due for renewal. The company also makes use of a number of microcomputer systems for costing and planning purposes. It is sometimes desirable to produce high quality graphical output for presentation at Board Meetings and for reports to shareholders. The company runs a thriving staff social club and produces its own staff magazine.

Task

You are employed as a trainee systems analyst/programmer by the company, and Judith Conlon, who has overall responsibility for systems development, has asked you to research the possibilities regarding the selection of new hard copy output devices, which may be used by the mini and microcomputer systems. The report should outline the types of device which may be considered for high volume text and/or high quality graphical output.

You should consider the benefits and drawbacks of each system selected and take into account their relative costs. Make your own argued recommendations.

Developmental Task

Visit an exhibition which includes demonstrations of the latest printing technologies or, if this is not feasible, research computing magazines and journals for descriptions of such equipment.

Chapter 6

☐ COMPUTER PROCESSING METHODS

Information Needs

There are many different methods of processing information by computer. A wide range of computer hardware and software is available for such processing. The different types of hardware and software are considered in some detail in Chapters 5 and 11 respectively, but this chapter examines how the needs of an organization determine the hardware and software which will be used, as well as the methods of processing employed. It begins with a brief review of the computer systems available before considering the methods of processing appropriate to different computerized information systems.

Types of Computer

Broadly, computers fall into 3 main categories and although the divisions are not always absolutely clear, they provide convenient labels to identify different systems. These are:

    (a)   Mainframe Computers

    (b)   Mini Computers

    (c)   Microcomputers

Each has particular features which will broadly identify a computer as belonging to one of the above types. However, computer technology is advancing so rapidly that some of the divisions between them begin to blur. For example, there are now powerful microcomputer systems (often referred to as super-micros) which far exceed the power and flexibility of earlier generation minicomputer systems.

a. Mainframe Computers

The mainframe computer has:

    (i) Large main memory;

    (ii) A very fast CPU and operating system software, which together allow many users and applications to be supported at apparently the same time;

    (iii) Facilities for large numbers of both magnetic tape and magnetic disk storage units;

(iv) The capability of supporting a large number and variety of
input and output devices.

Such computers are commonly used by large national and multi-national organizations such as
banks, airlines and oil companies.

b. Mini Computers

The mini computer is technically very similar to the mainframe with the following differences:

(i) It usually only has magnetic disk storage;

(ii) The main input/-output peripherals tend to be Visual Display
Units (VDUs).

Medium-sized organizations may use minicomputers for their main processing applications. Larger
organizations may apply them to Front End Processing (FEP). Employed in this way, a mini
computer handles a mainframe's communications traffic with remote terminals or other computers,
leaving the mainframe free to handle the main information processing tasks.

c. Microcomputers

The microcomputer is the smallest in the range and was first developed when the Intel Corporation
succeeded in incorporating the main functional parts of a computer on a single 'chip' using
Integrated Circuits (IC) on silicon. Subsequently, the technique of Large Scale Integration (LSI)
further increased the number of electronic circuits which could be packed onto one 'chip'. LSI has
been superseded by Very Large Scale Integration (VLSI) which packs even more circuitry onto a
single chip, thus further increasing the power and storage capacity of microcomputers and computers generally. This type of computer storage is known as Metal Oxide Semiconductor storage
(MOS) and has completely replaced the 'core store' used in earlier mainframe computers.

The miniaturization of the hardware, the vast increase in computer power and storage capacity, and
the drastic reduction in cost make it possible for small organizations to afford computer facilities.

Microcomputers have the following characteristics:

(i) Microcomputers were initially stand-alone units allowing a
single user to run a single application at one time;

(ii) Increasingly common is the multi-user system where a number
of microcomputers can be linked together or 'networked'. Such
networks often share hard disk storage with a storage capacity
measured in many millions of characters and allow different
users to run different applications at the same time;

(iii) Generally the main input/output is carried out via a keyboard
and monitor screen, although other devices such as light pens,
mice, concept keyboards and graph plotters can be used.

The range of microcomputer software is now extremely wide and the quality generally very high.
There are software packages available for most business applications. One area of recent rapid
growth has been in the development of graphics-based applications and most popular applications
software can now be operated via a graphical user interface and a 'mouse' (Chapter 5 Peripherals).
Many microcomputers are now sufficiently powerful to allow extremely sophisticated Computer
Aided Design (CAD) work, which until recently was only possible on a mini or mainframe computer
system. Further classifications of computer systems are given in Chapter 3 (Computer Systems).

Methods of Processing

There are three main types of information processing systems:

(a) Batch Processing;

(b)   On-Line Processing;

(c)   Database systems.

a. Batch Processing Systems

Such systems process 'batches' of data at regular intervals. The data is usually in large volumes and of identical type. Examples of such data are customer orders, current weekly payroll details and stock issues or receipts. Although associated with large organizations using mainframe or minicomputer systems, the technique can be used by a small business using a microcomputer.

The procedure can be illustrated with the example of payroll, which is a typical application for batch processing. Each pay date, whether it is every week or every month, the payroll details, such as hours worked, overtime earned or sickness days claimed, are gathered for each employee and processed in batches against the payroll master file. The computer then produces payslips for all employees in the company.

A major feature of this and similar applications is that a large percentage of the payroll records in the master file are processed during the payroll 'run'. This percentage is known as the 'Hit Rate'. In general high 'hit rate' processing is suitable for batch processing. If, as is usual, the master file is organized sequentially, then the transaction file will be sorted into the same sequence as the master file. In Chapter 4 it is explained that the sorting of transactions is essential if the master file does not allow direct access (as is the case for magnetic tape files).

The batch processing method closely resembles manual methods of data processing, in that data on transactions is collected together into batches, sent to the computer centre, sorted into the order of the master file and processed. Such systems are known as 'traditional' data processing systems. There is normally an intermediate stage in the process when the data must be encoded 'off-line'. This means that the data is transferred onto tape or disk. Such encoding may be carried out using another computer, such as in 'key-to-disk' systems (Chapter 8 Management Information Services), but the operation is carried out without the use of the main computer system.

A disadvantage of batch processing is the delay of often hours, or even days, between collecting the transactions and receiving the results of processing. This disadvantage has to be borne in mind when an organization is considering whether or not batch processing is suitable for a particular application.

Conversely batch processing has the advantage of providing many opportunities for controlling the accuracy of data and thus is commonly used when the immediate updating of files is not crucial.

The accuracy controls used in batch and other processing methods are explained in detail in Chapter 7.

b. On-Line Processing Systems

If a peripheral, such as a Visual Display Unit or keyboard, is 'on-line', it is under the control of the Central Processing Unit (CPU) of the computer.

On-line processing systems therefore, are those where all peripherals in use are connected to the CPU of the main computer. Transactions can be keyed in directly.

The main advantage of an on-line system is the reduction in time between the collection and processing of data.

It is important to note that on-line systems can also be used for batch processing, although the stages of intermediate encoding and sorting transactions are eliminated.

There are two main methods of on-line processing:

(i)   Real-Time Processing;

(ii) Time- Share Processing.

Real-Time processing

Process Control in Real-time.   Real-time processing originally referred only to process control systems where, for example, the temperature of a gas furnace is monitored and controlled by a computer. The computer, via an appropriate sensing device, responds immediately to the boiler's variations outside pre-set temperature limits, by switching the boiler on and off to keep the temperature within those limits.

Real-time processing is now used in everyday consumer goods. This has come about because of the development of 'the computer on a chip', more properly called the microprocessor. An important example of the use of the microprocessor is the Engine Management System, which is now standard on an increasing range of cars. A car's engine performance can be monitored and controlled, by sensing and immediately responding to changes in such factors as air temperature, ignition timing or engine load. Further examples of the use of microprocessors can be found on the automated production lines of engineering works and car plants where operations requiring fine engineering control can be carried out by Computer Numerical Controlled (CNC) machines.

The important feature common to all these applications is that the speed of the computer allows almost immediate response to external changes.

Information Processing in Real-time

To be acceptable as a real-time information processing system, the 'response-time' (that is the time between the entry of a transaction or enquiry at a VDU terminal,the processing of the data and the computer's response) must meet the needs of the user. The delay or response time may vary from a fraction of a second to 2-3 seconds depending on the nature of the transaction and the size of the computer. Any delay beyond these times would generally be unacceptable and would indicate the need for the system to be updated.

There are two types of information processing systems which can be operated in real-time. These are:

> (i) Transaction Processing;
>
> (ii) Information Storage/Retrieval

Transaction Processing. This type of system is one which handles clearly defined transactions one at a time. Each transaction is processed completely, including the updating of files, before the next transaction is dealt with. The amount of data input for each transaction is small and is usually entered on an 'interactive' basis via a VDU. Interactive means that the user's communication with the computer is carried out by question and answer. In this way, the user can enter queries via the keyboard and receive a response, or the computer can display a prompt on the screen to which the user responds. Such 'conversations' are usually heavily structured and in a fixed format and so do not allow users to ask any question they wish.

A typical example of transaction processing is provided by an airline booking system. The following procedures describe a client's enquiry for a seat reservation:

> (i) A prospective passenger provides the booking clerk with infor-
>   mation regarding his/her flight requirements;
>
> (ii) Following prompts on the screen, the clerk keys the details into
>   the system so that a check can be made on the availability of
>   seats;
>
> (iii) Vacancies appear on the screen and the client can confirm the
>   booking;
>
> (iv) Confirmation of the reservation is keyed into the system,
>   usually by a single key press and the flight seating records are
>   immediately updated;
>
> (v) Passenger details (such as name, address etc.) can now be en-
>   tered.

Such a system needs to be real-time to avoid the possibility of two clients booking the same seat, on the same flight and at the same time, at different booking offices.

Information Storage/Retrieval. This type of system differs from transaction processing in that, although the information is updated in real-time, the number of updates and the number of sources of updating is relatively small.

Consider, for example, the medical records system in a hospital. A record is maintained for each patient currently undergoing treatment in the hospital. Medical staff require the patient's medical history to be available at any time and the system must also have a facility for entering new information as the patient undergoes treatment in hospital. Sources of information are likely to include a doctor, nurses and perhaps a surgeon and new entries probably do not number more than one or two per day.

This is an entirely different situation from an airline booking system where the number of entries for one flight record may be 200-300 and entries could be made from many different booking offices throughout the world.

Time-Share Processing

The term 'time sharing' refers to the activity of the Central Processing Unit (CPU) in allocating 'slices' of its time to a number of users who are given access to a central computer, normally via Visual Display Units (VDUs).

The aim of the system is to give each user a good 'response time' - no more than 2 seconds. These systems are commonly used where a number of users require computer time for different information processing tasks. The CPU 'time slices' are allocated and controlled by a Time-share Operating System. The CPU is able to operate at such speed that, provided the system is not overloaded by too many users, each user has the impression that he or she is the sole user of the system.

A particular computer system will be designed to support a maximum number of user terminals. If the number is exceeded or the applications being run on the system are 'heavy' on CPU time the response time will become lengthy and unacceptable. Time-share systems are possible because of the extreme speed of the CPU in comparison with peripheral devices such as keyboards, VDU screens and printers. Most information processing tasks consist largely of input and output operations which do not occupy the CPU, leaving it free to do any processing required on other users' tasks.

c. Database Systems

Databases are based on the idea that a common 'pool' of data, with a minimum of duplicated data items, can be organized in such a way that all user requirements can be satisfied. Therefore, instead of each department or functional area within an organization keeping and maintaining its own files, where there are subjects of common interest, they are grouped to form a 'subject' database. Database systems are available for mainframe, mini and microcomputer systems.

The Physical and Logical Database

A database has to satisfy many users' differing information needs, generally through specially written applications programs. Because of this, it is often necessary to add further data items to satisfy changes in one or more user's needs. The software which controls the database must relate to the data at a data item level rather than at record level because one programmer's LOGICAL record requirements may contain some data items which are also required for another programmer's logical record description. The physical database must allow for both. It must be possible for data items to be connected into a variety of logical record forms.

Data Independence

In order that the physical database can be changed as necessary to accommodate user requirements, without the need to alter all applications programs (as is necessary with, for example, a COBOL program - if a file is changed, then any program accessing the file needs to be changed), the way the data is PHYSICALLY stored on the storage medium should be INDEPENDENT of the LOGICAL record structures required by applications programs.

Data Duplication

The fact that a database provides a common source of information for a number of user areas may suggest that each data item need only appear once. Although this is generally true, some data items need to be duplicated in order to establish necessary LOGICAL relationships between different records. Such limited duplication of data items is termed CONTROLLED REDUNDANCY.

A simple example will illustrate the need for some data duplication in a particular type of database system which is controlled by a Relational Database Management System.

Example of LOGICAL Data Structures in a RELATIONAL Database

The data is set up in table form and the example shows two, one for JOB and the other for EMPLOYEE:

JOB

Job Ref	Job Title	Department	Grade	Salary
P23MIS	Programmer	MIS	2	12000
A32ACC	Accountant	Finance	3	13000
A14ACC	Accounts Clerk	Finance	1	6200
S24SAL	Sales Clerk	Sales	2	6700

EMPLOYEE

Employee Ref No.	Name	Address	Job Code
12345	Jones, P.	12 The Grove	P23MIS
32453	Wilkins, J.	13 Daly Street	A14ACC
23413	Herbert, R.	10 Dunn Avenue	P23MIS
15893	Fender, T.	6 Henley Close	S24SAL
56990	Harris, B.	5 Fairways Drive	A32ACC
99251	Parker, N.	123 Thompson Road	A14ACC

It can be seen that the Job Ref in JOB and the Job Code in EMPLOYEE are, in essence, the same data item type, except that they are given different names. These duplicate data items can be used by the programmer to establish relationships between the data in each table. To discover, for example, which employees hold grade 2 Programmer posts, the Job Ref P23MIS could be used to retrieve the information from the EMPLOYEE table, namely Jones P., and Herbert R.

Creating the Database

A special language called a DATA DESCRIPTION LANGUAGE (DDL) allows the database to be created and changed and the logical data structures to be defined.

Manipulating the Database

A DATA MANIPULATION LANGUAGE (DML) enables the contents of the database to be altered by adding, updating or deleting records. This language is used by programmers to develop applications programs for users of the database.

Logical Views of Data

Different users may have different LOGICAL views of the same data. To illustrate this, consider the telephone number of a dentist. To his patients, the telephone number is that of their dentist. To the dentist's bank manager, it is the telephone number of a customer. It is the same data, but different people have different views of it.

To illustrate this idea further, here is another example. Consider the following customer order form:

HAWKINS SUPPLIES LTD.

Customer Order Form

Date: 3rd January 1987

Order No: 365746

Customer Name:
P. Jones Ltd
32 Slater Road
Newtown
NP3 4AS

Customer Account No: 13321

Item Code	Description	Quantity	Unit Price	Cost
AB312	Baked Beans 500g	35	0.20	7.00
AB316	Spaghetti 350g	20	0.25	5.00
				12.00
			VAT 15%	1.80
			Total	13.80

The first line (Item Code AB312) on the order form gives a quantity of 35 x Baked Beans 500g. The information may be required for different purposes by different users. In addition, each user department has a different 'key' to the information. The key will be one of the unique values which appear on the order form. They are:

Customer Account No. - which identifies the customer. Each customer is given a unique Account Number, so that it can be used to trace information on any orders relating to the customer in question;

Order No. - which identifies a particular order (each order must relate to only ONE customer);

Item Code. Each order will have a number of order lines but any item code will only appear ONCE on an order.

The information required is the Quantity (35) on the first order line of the order form. It may be required in the following ways:

    (a)   The Sales department (which knows the Order No) needs the information because of a customer query.

    (b)   The warehouse (which knows the Item Code) wishes to check stock issues.

    (c)   The Accounts department (which knows the Customer Account No.) needs the information (together with the rest of the information on the order) to produce an invoice.

The data must be structured so that each stock item quantity may be easily accessed when any of these departments require it.

Accessing a Database with Applications Programs

Because different user departments have different information requirements, there is a need for different Applications Programs. These are written by programmers using a Data Manipulation Language (DML). Applications programs allow the computer to be used to process data for particular purposes, for example, the production of payslips, invoices etc..

The following diagram illustrates this in simplified form:

An Overview of a Database System

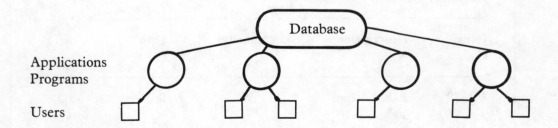

It should be noticed that two or more users may use the same application program.

Database Storage

Because the database must allow for various user applications programs accessing it at the same time, direct access storage must be used. There are many ways of physically organizing the data which are beyond the scope of this text, but whatever method is used it must allow for any variety of logical structures needed by applications programs.

To illustrate the variations in logical file organization, consider a personnel file with the following data item types in each record.

Employee No	Name	Salary

The Salaries Department may require the file in the sequence of the Employee No., whereas the Personnel Department may require the records in alphabetical order by Name.

The applications programmer does not need to know how the data is physically stored. His knowledge of the data held in the database is restricted to the logical view he requires for the program.

The complete or Global logical database is termed the SCHEMA.

The restricted or Local logical views provided for different applications programs are SUBSCHEMAS. (see next page)

Database Management Systems (DBMS)

In order that each application program may only access the data which it needs for processing or retrieval (in other words that data which is defined in its subschema), a Database Management System (software) controls the database and prevents accidental or deliberate corruption of data by other applications programs.

An application program cannot access the database without the DBMS. The following diagram illustrates the relationship between users, application programs, the Database Management System and the database:

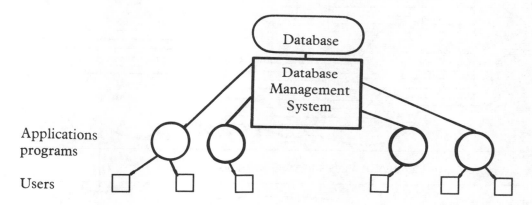

A database management system, therefore, is a piece of software which has the following functions:

1.   It is the common link between all applications programs and the database.

2.   It facilitates the use and organization of a database, and protects the database from accidental or deliberate corruption.

3.   It restricts a programmer's logical view of the database to those items of data which are to be used in the applications program he is writing.

Case Study - CODASYL Database Management System

One of the alternative approaches to the Relational method is one based on SET theory and developed by the Codasyl Committee, which also monitors standards in the COBOL programming language. The following diagram of a Codasyl logical SCHEMA (shown later) serves to illustrate this method of database organization:

DIFFERING VIEWS OF DATA

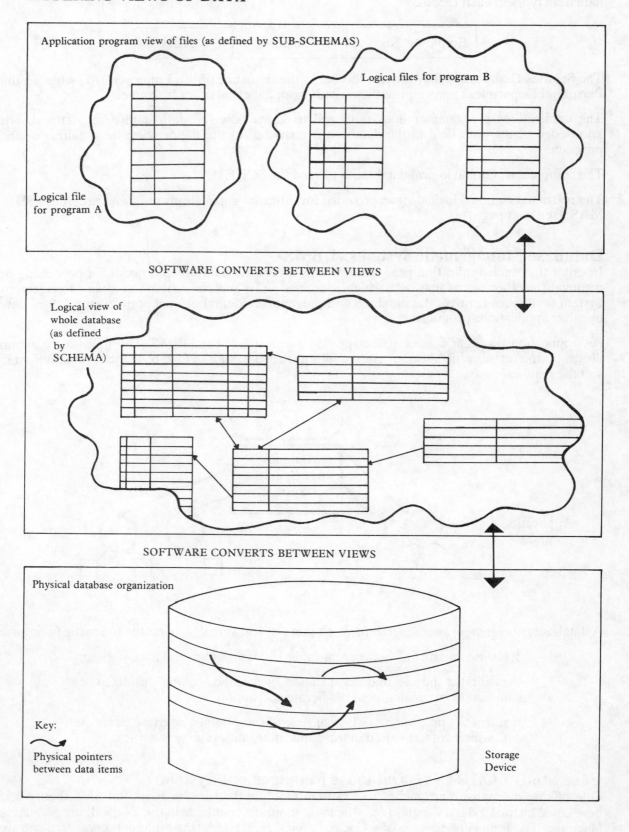

Application program view of files (as defined by SUB-SCHEMAS)

Logical files for program B

Logical file
for program A

SOFTWARE CONVERTS BETWEEN VIEWS

Logical view of
whole database
(as defined
by
SCHEMA)

SOFTWARE CONVERTS BETWEEN VIEWS

Physical database organization

Key:

Physical pointers
between data items

Storage
Device

Codasyl Database Schema for Large Company

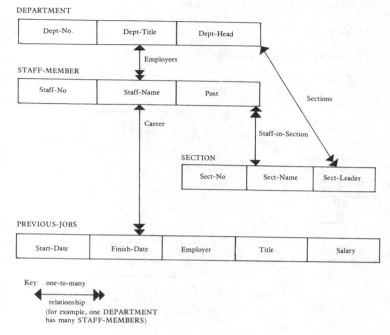

This schema can be explained in terms of SETS as follows:

There are 4 record types:

1. DEPARTMENT
2. STAFF-MEMBER
3. SECTION
4. PREVIOUS-JOBS

Each of 1, 2 and 3 can be retrieved directly by its record key, Dept-No, Staff-No and Sect-No respectively. Record type 4 is only accessible via the STAFF-MEMBER type record. This is reasonable as it would be unusual to search for a Previous-Jobs record without first knowing the identity of the Staff-Member.

There are 4 sets, each of which has an owner record and one or more member records. For example, one Department will have a number of Staff-Members (a one-to-many relationship). The sets are:

Employees (Owner, DEPARTMENT/ member, STAFF-MEMBER)

Sections (Owner, DEPARTMENT/ member, SECTION)

Staff-in-Section (Owner, SECTION/ member, STAFF-MEMBER)

Career (Owner, STAFF- MEMBER/member, PREVIOUS-JOBS)

Diagrammatically, a set can be pictured as on the following page.

For example, DEPARTMENT 4 as an owner record may have a number of SECTION member records.

Data Manipulation Language statements could be used to retrieve a Section record directly using its Sect-No or via its Sections Set (owned by Department Record). For example, if the section is in Department No 12:

1. MOVE 12 TO DEPT-NO

2. FIND ANY DEPARTMENT

3. SHOW SECTION

4. FIND NEXT SECTION

5. SHOW SECTION

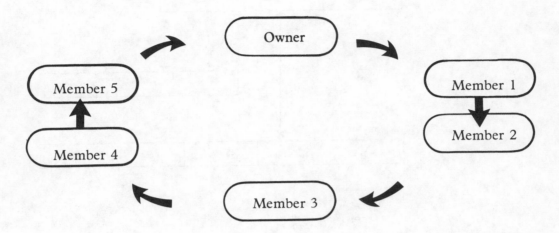

Steps 4 and 5 are repeated until the correct Section record is found or the end of set is reached. It should be noticed that a Previous-Jobs record can ONLY be found via the Career set and the appropriate Staff-member record.

As with any database, a Codasyl DBMS organizes and accesses the LOGICAL database via the SCHEMA description. The logical organization is in terms of SETS.

Query Languages

There are circumstances when the form of information needed from a database cannot be readily anticipated. Database management systems normally provide a specially designed language which allows a user who is trained in its use, to access a database without a specially-written applications program.

This type of language is called a QUERY LANGUAGE.

An example of a Query Language can be illustrated by the following data held in a database:

Order No.	Supplier No.	Date	Quantity
6345	163	210482	135
6612	286	230582	310
6422	163	090382	155

To retrieve those orders for Supplier No 163 may require the following statement:

LIST ORDER NO, DATE, QUANTITY WHERE SUPPLIER NO = 163

This is an extremely simplified example and does not include all the necessary requirements in using a query language. It is not a simple alternative to applications programs but can be extremely useful for on-demand enquiries.

Advantages of Databases

(a) Apart from Controlled Redundancy, there is no unnecessary duplication of data as occurs in traditional filing systems. Apart from the economic advantage, this means that transactions can update all affected areas of the database through a single input.

(b) Because of the single input principle, there is less chance of inconsistency as may occur if the same transaction is keyed in several times to different files. Equally, of course, an incorrect entry will mean that all applications programs using the data will be working with the wrong data value.

(c) The opportunities for obtaining comprehensive information are greatly improved with a central pool of data.

(d) On-demand or ad hoc enquiries are possible through the use of a query language.

Centralized And Distributed Systems

Centralized Systems

In a centralized system, all processing is carried out by a central computer. Even when terminals are remote from the central computer and connected by telecommunications links, if they are dependent on the central computer for all processing, it is a centralized system.

Distributed Processing Systems

A distributed processing system allows some processing to be carried out at remote terminal sites. The terminals have their own computing power, some file storage and some programs. Limited database facilities may also exist at each site. Usually, before being transmitted to the central computer for updating of files, transaction data will require some VALIDATION and other accuracy checks (see Chapter 7) and this can be done at the terminal. Terminals with this facility are called INTELLIGENT terminals. Microcomputers equipped with suitable software are often used to emulate mainframe intelligent terminals, with the added advantage of being usable as stand-alone systems when not communicating with the mainframe.

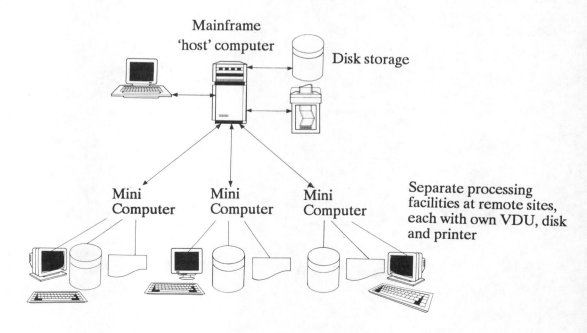

Mainframe 'host' computer

Disk storage

Mini Computer

Mini Computer

Mini Computer

Separate processing facilities at remote sites, each with own VDU, disk and printer

Reasons for Distributed Systems

Economy.   The transmission of data over telecommunications systems can be costly and local database storage and processing facilities can reduce such costs. Of course, to maintain such facilities at remote sites requires costly hardware, so the savings of distributed processing need to be set against the economies of scale provided by centralized systems. The radical reduction in computer hardware costs has favoured the expansion of distributed systems against centralized systems.

Minicomputers and Microcomputers.   The availability of minicomputer and microcomputer systems with data transmission facilities has made distributed processing economically favourable. An increasingly popular option in large, multi-sited organizations, is to set up Local Area Networks of microcomputers at each site and connect them via communications networks to each other and/or to a central mainframe computer at the Head Office. This provides each site with the advantages of local processing power, local and inter-site communications through Electronic Mail (Chapter 9 The Electronic Office) and access to a central mainframe for the main filing and database systems.

Local Management Control.   It is not always convenient, particularly where an organization controls diverse activities, to have all information processing centralized. Local management control will mean that the information systems used will be developed by people with direct knowledge of their own information needs. Responsibility for the success or otherwise of their section of the organization may well be placed with local management so it is desirable that they have control over the accuracy and reliability of the data they use.

Assignment   Transaction or Batch

Smith and Weston is a small plumbing and heating engineering firm, based in Scarborough. The partners, Ernie Smith and Brian Weston took over the business from Brian Weston's father in 1980 and are keen to expand it. The firm employs twenty five time-served plumbers and five apprentices. All employees are paid on the Friday each week. Ernie has been examining the possibility of computerizing a variety of the accounting tasks, including Sales Ledger and Wages. Much of the plumbing and heating work is carried on a sub-contracted basis for a number of larger contractors. About 60 per cent of the Sales Ledger accounts are updated on a weekly basis. Most of the available microcomputer software is designed for transaction processing, but some does have a batch processing facility.

Task

You are employed in a general clerical/office supervision role and currently carry out all the accounting tasks manually. Mr. Smith is unsure of the difference between batch and transaction processing and, being aware of your related studies at college, has asked you to explain the features of each method, pointing out the advantages and disadvantages of each to the firm.

1. Produce some notes to refer to when you explain the two methods of processing to Mr. Smith.

2. Role play an exercise in which you give an oral presentation to the lecturer of your explanations. Illustrate your talk with copies of documents (relevant to the business in question) used in batch processing. Make your own recommendations on the most appropriate processing method(s) for the applications mentioned above.

Assignment   A Fount of Knowledge

Borsettshire College of Further and Higher Education runs a wide range of vocational and non-vocational courses for both full-time and part-time students. It is generally accepted and generally stipulated by external course validating bodies such as BTEC, that full-time vocational courses should include a period of relevant work experience for each student. Borsettshire College offers full-time vocational courses in, for example, catering, hotel management and reception, computing, business studies, nursery nursing and social work. During the year, the total number of students requiring work placements of one sort or another is around 500. Approximately 30 academic staff are involved in organizing the work placements, many using the same employers. At present, there is little or no co-ordination of work placement planning, each member of staff dealing directly with employers. This has lead to some embarrassing moments. For example, when one member of staff from the Catering Department telephoned the Personnel Manager of a local hotel to arrange a placement, she was told that a colleague of hers from the Computer Studies Department was sitting in the Personnel Manager's office discussing a completely unrelated placement. Obviously, the Personnel Manager found it strange that neither member of staff, even though they worked at the same college, knew that the other was negotiating a work placement with the same employer.

At a recent staff meeting it has been agreed that, as a first step, information on work placements should be centrally available to all interested staff. In addition, it has been agreed that a non-academic member of staff should keep such an information store up-to-date. Before approaching an employer, a member of staff would be expected to refer the centrally-held information, to see who else used the employer and to determine if there were likely to be any clashes. If any further information is required, the other member(s) of staff responsible for work placements with the same employer, can be consulted directly. It has been suggested by the academic Computing staff that a relational database or card index package may provide two possible solutions, provided that money is available to pay for the services of a professional systems analyst/programmer. The person appointed to the task will be expected to consult the college staff on their requirements and to prepare for their approval a system specification, before development commences.

As a systems analyst/programmer employed by software house and a specialist in database systems on microcomputers, you have been given the task of developing the above system. The database is likely to contain information concerning the employer, the type of work placements offered, official contacts and details of college staff involved.

Task

1. In respect of the relational database alternative, identify the main database subjects which may warrant separate relations and suggest, with the aid of suitable diagrams, the data item types which could be included in each relation. Ignore any requirement for the identification of college tutors with particular employers. Indicate how connections between the relations are to be established and explain why there is a need for some data duplication.

2. Using a suitable relational database package, such as dBase IV, construct the relations designed in Task 1. Enter some sample data and use the query language to output at least two reports on work placement information.

Chapter 7

☐ CONTROL OF INFORMATION PROCESSING

The Need for Control

Computerized information systems present particular problems for the control of data entering the system, because for much of the time this data is not in human-readable form. Even when it is stored, the information remains in this state unless it is printed out or displayed on a VDU screen. If proper system controls are not used, inaccurate data may reach the master files or unauthorized changes to data may be made, resulting in decision-making which may be based on incorrect information.

System controls can be divided into three main types, according to the purposes they serve:

    (a)   Data Control;

    (b)   Auditing;

    (c)   Data Security.

a. Data Control

A number of data control mechanisms, including for example, the validation of input data, can be employed.

Controls should be exerted over:

- input;
- file processing;
- output.

Controls can be implemented by:

- clerical procedures;
- software procedures.

It is only through the combined application of both clerical and software controls that errors can be minimized. Their entire exclusion can never be guaranteed.

Input Controls

Transcription of data from one medium to another, for example, from telephone notepad to customer order form, or from source document to magnetic disk, provides the greatest opportunity for error. A number of strategies can be adopted to minimize input errors, including:

- minimizing transcription. This may involve the use of automated input methods such as bar code reading. Another solution is to use turnaround documents, which are originally produced by the computer and later become input documents. Examples of turnaround documents might be remittance advices which are sent to customers to be returned with their payments. Because these remittance advices already show customers' details, including account numbers, only the amounts remitted need to be entered for them to become complete input documents;

- designing data collection and input documents in ways which encourage accurate completion.

- using clerical checking procedures such as the re-calculation of totals or the visual comparison of document entries with the original sources of information;

- using codes of a restricted format, for example, customer account numbers consisting of two alphabetic characters, followed by six digits. Such formatted codes can easily be checked for validity;

- employing batch methods of input which allow the accumulation and checking of batch control totals, both by clerical and computerized methods;

- using screen verification before input data is processed and applied to computer files. Screen dialogue (the form of conversation between the computer and the user) techniques which allow data verification and correction at the time of entry can be used to provide this facility;

- checking input data with the use of batch or interactive screen validation techniques;

- ensuring that staff are well trained and that clerical procedure manuals are available for newly trained staff;

- controlling access to input documents. This is particularly important where documents are used for sensitive applications such as payroll. For example, input documents for changing pay rates should only be available to, say, the Personnel Manager.

File Processing Controls

Once validated data has entered the computer system, checks have to be made to ensure that it is;

- applied to the correct files;

- consistent with the filed data.

Header Records
Files can have header records which detail the function, for example, Sales Ledger, version number and 'purge' date. The purge date indicates the date after which the file is no longer required and can be overwritten. Thus, a file with a purge date after the current date should not be overwritten. Such details can be checked by the application program to ensure that the correct file is used and that a current file is not accidentally overwritten.

File Validation Checks
Some validation checks can only be made after data input when reference can be made to the relevant master file data. These are described in the later section on data control in batch processing systems.

Data Integrity
The printing of all master file changes allows the user department and auditors to check that all such changes are authorized and consistent with transaction documents. All data used by applications for reference purposes should be printed periodically. Such data, for example, price lists, may be held as permanent data on master files or in table form within computer programs.

Output Controls

It might reasonably be supposed that input and file processing controls are sufficient to ensure accurate output. Nevertheless, a number of simple controls at the output stage can help to ensure that it is complete and is distributed to the relevant users on time. They include:

- the comparison of filed control totals with run control totals. For example, when an entire sequential file is processed, the computer counts all records processed and compares the total with a stored record total held in a 'trailer' record at the end of the file;

- the reconciliation of control totals specific to the application with totals obtained from a related application. For example, the total sales transactions posted to the Sales Ledger in one day should agree with the total sales transactions recorded in the Sales Day book;

- the following of set procedures for the treatment of error reports;

- the proper checking and re-submission of rejected transactions.

Data Control in a Batch Processing System

It is extremely important that all relevant data is processed and that accuracy is maintained throughout all the processing stages. The controls which are used will depend on the type of processing method in operation, but batch processing provides the greatest opportunity for exerting control over the data, from the input stage through to the output stage. Amongst the control methods outlined above, there are two which are particularly important - Verification and Validation. These control methods can be used to maximum advantage in a batch processing system and typical procedures are described below.

The stages involved in a batch processing system cycle can be illustrated by the following example of a systems flowchart for a payroll run.

Systems Flowchart - Batch Processing of Payroll

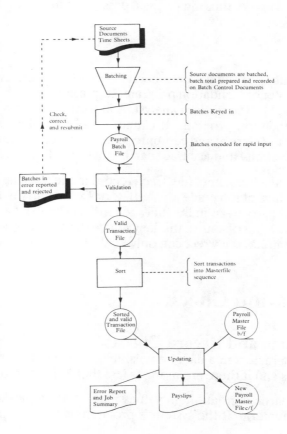

The following controls can be used at certain stages within the cycle:

Clerical Controls

These can be used at any stage in the cycle when the data is in a human readable form. The types of check include:

(i)   visual checking of source documents to detect missing, illegible or unlikely data values. An example of an unlikely data value could be a total of 100 in the weekly overtime hours entry for an individual worker;

(ii) the verification of entries by checking them against another source. An example of such referencing could be checking in the price catalogue for the price of a stock item on an invoice;

(iii) the re-working of calculations on a source document, for example, the checking of additions which make up the total quantity of an item on an order form.

Verification

Before processing, data has to be transcribed from the source documents onto a computer input medium. This usually involves a keying operation to encode the data onto magnetic tape or magnetic disk. This stage can be prone to error, particularly if large volumes of data are involved. Verification is a process, which is usually machine-assisted, to ensure that the data is encoded accurately. Magnetic tape encoders (key-to-tape systems) for example, can operate in two modes, record and verify. The operation involves one person keying the data in the record mode, after which a second person re-keys the data with the machine in verify mode. In effect the machine 'reads' the data from the first keying operation and then checks it against the second keying as it occurs. The machine signals if characters do not agree, thus indicating a possible transcription error. Key-to-disk systems operate on a similar principle.

Validation

This process is carried out after the data has been encoded onto the input medium and involves a program called the Data Vet or Validation program. Its purpose is to check that the data falls within certain parameters defined by the systems analyst. A judgement as to whether or not data is valid is made possible by the validation program. It cannot ensure absolute accuracy. That can only be achieved by the use of all the clerical and computer controls built into the system at the design stage. The difference between validity and accuracy can be illustrated by the following example.

A company has established a Personnel file. Each record in the file may contain a data item, the Job Grade. The permitted values of job grade are A, B, C or D. An entry in an individual's record of job grade is A, B, C or D. An entry in an individual's record may be valid and accepted by the system if it is recorded as A,B,C or D, but of course this may not be the correct grade for the individual worker concerned. Whether the grade is correct can only be determined by accuracy checks such as those discussed earlier.

Types of Validation Check

Character, Data Item and Record Checks

Size. The number of characters in a data item value is checked. For example, an account number may require 6 characters and if there are more or less than this, then the item is rejected.

Mode. It may be that particular data item values must contain particular types of character, for example alphabetic or numeric. If the system is programmed to accept only numbers then letters would be rejected.

Format. This refers to the way characters within a value are organized. For example, an Item Code may consist of 2 alphabetic characters followed by 6 numeric characters. The system would reject any entry which did not correspond to this format.

Reasonableness. Quantities can be checked for unusually high or low values. For example, a gas consumer with one small appliance may have a meter reading which would only be appropriate to a consumer with a large central heating system. If such a value was entered, the system would not accept it.

Presence. If a data item must always have a value then it can be checked for existence. For example, the data item 'Sex' in a Personnel record would always have to have an M or F entry.

Range. Values are checked for certain upper and lower limits, for example, account numbers may have to be between 00001 and 10000.

Check Digits. An extra digit calculated on an account number can be used as a self checking device. When the number is input to the computer the validation program carries out a calculation similar to that used to generate the check digit originally and thus checks its validity. This kind of check will highlight transposition errors caused by, for instance, keying in the digits in the wrong order.

The following example serves to illustrate the operation of one such check digit method.

Example Modulus 11 Check Digit.

Consider a stock code consisting of six digits, for example 462137.

The check digit is calculated as follows:

Firstly, each digit of the stock code is multiplied by its own WEIGHT. Each digit has a weight relative to its position, assuming the the presence of a check digit in the rightmost position. Beginning from the check digit position (x) the digits are weighted 1,2,3,4,5,6 and 7 respectively.

Stock code	4	6	2	1	3	7	(x)
Multiplied by Weight	7	6	5	4	3	2	(1)
Product	28	36	10	4	9	14	

Secondly, the products are totalled. In this example, the sum produces 101.

Thirdly, divide the sum by modulus 11. This produces 9, remainder 2.

Finally, the check digit is produced by subtracting the remainder 2 from 11, giving 9.

Whenever, a code is entered with the relevant check digit, the validation software carries out the same algorithm, including the check digit in the calculation. Provided that the fourth stage produces a remainder of zero the code is accepted as valid. This can be proved using the same example as above.

Stock Code	4	6	2	1	3	7	9
Multiplied by Weight	7	6	5	4	3	2	1
Product	28	36	10	4	9	14	9

Sum of Products 110

Divide sum by 11 giving 10 remainder 0.

If some of the digits are transposed the check digit is no longer applicable to the code and is rejected by the validation program because the results of the algorithm will not leave a remainder of zero.

This is shown below.

Stock code	6	4	1	2	3	7	9
Multiplied by Weight	7	6	5	4	3	2	1
Product	42	24	5	8	9	14	9

Sum of Products 111

Divide sum by 11 giving 10 remainder 1.

All the above checks can be carried out prior to the master file updating stage. Further checks on data can be made through the use of a validation program at the update stage, by comparison with the master file. They are as follow:

New records. When a new record is to be added to the master file, a check can be made to ensure that a record does not already use the entered record key .

Deleted records. It may be that a transaction is entered for which there is no longer a matching master record.

Consistency. A check is made that the transaction values are consistent with the values held on the master record which is to be updated. For instance a deduction for pension contributions by an employee who is not old enough to be in a pension scheme would obviously be inconsistent.

Validation using Batch Controls

These checks are only possible in a batch processing system.

Batch Totals

The purpose of batch totals is to allow a conciliation of manually produced totals for a batch with comparable computer produced totals. Differences are signalled and the batch is rejected for checking and re-submission.

Preparation of Batch Totals. Following the arrangement of source documents into batches of say 30 in each batch, totals are calculated on add-listing machines for each value it is required to control. On an order form, for example, quantities and prices may be separately totalled to provide two control totals. Totals may also be produced for each account number or item code simply for purposes of control although they are otherwise meaningless. For this reason such totals are called 'hash' or 'nonsense' totals. The totals are recorded on a batch control slip attached to the batch, together with a value for the number of documents in the batch and a batch number. The batch number is kept in a register held by the originating department so that missing or delayed batches can be traced.

A typical Batch Control Slip may be as follows:

Dept Ref: Sales	Date 30/01/86
Data Type: Orders	Batch No. 23
Number in Batch: 40	
Quantity Total: 30450	
Price Total: 13223.66	Prepared by: JE Checked by: PMC
Item-code Total: 576126	Entered by: DR

It should be noted that hash totals may produce a figure which has a large number of digits, so extra digits over and above the original length of the data item are truncated.

Reconciliation of Batch Totals. The details from each batch control slip are entered with each batch of transactions at the encoding stage. The serial transaction file which results will be arranged thus:

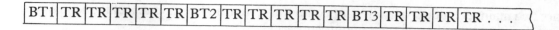

$$BT = \text{Batch Total} \qquad TR = \text{Transaction record}$$

The serial transaction file is processed from beginning to end by the validation program. The sum of the transaction records relating to each batch should match the batch total. If any validation error is detected, either by differences in batch totals or through the character or data item checks described earlier, the offending batch is rejected to be checked and re-submitted. The rejected batches are reported on a computer printout.

Validation During Updating

Checks can be made in the manner described earlier on transactions for deleted or new records, or data which is inconsistent with the relevant record on the master file.

The above controls can be used in conjunction with proper clerical procedures to ensure that as far as possible, the information stored on the master files is accurate.

File Controls

In addition to controlling the accuracy of data entering the system it is essential to check both that the data is complete and that all relevant data is processed. This can be done through the use of file controls on the transaction file.

Following the validation of the batches of transactions, correct batches are written to another file to be sorted and used for updating the relevant master file. During validation, the validation program accumulates totals for all the correct batches. These can be used during the update run to ensure that the whole transaction file is processed.

Validation in On-Line Systems

On-line systems as described in Chapter 6 tend to be interactive and transactions are processed immediately with the master files at the data entry stage. The main controls which can be introduced to such systems include:

    (i) the character, data item and record validation checks described earlier. Error messages are displayed on the screen at the time data is entered and require immediate correction at that time;

    (ii) visual verification. At the end of each transaction entry, the operator is given the opportunity to scan the data on the screen and to re-enter any incorrect entries detected. This usually takes the form of a message at the bottom of the screen which is phrased in a way such as "Verify (yes or no)";

    (iii) the use of well-trained data entry operators. They should have sufficient knowledge of the data being entered and the application it serves, to respond to error messages and make corrections to data accordingly.

Of course in a batch processing system, data entry is simply a keyboard skill, requiring little knowledge of the data and little use of initiative and this contrasts with the need for well trained data operators mentioned in (iii) above.

b. Auditing

There are two main techniques available for computer system auditing. One technique involves the use of test data and the other of audit enquiry programs.

The Test Data Method

With this method, the auditor runs the target application with test data, the expected processing results of which are already known. In this way, the computation of for example, payroll figures, can be tested for accuracy in a variety of circumstances. The logical outputs of the program can also be verified. In fact, the method is similar to that used by systems designers prior to a system's implementation (Chapter 14 Systems Development and Implementation). The test data may be recorded on a batch of source documents. In this case, the input will not only test the application's computerized processing and controls, but also the suitability of the source document design for input purposes. The auditing process may also include the testing of batch preparation and input data verification procedures. Software validation checks should be subjected to testing with normal and exceptional data. Normal data includes the most general data which the software is designed to handle. Exceptional data includes any which the software is not designed to accept. The software should demonstrate that it can reject all such data and continue its normal operation. Test data runs may take one of the following forms:

Live Data Testing. The auditor selects examples of live data from the system which fulfil the conditions to be tested. The results are calculated manually and checked against the computer-produced outputs. It is essential that manual calculations are made, as a casual assessment of the accuracy of processing can often lead to errors being overlooked. A severe disadvantage of this approach is that the auditor may be unable to find examples of all conditions to be tested in the available live data. It is also quite possible that examples of exceptional or nonsensical data will not be found at the time of the audit and it is important that such conditions are tested. 'Murphy's law' will probably ensure that such exceptional data appears the day after the audit. The testing can only give a 'snapshot' of the system's performance which may be radically different on other occasions;

Historical Data Testing. Sampling of transactions which have already passed through the system is an important part of internal auditing. It is important that the original transaction documents are made available for inspection to allow the auditor to check their validity, authorization and consistency with associated results. Results can be calculated manually and then compared with any printed results. If results were not printed at the time, then use may be made of a file dump utility to access the appropriate historic file;

Dummy Data Testing. With this method, the auditor constructs fictitious or dummy data which contains the conditions to be tested. To ensure that such test data is not applied to the application's operational files, it is also usual to set up dummy files, for example, customer or supplier files, specifically for audit purposes. If such data is used in an actual processing run, and the entries are not reversed out in time, there is a danger that the results will be taken as real by users. There are a number of apocryphal stories concerning lorries which delivered goods to non-existent addresses as a result of such fictitious entries. For this reason, it is always advisable to make use of specially created audit files or copies of the master files.

In summary, the test data method is useful for the audit of:

- data preparation procedures, such as batching;

- data verification and validation controls;

- an application's computational and logical processes. A number of drawbacks and limitations of the test data method of auditing can also be identified:

- it only provides a snapshot view of the system at the time of the audit. On the other hand, it may be used repeatedly in order to cover a more extended period of assessment;

- it may involve the setting up of dummy files if fictitious data is to be used;

- source documents and batch totals have to be prepared for fictitious data which is not of operational use to the business;

- the computer system has to be made available to the auditor for the period of the test. During this time it is not available for operational use.

Audit Enquiry Programs

These programs overcome many of the disadvantages inherent in the test data method and are an essential audit tool, particularly for external auditing which requires the examination of live data already processed. Audit enquiry programs vary in sophistication but generally provide facilities to:

- examine the contents of computer files;

- retrieve data from computer files;

- compare the contents of files. Thus, for example, two versions of identical files may be compared to ensure that the structure has not been altered, perhaps to include an extra field or record type;

- produce formatted reports according to the auditor's requirements.

A major benefit to the auditor is that any data stored on computer file can be retrieved. Many financial packages update files 'in situ', so that each updating transaction causes the overwriting of the relevant master record with new values. Thus, there may be circumstances when the results of processing individual transactions can only be established in terms of the cumulative effect of a group of transactions on a particular record. For example, during one day, a stock record may be updated by several transactions but the values held in the stock record at the end will not show their individual effects. However, provided that the source documents are retained or the transactions are logged onto a separate file (see Transaction Logging in the next section on Security), the auditor can still reconcile their expected effect on the master file with the actual values held there.

Audit Trails

An audit trail should allow the tracing of a transaction's history as it progresses from input through to output. Computerized systems present particular difficulties in that the trail disappears as it enters the computer system. The auditor may ignore the computer system and pick up the trail at the output stage (auditing around the computer). This has obvious limitations in that the auditor cannot trace a transaction which does not result in printed output. Although audit enquiry programs allow the auditor to examine the contents of files, not every transaction effect is recorded permanently on computer file. Audit trails have to be designed into the system in such a way that intermediate stages of a transaction's progress are recorded for audit purposes.

c. Data Security

The controls used have several main functions:

(i)   to prevent loss of data files caused by software or procedural errors, or by physical hazards;

(ii) to protect data from accidental or deliberate disclosure to unauthorized individuals or groups;

(iii) to protect the data from accidental or deliberate corruption or modification. This is known as maintaining 'Data Integrity';

(iv) to protect the rights of individuals and organizations to restrict access to information which relates to them and is of a private nature, to those entitled or authorized to receive it. This is known as 'Data Privacy'.

Security Against Data Loss

The loss of master files can be an extremely serious occurrence for any organization so properly organized security procedures need to be employed. Among commercial organizations that have lost the major part of their information store, a large percentage subsequently go out of business.

Master Files

The main causes of data loss are as follow:

Environmental hazards such as fire, flood and other natural accidents;

Mechanical problems, for example the danger of disk or tape damage caused by a drive unit malfunction;

Software errors resulting from programming error;

Human error. A wrong file may be loaded, the wrong program version used, a tape or disk mislaid, or physical damage caused to tape or disk;

Malicious damage. It is not unknown for staff to intentionally damage storage media or misuse a program at a terminal.

The standard solution to such problems is to take regular copies of master files and to store the copies in a separate secure location. It is also necessary to maintain a record of transactions affecting a file since the last copy was taken, so that if necessary they can be used to reconstruct the latest version of the file. The method used to achieve this is referred to as the Grandfather, Father and Son (Generation) System.

Magnetic Tape Files

When a tape master file is updated by a tape transaction file the physical nature of the medium makes it necessary for a new tape file to be produced (This is discussed in Chapter 5). As the following systems flowchart illustrates, the updating procedure provides a built-in security system.

Tape File Security - Generation System

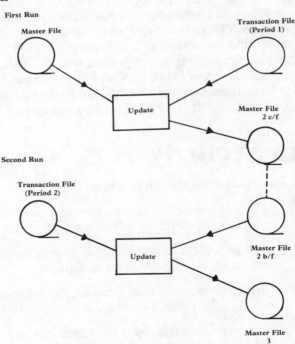

In the First Run, Master File 1 is updated by the transactions file to produce Master File 2 as its 'son'. Master File 1 is the 'father'. Should the 'son' file be damaged and the data lost, it can be recreated from the 'father' master file and the relevant transactions.

At the end of the Second Run, Master File 1 becomes the 'grandfather', Master File 2 becomes the 'father' and Master File 3, the son.

Each 'generation' provides security for subsequent files. The number of generations used will depend on the policy of the organization. Three generations is usually regarded as providing sufficient security and the oldest files are re-used by being overwritten as each cycle of generations is completed.

Magnetic Disk Files

Security Backups. Disk files can be treated in the same way as tape files in that the updating procedure may produce a new master file leaving the original file intact. On the other hand, if the file is updated 'in situ' (which in so doing overwrites the existing data), then it will be necessary to take regular backup copies as processing proceeds. The frequency with which copies are taken will depend on the volume of transactions affecting the master file. If the latest version of the master file is corrupted or lost, then it can be recreated using the previous backup and the transaction data received since the backup.

Transaction Logging. In an on-line system, transactions may enter the system from a number of terminals in different locations, thus making it difficult to re-enter transactions to re-create a damaged master file. One solution is to 'log' all the transactions onto a serial transaction file at the same time as the master file is updated. Thus the re-creation process can be carried out without the need for keying in the transactions again.

The following systems flowchart illustrates this procedure.

System Flowchart - Master File Backup and Transaction Log

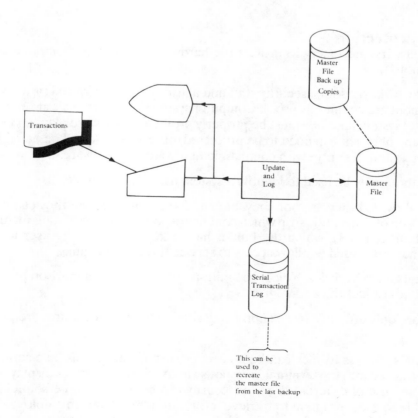

Data Security to Prevent Unauthorized Access

Unauthorized access to a system may:

- provide vital information to competitors;

- result in the deliberate corruption of the data. There is a documented case in the USA of young 'hackers' filling a database with graffiti resulting in a cost of thousands of dollars to reconstruct the data base;

- allow fraudulent changes to be made to data by employees or others;

- result in loss of privacy for individuals or organizations if the information is confidential.

To avoid such hazards an information system should be protected:

- physically;

- by administrative procedures;

- by software;

To detect any unauthorized access or changes to the information system:

- Users should require authorization (with different levels of authority depending on purpose of access);

- User actions should be logged and monitored;

- Users should be identifiable;

- The files should be capable of being audited;

- The actions of programmers should be carefully controlled to prevent fraud through changes to software.

Methods of Protection

Physical Methods. It is necessary to protect the hardware in the main computer installation and terminals at remote sites.

Methods include, locks on doors, security staff and alarm systems (infra-red systems to detect body heat and movement are commonly used). Computer systems with terminals at remote sites present a weak link in any system and they must be properly protected. Software plays an important role in this. Disk and tape libraries also need to be protected, otherwise it would be possible for a thief to take file media to another centre with compatible hardware and software.

A variety of methods may be used to identify a system user. They include:

Identity Cards. Provided they are not copyable and have a photograph they can be effective and cheap. The addition of a magnetic strip which contains encoded personal details including a personal identification number (PIN), which the holder has to key in, allows the user to be checked by machine. This method is used to allow access to service tills outside banks.

Personal Physical Characteristics. Voice recognition or fingerprint comparison provide effective, if expensive, methods of identification.

Such methods are only effective if the supporting administrative procedures are properly adhered to.

Software Methods. Access to files can be controlled at different levels by a series of passwords, which have to be keyed into the terminal in response to a series of questions displayed on the screen. An example of the use of different levels of security can be found in a Personnel Department. A typist may be able to use a program to retrieve information regarding an employee's career record but only the personnel manager is authorized to use a program to change the information held in the record.

'Hackers' are people who specialize (for fun or fraud) in breaking through the software protection to gain access to an information system's files. The passwords used therefore, should be carefully chosen, kept secure (memorized and not divulged) and changed frequently.

Using people's names for example, may allow entry by guessing or by trial and error.

Even if the terminals linked to a system are protected, an experienced hacker equipped with telephone, microcomputer and modem (a device to allow transmission of computer data over telephone lines) may gain access to a computer system's files while the system is in operation. The password controls may prevent access but if the data signals being transmitted along the telephone lines or via satellite are not properly protected, hackers can pick up the signals and display them on their own machines. To prevent such intrusion, DATA ENCRYPTION methods are used to protect important and confidential information during transmission from one centre to another. As the power and speed of computers has increased, so the breaking of codes has been made easier.

Code designers have produced methods of encryption which are currently unbreakable in any reasonable time period, even by the largest and most powerful computers available. An example of such an elaborate coding system is illustrated by the operation of the Electronic Funds Transfer (EFT) system. This is used by banks and other financial institutions to transfer vast sums of money so these transmissions are protected by the latest data encryption techniques.

Security to Maintain Data Integrity

Data integrity refers to the accuracy and consistency of the information stored and is thus covered by the security methods outlined above.

Security to Maintain Privacy of Data

The rights of individuals and organizations concerning their confidential records are similarly protected by the methods outlined earlier. In addition, legislation by parliament (the Data Protection Act 1984) attempts to exert some control by requiring any persons or organizations holding personal information on computer files to register with the Data Protection Registrar. Some countries have 'Freedom of Information Acts' which allow the individual to see any personal information stored in their own files, except where national security is thought to be threatened. It is generally accepted that the Data Protection Act falls far short of complete freedom of information.

Assignment   The Client's Systems

Foreman and Gilchrist is a firm of Chartered Accountants based in Norwich. It is a long established practice, having been founded in 1912 by Bernard Foreman, and has developed a reputation for being efficient, although rather staid, in its approach. The firm deals with a wide range of clients, concentrating on audit and tax work, but also providing comprehensive book-keeping, VAT and wages services to its clients. The practice has two senior partners, Alan Foreman and John Gilchrist and one junior partner, Peter Wilkinson. Many of the firm's clients now use computerized accounting systems.

You are employed as an articled clerk to the firm and have gained some experience in the auditing of computerized accounting systems. The two senior partners are a little 'out of touch' in this respect and Mr. Wilkinson has the main responsibility for the auditing of computerized accounting systems. He has asked you to prepare a booklet, for the use of new clerks entering employment with the firm, on the principles of data control used in computerized systems. The booklet should enable them to have some idea of the principles behind any particular system operated by a client. This is particularly important when they visit a client's premises for auditing purposes.

Task

Produce an introductory booklet suitable for a person who has a knowledge of financial accounting, but lacks experience of computerized systems. The booklet should include:

1. an outline of the particular problems of financial control which are posed by a computerized information system:

2. a description of the main subdivisions within an information processing system which require control and the methods of control used at each stage.

3. an explanation of the term 'audit trail' and the tools available to the auditor for determining the validity and acccuracy of computer processing.

Developmental Task

Visit local firms to identify the system controls they use and obtain sample data control documents. Examine a software package for accounting and determine the degree of detail available for an audit trail.

Assignment

Entering the Exams

Barneswell College of Further Education has a student population of approximately 1500 part-time students and 500 full-time students and offers a wide range of courses for single subject examinations offered by the GCSE Boards and other bodies, such as the City and Guilds Institute and the Royal Society of Arts. In addition, there are many vocational courses relating mainly to 'white collar' work in commerce, local and national government and industry. Although the college has an academic Computing section, staff from the section are not expected to be involved in any computerized administration systems.

The college is currently developing computerized systems to cover a variety of applications including, amongst others, examination entries, student records, and resource management, as part of an Educational Management Information System.

The college office already possesses two stand-alone, hard disk, PS/2 microcomputer systems, which the examinations officer, Dave Gubbins, has already used for the recording of examination entries for City and Guilds students. These will be linked into a college-wide, multi-user system, to be installed in the college in the near future.

The examination officer's experiences with computer systems so far, have not been entirely happy. Following the keying of exam entry details, 350 in all, the relevant disk file was corrupted and all data relating to the exam entries was lost. At this stage, no hard copy had been produced and the only solution was to re-enter all the examination details. Dave Gubbins was extremely upset because the keying exercise had to be carried out the evening before the submission date to the City and Guilds Institute. He is keen to ensure that such occurrences are not repeated in any new system.

Task

You are employed by the college to advise management on the administrative applications required of the new computerized system and your current concern is to produce a report on data security for the Project Development Group.

Produce a formal report, giving your reasoned recommendations for the following:

1. the prevention of loss of data from computer files;

2. the maintenance of security against unauthorized access to computer files.

Your recommendations should identify procedural and computer controls which may be of service.

Developmental Task

Examine the college's responsibilities under the 1984 Data Protection Act.

Assignment   Belt and Braces

Mountian Ash Garden Centre is a thriving business, producing top quality plants, shrubs, trees and so on for the garden. The business employs three full-time horticultural staff. The owner, Gordon Anderson is fanatical about the care of his stock and adopts a 'belt and braces' approach to life in general. The business's accounts have, until recently, been manually maintained by his wife. They are externally audited by a local firm of Chartered Accountants. The business has grown rapidly in recent years and the manual bookkeeping systems are not adequate for the efficient management of the business's finances. The Chartered Accountants have suggested to Mr. Anderson, that he needs to computerize his accounting and stock control systems. His wife is spending more time helping in the garden centre shop and hasn't the time to learn the necessary skills. They both decide that a specialist, with computing skills and accounting knowledge, will have to be employed. Mr Anderson is aware that computerized processing can result in some loss of control over the data and as his wife will no longer be involved, this is one aspect of the proposals on which he needs reassurance. He has approached a firm of software consultants, SoftSystem, for advice. You are employed by SoftSystem as a Sales Representative and part of your role is to deal with initial customer contacts. You have arranged to visit Mr. Anderson at the garden centre to assess his requirements and to advise him on possible solutions.

Task

You are aware of Mr. Anderson's reservations concerning the control and security of data and decide to make some notes on the subject to help you in your talk with him. The notes should cover the following topics:

1. the various meanings of the term 'security' and more detailed explanations of those which are particularly relevant to Mr. Anderson's circumstances;

2. the controls which may prevent such breaches and losses of security. You will obviously wish to highlight those which are going to be feasible and cost-effective in Mr. Anderson's particular circumstances;

3. the controls which may be sensibly employed to prevent inaccurate and invalid entries to the files;

4. audit trails. Give a simple explanation of the term and practical advice on the software packages which provide audit trails and the extent of control they provide.

N.B. Use an application, which is likely to require computerization, for illustration purposes.

Chapter 8

☐ MANAGEMENT INFORMATION SERVICES

Introduction

This chapter outlines the role and function of the Data Processing or Management Information Services Department. Some organizations still use the former title, but because of its changing role in producing management information as well as carrying out the routine data processing tasks, the latter title is used in this text.

As its title implies, this department has a servicing function to the organisation as a whole. Most such departments in large organizations have some centralized computer facility which carries out most of the computerized data processing. Smaller organizations may not have a central facility but instead have microcomputer systems in each department which uses a computer. In this context however, it is proposed to concentrate on the management information services of larger organisations.

Functions

Management Information Services has two principal functions:

(a) To provide a facility to satisfy the OPERATIONAL information needs of the main functional areas of the organization by computerized processing.

Each functional area has its own operational information needs. Examples are, the need for payroll details and payslips by Wages and Salaries and the need for customer invoices by Sales Order Processing. The topic of Operational Information is discussed further in Chapter 2. Here is a typical list of such routine operations:

(i) Keeping stock records;

(ii) Payment of suppliers;

(iii) General ledger, sales and purchase accounting;

(iv) Payroll;

(v) Invoicing;

(vi) Production of delivery notes;

(vii) Routine costing;

(viii) Filing of customer orders

This routine data processing work forms the bulk of the activity within Management Information Services, but there is an increasing demand for management information which introduces the second principal function.

(b)   To assist with operations which require management involvement and thinking but which can be partially automated or assisted by computers.

Examples of such functions include:

(i) Production planning;

(ii) Short term and long term forecasting;

(iii) The setting of budgets;

(iv) Decision making on financial policies;

(v) Marketing decisions;

(vi) Sales management;

(vii) Factory maintenance and management;

(viii) Price determination;

(ix) The selection of suppliers.

Although Management Information Services plays a central role, the advent of microcomputers and remote terminals (terminals connected to the computer by a telecommunications link) has meant that some of the above operations can be carried out by executive staff, with or without the use of the centralized facility.

Example

Consider the situation of a Sales Manager who is planning a sales strategy in terms of which geographical locations to increase sales representatives' visits. With the use of a microcomputer and database software package he or she could keep records of sales staff on 'floppy disk'. To obtain the required results, the Sales Manager may also need information stored with Management Information Services. Using a telecommunications link, he or she could call up the information from the central computer, combine it with the information on sales staff and use the database query facilities to obtain the required results. This example assumes that the organization uses a Database Management System which allows such enquiries. However, in this context it is not the particular methods of computer processing which are of interest. It is sufficient to know that such facilities exist. Database Management Systems are described more fully in Chapter 6.

Staffing

The chart on the following page illustrates the staffing structure of a typical Management Information Services department.

The department is normally headed by a Management Information Services Manager or Data Processing (DP) Manager. His or her major responsibility is to ensure that the department functions efficiently. He or she is responsible for ensuring that the information processing needs of the various functional areas and corporate management are met.

Beneath the control of the manager are staff involved in specialist areas of work within the department. There are broadly two areas of specialism:

(a)   Systems Development and Maintenance;

(b)   Operations.

Management Information Services

```
                              Manager
        ┌────────────────────────┼────────────────┐
    Systems              Programming        Operations
    Manager                Manager            Manager
       │          ┌───────────┘                  │
       │          │                              │
    Senior      Senior                ┌──────────┼──────────┐
    Systems   Programmers             │          │          │
    Analysts     │                  Senior      Data        Data
       │         │                 Operator   Control    Preparation
       │         │                    │      Supervisors  Supervisors
       │         │                    │          │          │
    Systems   Programmers          Operators     │          │
    Analysts                                    Control      │
                                                Clerks     Keyboard
                                                          Operators
```

a. Systems Development and Maintenance

The development of new computerized systems and the maintenance of existing systems involves specialist staff trained in Systems Analysis and Programming.

Systems analysis is concerned with the design of new computerized systems according to requirements laid down by corporate management. Prior to the design stage there is an investigative stage which necessitates close consultation with potential users in the various functional areas of the organization, to discover their information needs.

The result of the design stage is a System Specification which, rather like an architect's plans for a house, details all necessary materials and procedures to fulfil the specification. The specification will detail the clerical procedures necessary, the hardware required and most importantly what the computer has to produce for the users.

Once a system has been implemented it will require continual monitoring and modification as the information needs of the users change. The task of monitoring and modification remains with the systems analysts.

Programming is a task which perhaps lacks the creative element present in systems analysis and design. The programmer's job is concerned with coding the necessary computer instructions in a programming language such as COBOL or DbaseIV, in order to implement the requirements laid down by the systems analysts in the Program Specification (this forms part of the System Specification). Programmers involved in writing computer programs for user applications such as Invoicing or Payroll are known as Applications Programmers.

b. Operations

The Operations section is usually led by an Operations Manager and within his control are 3 sub-sections:

      (i) Data Control;

      (ii) Data Preparation;

(iii) Computer Operations.

Data Control

The staff in this section are responsible for the coordination and control of data flowing through the Operations section. The data received from, for example, Wages and Salaries, to enable the payroll master file to be updated and for payslips to be produced, has to be controlled to ensure its accuracy at all stages of processing. Chapter 7 describes the methods of control in detail.

Data Preparation

The work in this section involves the encoding of data from source documents such as customers' orders onto a 'machine-sensible' medium. Currently, this is usually magnetic tape or disk. Key-to-tape systems are dedicated, off-line devices, which allow data to be encoded directly onto cassette tape, without the use of a central computer. Prior to processing by computer, the cassettes from the magnetic tape encoders (it is likely that many will be in use) are gathered together and the data is merged onto a large reel for input to the computer. This form of encoding is rather outmoded and key-to-disk systems are generally more popular for large volume encoding. The latter system makes use of a minicomputer and a number of on-line keying stations. The processing power of the minicomputer allows much greater control, both in terms of verification and validation (Chapter 7 Control of Information Processing) of the data, than is possible with key-to-tape systems. The data entered via the keying stations is stored on magnetic disk and can be input to the main computer directly from there, or after transfer to magnetic tape.

Computer Operations

The staff in this section are essentially Computer Operators. They are responsible for the day-to-day running of the hardware, including the loading and unloading of input and output media, such as disk and tape. The computer hardware is under the control of software which constitutes the Operating System (which is discussed in Chapter 11 Software), but the operator needs to communicate with the operating system regarding jobs to be processed and to deal with error conditions which may arise. Communication between the operator and the operating system software is effected through a terminal dedicated to that purpose.

Storage of Magnetic Tapes and Disks

Depending on the size of the organization, the tape or disk library (the cataloguing and storage area for computer file media) may be staffed by a librarian or by the operators. In any event it is vital that information files are properly indexed and kept in a SECURE environment. 'Secure' means that the media need to be protected from physical hazards and unauthorized access. More detailed descriptions of SECURITY procedures are given in Chapter 7.

Staffing in Small Firms

In large organizations, computer installations are run by teams of specialists, comprising systems analysts, programmers and operators. In a small business, there may be one person with special responsibility for a number of aspects of computer usage. Even if there are other computer specialists in the business, each is likely to have a wider range of responsibilities than is the norm for large computer installations. These responsibilities may include, for example, hardware assessment, system design and implementation, software assessment and purchase, routine hardware maintenance, network management and staff training.

Assignment **Information for the Council**

Newborough County Council accommodates its various local authority departments in a purpose-built Civic Centre near the centre of Newborough. It uses a mainframe computer system for large volume processing tasks such as the payroll for local authority employees and the preparation of Community Charge demands.

Although some computing facilities are available in the various departments, through the use of microcomputer systems or on-line terminals, most of the processing is centralized. The large computer centre accommodates the mainframe computer and peripheral equipment and adjoining work rooms are used by the specialist staff working in the Management Information Services Department. Its staffing structure is illustrated in this chapter.

Task

You are employed as a Personnel Officer and the Personnel Manager has asked you to prepare a booklet outlining the role of Management Information Services in the Civic Centre and the jobs of the specialist staff who work there. The Department's manager is concerned that the work of the department as a servicing unit for the whole organisation is recognized by other staff in the Civic Centre. It is intended that newly appointed staff are given a 'tour' of the various departments so that they can gain a wider view of the work of the council. The booklet of the work of Management Information Services seeks to support this aim.

Prepare the booklet.

Chapter 9

☐ THE ELECTRONIC OFFICE

Electronic Office Systems

The concept of the electronic office aims to improve and partially automate office activities within an organization. Through the use of electronic equipment, changes can be introduced in 3 main ways:

a. Document Preparation

- by replacing, or at least supplementing the more traditional methods of recording information. At present, for example, preparation of documents such as an internal memorandum, may involve the office manager using a dictaphone (tape recorder for dictation and transcription) and the audio typist using a manual, electric or electronic typewriter. Additionally, documents with diagrams may involve an artist or draughtsman in their preparation.

b. Document Storage and Retrieval

- by improving the methods of storing and retrieving documented information. The existing methods may involve the use of indexed filing cabinets.

c. Information Transmission

- by improving the integration of office activities through more efficient information transmission. At present, for example, the main methods of communication may be by typed paper documents or the telephone.

The main components of an electronic office system consist of a variety of electronic products used in each area of activity listed above.

a. Document Preparation

Text Preparation
In text preparation, the main electronic component is the word processor. A word processor consists of a processor (CPU), memory, keyboard, screen, diskette storage and printer, together with appropriate software. The text appears on the screen where it can be manipulated and edited prior to printing or storing on diskette. The equipment also possesses many automatic features, including those for adjusting margins, tabulation points, headings and change of typeface (Chapter 11 Software).

Diagrams and other Graphical Material
Diagrams and other graphical representations can be included in the text in two ways:

    (i)   The text layout can be left with gaps for insertion of graphical material at the printing stage, or

(ii)   Integrated software may allow the insertion of the graphical material while the text is still on the screen. In addition pictures from printed material can be reproduced within the document, through the use of a digitizer (hardware) connected to the computer and a graphics program. This is a technique now commonly used in newspaper production. The publishing industry now makes widespread use of Desk Top Publishing (DTP) systems, which are designed for the more powerful microcomputers. These systems make use of laser printers to produce the high speed, high quality output required by the publishing process.

Types of Word Processor

Dedicated Word Processor. By dedicated, we mean that it is solely concerned with word processing and is programmed for that purpose only. A dedicated word processor provides a more sophisticated facility than a computer 'package'. Generally expensive, it can only be justified where there is a sufficient volume of text preparation to occupy a full-time operator. It may be linked to other equipment in the office, for example to the photocopier so that a number of copies of a document could be produced by a command from the word processor.

Computer with Word Processing Package. Using a computer with a package such as Word Perfect is an advantage where there is a lower volume of text preparation and the computer is used for other applications as well. Apart from being less sophisticated than the dedicated word processor, it has the disadvantage of a general purpose computer keyboard without specialist word processing function keys. However, the programmable function keys (Chapter 5 Peripherals) are used by all word processing packages. Normally, a card or plastic template is provided, which fits over the function keys, thereby explaining the particular purpose of each key for that package. Some manufacturers of mini and mainframe computer systems will provide special keyboards to accompany the particular word processing package they sell.

b. Document Storage and Retrieval

The storage of documents with a high graphical content on computer storage is not particularly efficient, in that such documents occupy an excessive amount of computer memory. There are two main alternatives to computer storage available for the electronic office. They are:

(i)   Microforms (microfilm and microfiche);

(ii)   Optical disk (including Compact disk).

Microforms

As a celluloid medium, microform can store documentary information including graphical material. The structure of the microform can be either Microfilm (a continuous reel) or Microfiche (a grid pattern).

Microform reduces storage space requirements by approximately 95 per cent of that required by paper documentation.

There are two methods by which documentary information can be recorded on microform:

(i)   by direct computer output (COM - computer output on microform). In this way, for example, text on screen could be recorded on microfilm using a microfilm recorder.

(ii)   by photographic miniaturization.

To read information stored on microform, a special projector can be used to magnify the image and display it on a screen.

Retrieval of documents stored on microfiche can be made more efficient, particularly where large numbers are involved, by using a computer to locate and retrieve individual documents identified by unique codes. The computer will use indexing techniques to ensure an efficient search and retrieval process.

These document storage and retrieval techniques can be combined with computerized information systems used by other sections of an organization, to allow the combination of information from a variety of sources into a document.

Optical Disks

The optical disk uses laser beam technology to allow data to be recorded and read using bit-densities several times greater than a typical magnetic disk. Data are recorded as bit-patterns using high-intensity laser beams to burn tiny holes into the surface of the disk. The data can then be read from the disk using a laser beam of reduced intensity. A similar technology is used for Compact Disk (CD) digitized recordings of music and film. Its application in computing is still in the early stages of development but it is likely to have a profound impact on backing storage usage.

There are two main types of optical disk system presently available.

CD-ROM (Compact Disk-Read-Only Memory) Systems. As the title suggests this type of disk only allows the computer to read data from the disk. The disk is pre-recorded by the manufacturer. It is of no use for the storage of data which require updating. Its main application is for Interactive Video Disk systems. A video disk can store text, images and audio signals and is of use in advertising, training and education. Sequences of film and sound can be retrieved under computer control.

WORM (Write Once, Read Many). The large storage capacity of optical disks means that the writing facility can be used for a considerable period before all space is used up. Storage capacities are measured in gigabytes (thousands of millions of characters), which is way beyond the capacity of any magnetic disk system. Optical disk systems which provide an erase facility are available, but are still too expensive for most users.

Apart from its vast storage capacity, the optical disk is less prone to environmental hazards such as dust.

c. Information Transmission

Documents produced in the electronic office may be transmitted to those who should receive them by a variety of methods which all involve the conversion of text and graphical material into a digital form which a computer can handle. A global term for the variety of systems in use is ELECTRONIC MAIL. The concept of electronic mail stems from its manual counterpart except that the medium of paper is made redundant during the transmission process and is not even essential if hard copy is not required by the receiver.

Until recently the standard methods of text transmission were:

> (i) Telex (teleprinter exchange);
>
> (ii) Facsimile Transmission.

Telex

Telex is a well established communications system which, rather like the public telephone network, allows subscribers to communicate with one another. There are over a million subscribers in this country at present.

Each subscriber is given a telex code (you will often see it at the top of business letter headings next to the telephone number) and must have a teleprinter which is a combination of keyboard and printer. There is no screen, so all messages sent or received are printed onto hard copy. The transmission rate of approximately 6 characters per second is slow compared with more modern telecommunications systems, but the limitations of keyboard entry and printer speed on the teleprinter, make any faster speed unnecessary.

The main benefit of telex is that a permanent record of communications is kept and the receiver does not have to be 'on the spot' when the message arrives.

Its main disadvantage is that there is no storage facility for messages. Any transmission has to be printed as soon as it is transmitted so that if the receiver is faulty, the system comes to a halt. However, systems now exist to allow Telex to be accessed via Prestel, using a microcomputer system with full word processing facilities (see the section on Prestel at the end of this chapter).

Facsimile Transmission

This system can utilize either the telephone or telex networks to allow users to transmit an accurate copy of a document. The information (text or picture) is digitized by a facsimile machine which scans the page automatically to produce the required signals. Computer storage is used within the network so that signals can be queued if there is a hold-up in the system. Modern systems can transmit an A4 page in less than a minute.

Computer Networks

Networking or linking together computer systems has the effect of decentralizing computer processing and improving communication within an organisation. The topic of computer networks is discussed fully in Chapter 10 but their use for ELECTRONIC OFFICE systems is described after the following brief outline of network features.

There are broadly two types of computer network:

a. Local Area Networks (LAN)

These are used to connect computers in a single room or within a building or buildings on one site. Its main feature is that, unlike Wide Area Networks, no special telecommunications hardware is necessary.

b. Wide Area Networks (WAN)

WAN are used to connect computers on different sites or even in different parts of the world. They make use of telecommunications systems (in this country the principal provider is British Telecom) including satellite links. These networks extend beyond the concept of the office as a single room or group of rooms. A user can be 'at the office' at home if he has the necessary terminal link. Organizations with offices abroad can benefit from the immediate communication facility normally available to people in the same room.

Computer networks provide several advantages for their users:

(i) In Local area networks there is the opportunity to share disk storage and possibly printer facilities. In all networks there is the facility for sharing information, perhaps in a central database.

(ii) Improved communication facilities. Within a network a facility exists for terminal users to communicate with one another via the network. Therefore the results of processing, or perhaps a document prepared by word processing, could be immediately communicated to one or more of the other users on the system.

(iii) Processing facilities can be provided for each user but an element of central control can still exist.

(iv) The breakdown of one computer in the network does not effect the others in the system, except where a central 'host' computer handles all communications. In the latter case, although some independent processing power may remain, inter-network communication is not possible. In a centralized system, if the central computer is 'down', all connected terminals lose their processing power.

Computer Networks for Communication

Three main electronic communication systems can be identified, although in practice they may be integrated. They are:

    (a)   Electronic mail and message systems;

    (b)   Electronic diaries and calendars;

    (c)   Electronic notice boards.

a. Electronic Mail

Unlike telex and facsimile transmissions, which require paper for input and output, electronic mail systems based on computer networks are paper-less (except when a user requires hard copy). A major advantage is the facility for message storage if a destination terminal is busy, or has a temporary fault. When it is free, the message can be transmitted.

Certain basic features can be identified as being common to all electronic mail systems:

    (i)   a terminal for preparing, entering and storing messages. The terminal will be 'intelligent', possibly a microcomputer, mainframe terminal or dedicated word processor. In any event, it should have some word processing or text editing facilities to allow messages to be changed on screen before transmission. A printer may also be available for printing out messages received over the system;

    (ii)   an electronic communication link with other workstations in the network and with the central computer controlling the system;

    (iii)   a directory containing the electronic addresses of all network users;

    (iv)   a central mailbox facility (usually the controlling computer) for the storage of messages in transit or waiting to be retrieved.

Ideally, the following facilities are available to electronic mail users:

    (i)   messages are automatically dated upon transmission;

    (ii)   messages are automatically acknowledged as being received when the recipient first accesses it from the terminal;

    (iii)   multiple addressing; that is the facility to address a message to an identified group, without addressing each member of the group individually;

    (iv)   priority rating to allow messages to be allocated different priorities according to their importance.

Networks require two particular features in order to support electronic mail:

    (i)   a message storage facility to allow messages to be forwarded when the recipient is available. This means that the recipient does not have to be using the system at the time the message is sent;

    (ii)   compatibility with a wide range of manufacturers' equipment. Devices attached to a network have to be able to 'talk' to the communications network using 'protocols' or standards of communication. Network protocols are explained in Chapter 10.

Benefits of Electronic Mail

The following major benefits are generally claimed for electronic mail systems:

    (i)   Savings in stationery and telephone costs;

(ii)   More rapid transmission than is possible with conventional mail;

(iii) Electronic mail can be integrated with other computer-based systems used in an organization;

(iv)   All transmissions are recorded, so costs can be carefully controlled;

(v)   Electronic mail allows staff to 'telecommute', that is, to work from home via a terminal;

(vi)   The recipient does not have to be present when a message is sent. Messages can be retrieved from the central 'mailbox' when convenient.

Electronic mail refers to communication over long, as well as short distances via Wide Area Networks, but internal office communication via a Local Area Network is referred to as Electronic Messaging.

b. Electronic Diaries and Calendars

An ordinary desk diary is generally used by managerial or executive staff to keep a check on important meetings and much of the time it is quite adequate for the purpose. A conventional calendar is usually pinned to a wall for staff to check the date. Electronic diaries and calendars do not attempt to replace these traditional facilities. To begin with, it would be extremely tedious if it were necessary to sit at a computer terminal simply to discover the date.

An electronic diary and calendar system may provide the following facilities:

Diary Entries

Entries are made under a particular date and can be retrieved using the relevant date. Used in this way, the system 'apes' the conventional diary by producing a list of entries for any date entered. At this level, it could be argued that a desk diary does the job just as well;

Search and Retrieval on Event

Instead of entering the date, the user requests a list of entries conforming to particular criteria. For example, a request for a list of Board meetings over the next six months would produce a list with the relevant dates. Similarly, for example, a request for a list of those supposed to be attending a Board meeting on a particular date would produce a list of attendees names;

Flexible Search and Retrieval

This facility can be used to produce a number of alternative strategies based on specified criteria. Suppose, for example, that a Board meeting has been called, but the exact date has not been set. The problem is to set a date which falls within the next three weeks and is convenient for all Board members. The search and retrieval facility allows the searching of each member's electronic diary for dates when all are available. The system may produce a number of possible dates. Such tasks can be extremely time-consuming to carry out manually.

At this point, it is important to note that the above examples assume a comprehensive diary system which is kept up to date. The system fails if, for example, one director's diary entries are incomplete.

c. Electronic Notice Boards

Electronic notice boards are essentially a localized version of the viewdata systems described in the next section. The system may be used by an organization to advertise staff promotions, training courses, new staff appointments and retirements.

Teletext and Viewdata Systems

The combination of the telecommunications and computer technologies has produced an 'information explosion' and there are now many services providing specialist information, which organizations can use either independently or in conjunction with their own computerized information systems.

Public Systems

Teletext

Teletext systems, such as Ceefax and Oracle, provide a public service based on a central computer database, which users can access via an ordinary television set with special adapter and keypad. The database consists of thousands of 'pages' or frames of information which are kept up to date by Information Providers. Pages can be accessed and displayed on the television screen through the use of the keypad, directly via page number or through a series of hierarchical indexes. Major subject areas include Sport, News, Business, Leisure and Entertainment, Finance and Travel. Pages are transmitted using spare bandwidth unused by television pictures, in 'carousels' or groups. The user may have to wait some time while the carousel containing the required page is transmitted.

Its major drawback is that communication is ONE WAY. The user cannot send messages to the database, only receive.

Viewdata or Videotex

The principle of a central database and frames of information forms the basis of viewdata systems. The major public viewdata system in the UK is Prestel. Each user requires a telephone, TV monitor or television set, electronic interface, a modem (for modifying computer signals for transmission over the telephone network), an auto-dialler (for contacting the database and identifying the terminal user) and an electronic device to generate the picture from the received data.

Its major benefit is that it provides an INTERACTIVE system. Communication is TWO WAY. A user can transmit messages to the database.

Private Communications on Prestel

Prestel provides a facility for Closed User Groups (CUG) so that, for example, a group of estate agents could rent several pages which were for their own exclusive use and could not be accessed by ordinary users.

Access to other Databases via Prestel

A facility exists called Gateway which allows Prestel users to access their own bank's database, to carry out transactions on their personal or business accounts via the Prestel network. The user will register with their bank, pay an annual subscription and receive personal security details such as a password and sign-on code. The Bank of Scotland operate such a service called Home Banking.

Telex can now be accessed, from a microcomputer, through a Prestel gateway. LAN gateway products also exist to allow access to the Telex system by any user node on a LAN. Electronic mail facilities, such as those described in the previous section are not inherent in Telex. However, gateway software, such as Torus's Telex Gateway, can provide them instead. For example, incoming telex messages can be stored on disk at the gateway LAN station, be sent to any shared printer on the LAN if hard copy is required or, be distributed to other nodes electronically. Personal user directories can be set up and messages can be queued or assigned a particular time for transmission.

Other Network-based Systems

Other facilities accessible via networks, include:

Electronic Data Interchange (EDI). Similar to electronic mail, EDI allows users to exchange business documents, such as invoices and orders, over the telephone network;

Bibliographic Databases. These databases provide information on specialized and widely ranging topics. For example, BLAISE, which is provided by the British Library, gives information on British book publications. Euronet Diane (Direct Information Access Network in Europe) provides information extracted from publications, research documents and so on, which may be of interest to specialists, such as scientists, engineers, economists and lawyers. Each extract provides the relevant bibliographic references to allow users to access the original sources more fully.

Assignment   **The Royal County**

The Royal County Hotel is situated in Princes Street, Edinburgh and has 350 rooms, each with en-suite shower and toilet facilities, colour television and video recorder. It has a reputation for haute cuisine and has an AA 5-star rating. It is not a member of any large hotel group, being the pride and joy of a self-made millionaire, Charles Pender, who started his career in the restaurant industry after some years as a chef with the Cunard shipping line. Mr. Pender has always tried to maintain a friendly but efficient service in the hotel and up to now has not made use of computer facilities for hotel administration. Recently, Mr. Pender has opened two new hotels of similar rating in Newcastle upon Tyne and Norwich. There are thirty administrative staff employed at the Edinburgh hotel, including a hotel manager, an assistant manager, a restaurant manager and three receptionists. The excessive workload on staff and the number of recent administrative errors affecting guests have persuaded Mr. Pender that computer facilities are needed.

You are currently employed as a trainee systems analyst by Datasoft, a software consultancy firm based in Edinburgh and the firm has been approached by Mr. Pender concerning the computerization of hotel office procedures. The idea is that hotel reception should be electronically 'part of' the main office, which is situated on the top floor of the building. In addition, inter-hotel communication would allow Mr. Pender to exert greater control over all three hotels. The use of 'electronic office' facilities would seem to be appropriate. The senior systems analyst, Judith Stewart, has asked you to visit the hotel and carry out a preliminary investigation of Mr. Pender's requirements. She has also asked you to provide a preliminary report on your findings for Mr. Pender.

Task

Prepare an informal report for Mr. Pender outlining the facilities which constitute an 'electronic office' and suggesting ways in which the facilities could be used in the hotels. Also explain, in simple terms, how the inter-hotel communication is to be accomplished.

Developmental Task

Research available software packages for hotel management, from hotel industry and computing magazines.

Assignment   Mr. Pender's Electronic Office

Referring to The Royal County Hotel case study on the previous page, identify the components which may be needed for the electronic office facilities.

Task

Produce a sample specification, detailing the components which may need to be purchased, their function within an electronic office system and the approximate costs.

Developmental Task

As a group effort, write to a number of manufacturers requesting a copy of their product catalogues. Alternatively, research the subject from computing and office machinery magazines. Try and organize a visit to an organization with a computer network and/or electronic office facilities.

Assignment

The Personal Touch

Hailes Bookshop in Cambridge is internationally reputed to be one of the finest and largest bookshops in the world. The shop occupies a complete block of terraced Victorian buildings. There are three floors and each floor has several sections, divided according to subject. If a book is in print, Hailes will have a copy. Despite its volume of business, its only concession to automation to date, has been to use electronic tills. All other tasks are carried out manually and communications between staff are generally face-to-face. There is a family atmosphere amongst the staff and management and the firm even employs a tea lady who wheels her trolley of tea and biscuits from department to department at break times. However, there is increasing competition from bookshops which adopt a supermarket approach. These 'book supermarkets' are highly automated and make extensive use of computers for almost all their data processing applications. Their staff have little or no knowledge of the products they sell and customers are left to sort out their own needs. In contrast, Hailes employs staff with specialist knowledge of books in a number of subject areas, but not in popular fiction. It is in this area that Hailes is experiencing severe competition.

The directors of Hailes are willing to accept the idea that some applications and particularly stock control, could benefit from computerization. A software consultancy, DataSoft, has been approached by the Hailes directors for advice on the best approach to computerization. DataSoft have recommended the use of a Local Area Network, which they point out, will allow automation of a range of routine office tasks, apart from the standard data processing tasks envisaged by the Hailes directors. DataSoft have also emphasized the potential benefits of electronic messaging between the various departments of the shop and the provision of access to external electronic mail systems. The Hailes directors are proud of the friendly atmosphere amongst staff and the frequent personal contacts. They are unwilling to sacrifice the 'personal touch' to the objective of automated efficiency, but are very conscious of the need to improve their competitiveness.

Task

As a sales representative for Datasoft, you specialize in automated office systems and the directors of Hailes Bookshop have asked you to give them a talk, outlining the office automation facilities from which they may benefit. Prepare notes to help you.

Chapter 10

☐ COMPUTER NETWORKS AND DISTRIBUTED SYSTEMS

This chapter looks at how computer networks have developed, some technical aspects of their construction and how they can be used to decentralize or distribute the data processing function.

Factors Favouring the Decentralization of Computing Power

Three main factors have encouraged many organizations to adopt a decentralized policy:

(i) Many organizations already have a number of computers installed at geographically separated sites. At first these systems tended to be used in isolation, but the need to extract and analyse information from the company as a whole, led to their connection via the telecommunication network;

(ii) The cost of computers has fallen dramatically, making it cost-effective for organizations to process and analyse data at the various points of collection;

(iii) The development of Local Area Networks of low-cost microcomputers with electronic office facilities (Chapter 9), has encouraged demand for local computer power and these networks can be readily connected to any central facility via telecommunications networks;

Data Communications and Computers

The combination of computer and telecommunications technologies has had a profound effect on the way computer systems are organized. The idea of a computer centre handling all computer processing, without any user involvement, is rapidly becoming obsolete. A computer network aims to distribute the processing work amongst a number of connected computers and to allow users direct control over processing.

A system which uses a central computer to control all processing, with a number of 'slave' terminals is not necessarily a computer network. The following section describes two pre-network systems which make use of the telecommunications and computer technologies. They are:

(a)   Non-Interactive Systems;

(b)   Interactive 'Dumb' Terminal Systems.

a. Non-Interactive Systems

Systems for the transmission of data from remote terminals to a central computer, have been in widespread use since the mid-1960s. Used for transfer of large volumes of data, they were known as Remote Job Entry (RJE) systems. At first, they tended to use terminals which only allowed one-way transmission. The way in which many banks used the system is described below as an example.

Example: The Transmission of Bank Transactions

Details of the customer transactions were transmitted by a 'dial-up' telephone connection to the computer centre, at the end of the day. During the day, the transactions were keyed into 'off-line' accounting machines which automatically punched the details onto paper tape. The paper tape was then loaded onto a paper tape reader, the computer link made and the data transmitted to the computer centre.

The system was extremely limited. It only provided a facility for transmitting data TO the computer. The system did not allow the link to be used to retrieve information from the computer and no separate processing power was available at the transmitting branch. The system can be illustrated diagrammatically as follows:

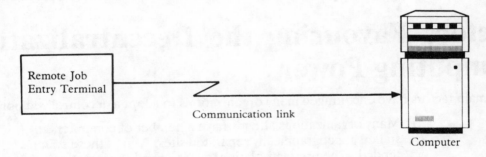

Similar systems developed using key-to-tape or key-to-disk systems for the data encoding process, but processing control was still completely centralized.

b. Interactive 'Dumb' Terminal Systems

Through the use of a teletypewriter (TTY) terminal or more recently, a VDU terminal, it became possible for the communication link to be two-way.

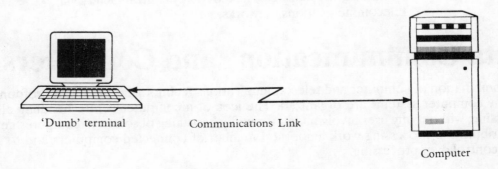

Both the TTY and VDU terminals acted as input and output devices and supported two-way communications. However, these devices had no processing power or storage facility of their own ('dumb') and were entirely dependent on the central computer. Whenever the central computer was 'down', all users were deprived of any processing facility.

Neither of the above systems can be described as a network because all processing control is with a central computer system.

Computer Networks

Some computer networks use 'intelligent' VDU or microcomputer terminals to permit some independent processing power at sites remote from the central computer. Other networks distribute even more processing power by linking together microcomputer or minicomputer systems. In this case, the 'terminals' are computer systems in themselves. Because such networks distribute some processing power to a number of different sites, they are also known as DISTRIBUTED processing systems.

Applications of Computer Networks

Networks can be configured to suit almost any application, from the provision of a world-wide airline booking service to home banking. Terminals may be only a few hundred feet apart and limited to a single building, or they may be several thousand miles apart. Some major areas of use, or potential use, are as follow:

  (i)   Computer-aided education can be supported by a network which provides Computer-Assisted Learning (CAL) packages to suit a wide range of subject and course areas;

  (ii)   Public data bases can allow people to make, for example, airline, restaurant, theatre or hotel reservations from anywhere in the world, with instant confirmation. Home banking services, such as that provided by the Bank of Scotland can be accessed by Prestel subscribers. A potential area of use could be the newspaper industry. Subscribers could arrange for personalized newspapers which contained only those subjects of interest to them. Information could, of course, be completely up-to-date;

  (iii) Electronic mail has the potential to make hand-delivered communications virtually obsolete and this is discussed in Chapter 9;

  (iv)   Teleconferencing allows discussion amongst individuals without their physical presence in one room. A meeting can be conducted by the typing of messages at terminals. All contributions to a discussion are automatically recorded for later reference .

Local Area and Wide Area Networks

Computer networks can be classified according to their geographical spread. A network confined to, say, one building with work-stations which are usually microcomputers distributed in different rooms, is known as a 'LOCAL AREA NETWORK' (LAN). One particular type, known as a 'RING NETWORK' can extend over a diameter of two or three miles. A computer network distributed nationally or even internationally makes use of telephone and sometimes, satellite links, and is referred to as a 'WIDE AREA NETWORK' (WAN). In large organizations with several branches, it is becoming popular to maintain a LAN at each branch for localized processing and to link each LAN into a WAN covering the whole organization. In this way, branches of an organization can have control over their own processing and yet have access to the organization's main database at headquarters. In addition, inter-branch communication is possible.

Network Topologies

Computer networks can be categorized according to their 'shape' or TOPOLOGY. Each terminal in a network is known as a NODE. If a central computer controls the network it is known as the HOST computer. The topology of a network is the arrangement of the nodes and the ways they are interconnected. The communication system within a network is known as the 'SUBNET'. Data can be transmitted around the subnet either on a point-to-point basis or via a broadcast channel.

- If POINT-TO-POINT transmission is used, the data passes through each device in the network. Thus, if two devices wish to communicate, they must do it indirectly, via any intervening devices. Each device must have the facility to store the entire message and forward it when the output channel is free.

- If a BROADCAST channel is used, a common communication channel is shared by all devices in the network. This means that any message sent by a device is received by all devices. The message contains the address of the device intended to receive it, so that the other devices can ignore it.

There are a number of recognized network topologies and some of the most common are described below.

a. Star Network

A star network generally has a central host computer at the hub, with the terminals or nodes connected directly to it. The following figure illustrates one particular type of star topology.

Switched Hub Star Network

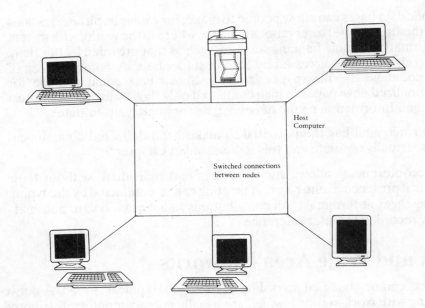

Host Computer

Switched connections between nodes

In this structure, all messages pass through the host computer, which interconnects the different users on the network. Thus, in this topology the host computer at the hub has a message switching function. Messages are transmitted point-to-point. The topology is particularly useful for intercommunications between pairs of users on the network (via the host). The network may consist of several computer systems (the nodes), connected to a larger host computer which switches data and programs between them. The star topology is less suitable where several nodes require access to another node.

Star Computer Network

The following star topology illustrates a popular form of network where the hub performs processing on information fed to it via the telephone system. In this case, the host computer has a processing rather than a message switching function.

Star Network

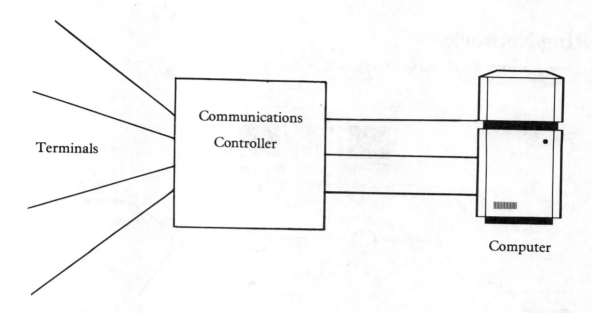

The star computer network is by far the most popular for WANS, because most large organizations start with a central computer at the head office, from which branch computer facilities are provided via the telephone network. The main aim is to provide computer communication between the branches and head office. Most other network topologies aim to provide communication between all devices on a network.

The advantages of a star network topology are as follow:

(i)   It is suitable for WANs where organizations rely on a central computer for the bulk of processing tasks, perhaps limiting the nodes to their local processing needs and the validation of data, prior to transmission to the central computer;

(ii)   Centralized control of message switching allows a high degree of security control;

(iii) Each spoke in the star is independent of the rest and a fault in a link or device in one spoke, can be identified by the computer at the hub;

(iv)   The data transmission speeds used can vary from one spoke to another. This is important if some spokes transmit using high speed devices, such as disk, whilst others transmit from low speed keyboard devices. The method of transmission may also vary. For example, one node may only require access to the network at the end of each day, in which case a 'dial-up' connection may be sufficient. A dial-up connection uses the public telephone network and the user only pays for the time taken for transmission. Alternatively, other nodes may require the link for most of the working day, in which case a permanent leased line is appropriate. Leased lines provide a more reliable transmission medium and also allow higher speeds of data transmission.

The main disadvantages inherent in star networks are as follow:

(i)   The network is vulnerable to hub failures which affect all users. As a distributed processing system, some processing is still possible at the nodes but inter-node communication is lost when the host computer fails;

(ii)   The control of communications in the network requires expensive technology at the hub, probably a mini or mainframe computer. Complex operating and communications software is needed to control the network.

b. Ring Network

A ring network connects all the nodes in a ring, as illustrated below.

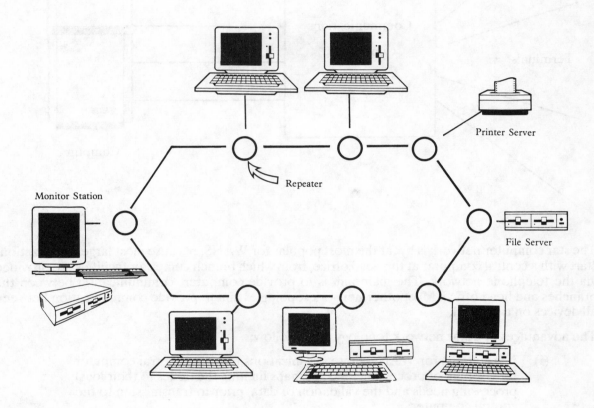

There is no host computer and none of the nodes need have overall control of access to the network. In practice, a monitoring station is used for the control of data transmission in the network. The topology is designed for LANs and the Cambridge Ring is a popular configuration.

The ring consists of a series of REPEATERS which are joined by the physical transmission medium. Repeaters regenerate messages as they pass around the network. The user devices are connected to the repeaters. Thus, a message from one node, addressed to another, is passed continually around the ring until the receiving node flags that it is ready to accept it. Data is transmitted in mini-packets of about 40 bits and contains the address of the sending node, the address of the receiving node and some control bits.

The ring network presents particular advantages:

(i)   There is no dependence on a central host computer as data transmission around the network is supported by all the devices in the ring. Each node device has sufficient 'intelligence' to control the transmission of data from and to its own node;

(ii)   Very high transmission rates are possible;

(iii) Routing between devices is relatively simple because messages normally travel in one direction only around the ring;

(iv) The transmission facility is shared equally amongst the users.

The main disadvantages are as follows:

(i) The system depends on the reliability of the whole ring and the repeaters;

(ii) It may be difficult to extend the length of the ring because the physical installation of any new cable must ensure that the ring topology is preserved.

c. Loop Network

A loop network is similar in shape to a ring network, but priority of access to the network is controlled by a loop controller. Thus access to the network may not be equally shared amongst the nodes. Transmission rates also tend to be lower than for the ring. This is because communications are generally via the controller rather than direct from device to device. Communication is point-to-point. The topology is commonly used for the local handling of terminals by a large computer system.

d. Bus Network

The bus or highway network can be likened to a bus route, along which traffic moves from one end to the other. To continue the analogy, the stations are like 'bus stops' and the data like 'passengers'. Data can be placed on to the route or 'picked up' as it passes. The term 'station' is used rather than 'node' for this type of network. The communications subnet uses a broadcast channel, so all attached nodes can 'hear' every transmission. The topology is illustrated below and is typical of many LAN configurations.

As is the case in the ring network, there is no host computer and all stations have equal priority in using the network to transmit.

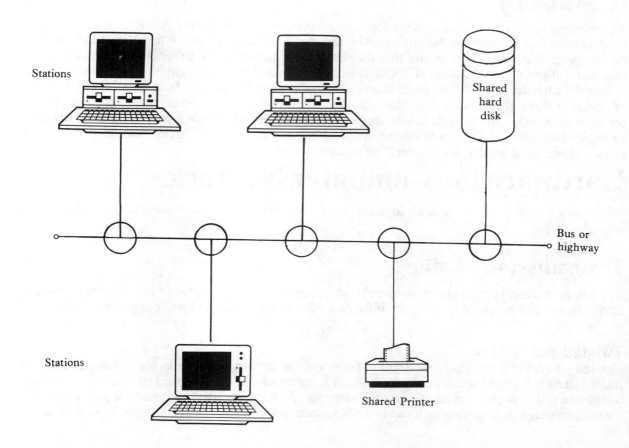

Stations

Shared hard disk

Bus or highway

Stations

Shared Printer

Local Area Network Access Methods

The three main methods of controlling access to a LAN are as follow:

a. Empty Slot Technique

This system is appropriate for networks in the shape of rings or loops, where messages are passed point-to-point in one direction. One or more empty slots or packets circulate continuously around the ring. When a device has information to transmit, it loads it into the slot, which carries it to its destination. At the time of loading, the destination address is placed in the slot and a 'full-empty' flag is set to 'full'. As the slot is passed from one repeater to another, no attempt will be made to load the slot as long as the flag is set to 'full'. When the slot reaches the destination device, the device's repeater reads the information without clearing the slot. Before passing it on, the repeater sets a 'received message' flag in the slot. When the slot again reaches the sending device, the flag is set to 'empty'. The destination device can check that the message was received by checking the 'received' flag. If the message was not successfully received, perhaps because the destination device was not 'listening', the sender device can check the acknowledgement flag and re-transmit in the next slot.

b. Token Passing Technique

This technique is also used for ring networks. An imaginary 'token' is passed continuously around the ring. The token is recognized as such by the devices, as a unique character sequence. If a device is waiting to transmit, it catches the token and with it, the authority to send data. As long as one device has the token, no other device can send data. A receiving device acknowledges the receipt of a message by inverting a 1-bit field.

c. Carrier Sense Multiple Access with Collision Detector (CSMA-CD)

This method of access control is used on broadcast systems such as the bus network. Each device is theoretically free to transmit data to any other device at any time. Before attempting to transmit, a device 'polls' the network to ensure that the destination device is free to receive data and that the communications channel is free. A device wishing to transmit must wait until both conditions exist. Generally such delay will be no more than a few millionths of a second. Because of the possibility of collision through simultaneous transmission, a collision detection mechanism is used. When collision does occur, the devices involved cease transmission and try again some time later. In order to avoid the same collision, each device involved is made to wait a different time. If a number of retries prove unsuccessful, an error will be reported to the user.

Hardware for Computer Networks

When data is transmitted between two hardware devices in a network, a communication MEDIUM is used.

Transmission Media

The commonly used media are, twisted-pair cable, coaxial cable and optical fibre. Where a physical connection is not practical, then radio, infra-red, microwave and laser technologies may be used.

Twisted-pair Cable

Twisted-pair cable is formed from strands of wire twisted in pairs. It predates any other method and is still extensively used for standard telephone or telex terminals. Each twisted pair can carry a single telephone call between two people or two machines. Although twisted-pair cable is generally used for analogue signal transmission, it can be used successfully for digital transmission. Variation in the lengths of wire within pairs can result in signals being received out of phase, but this can be overcome by the frequent use of repeaters. The repeaters 'refresh' the signal as it passes to maintain its consistency. Although transmission rates permitted by such cable are lower than for some other media, they are acceptable for many computer applications.

Coaxial Cable

Coaxial cable is resistant to the transmission interference which can corrupt data transmitted via twisted-pairs cable. It thus provides a fast, relatively interference-free transmission medium. Its construction consists of a central conductor core which is surrounded by a layer of insulating material. The insulating layer is covered by a conducting shield, which is itself protected by another insulating layer. During network installation, the cable can be cut and connections made, without affecting its transmission quality. The quality of cable can vary and some low quality cable is unsuitable for data transmission over long distances. On the other hand, high quality cable can be quite rigid and difficult to install in local networks, where space is limited. Despite this difficulty, it is an extremely popular choice for LANs.

Optical Fibre Cable

Optical fibre cable consists of thousands of clear glass fibre strands which transmit light or infra-red rays instead of electrical signals. The data is transmitted by a light-emitting diode (two-state signals) or injection-laser diode. Transmission speeds of billions of bits per second are achieved. Repeaters are only required after several miles. The other end of the cable has a detector which converts the light pulses into electrical pulses suitable for the attached device.

Optical fibre cable is more expensive than electrical cable but is finding increasing use in LANs. However, its main application is for long-distance communications.

Radio Transmission

Infra-red Radiation

Infra-red radiation can be used within a single room with the use of an infra-red transmitter-receiver. Each device within range would also contain an infra-red transmitter-receiver. Infra-red communication provides a useful alternative to conventional cable in situations where cable would be a nuisance or hazard. As long as devices are in 'sight' of one another, infra-red provides a possible medium of communication.

Microwaves

Microwaves are high-frequency radio signals and can be used where transmitter and receiver are not 'in sight' of one another. The communication path must be relatively obstruction-free. Microwaves can be transmitted via earth transmitters or via communications satellites. Earth stations must be no more than 25-30 miles apart, because humidity in the atmosphere interferes with microwave signals. Each station in a communication path acts as a repeater station. Obviously, it is impractical to build sufficient repeater stations to deal with all transmissions, so communications satellites are used. Satellite communications are now fairly common and provide a cheaper and better trans-ocean transmission medium than undersea cable.

Data Transmission Techniques

Transmission Modes

Communications media can be classified according to whether or not two-way transmission is supported.

Simplex mode allows communication in one direction only and as such, is inappropriate for use in WANs.

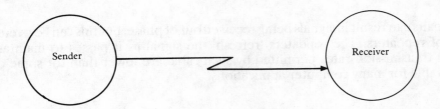

Half-duplex mode supports communications in both directions, but not at the same time.

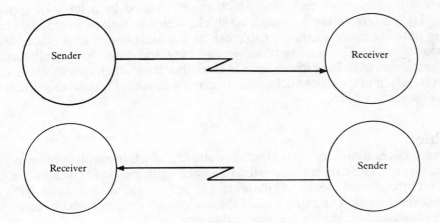

Duplex mode allows communication in both directions at the same time. In interactive systems, when on-demand enquiries are needed this mode is appropriate.

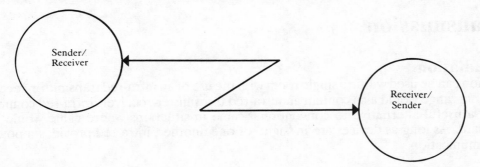

Types of Signal

There are two forms of signal which can be transmitted along a medium, ANALOGUE and DIGITAL. The telephone network is designed to carry the human voice and carries signals in continuous sine wave form. Computers handle data in digital form. The two wave forms are illustrated below.

Analogue and Digital Transmission

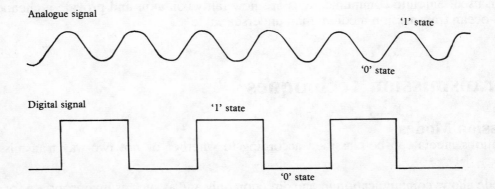

Any telephone link between computer devices requires a device to modify the signals transmitted. Developments are taking place to digitize all telephone transmissions and this will allow the telephone network to support computer transmissions directly. In the meantime a device called a MODEM is needed to MOdulate and DEModulate the signal. The modem for the transmitter device has to modulate the digital signal into analogue form for transmission along the telephone line. The modem at the receiver device has to carry out the reverse operation.

Modem in Telecommunications Link

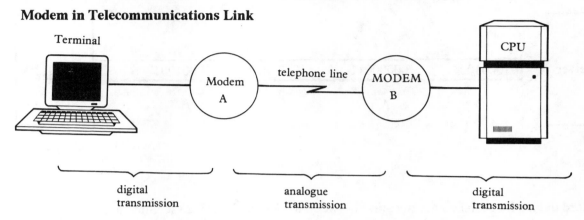

Modems are capable of both functions, so that two way communications are supported.

Types of Modem

Modems can be held externally in a separate unit, or on a system board plugged into one of the expansion slots inside the computer. Although space is saved when the modem is held internally, the plug-in board takes up one of the limited number of expansion slots in the computer. For example, other plug-in boards may be needed for an extra programming language or to support graphics.

Acoustic-coupler modems are connected to the telephone handset and convert the computer's digital signal into audible tones, for transmission as analogue signals down the telephone line. The receiving device converts the signal back to a digital form for processing. The user has to dial the number of the computer system, wait for a high pitched signal, and then connect the handset to the modem. The data transmission rate is lower than for other types of modem, but acoustic-coupler modems provide a simple computer connection for anyone with a terminal and a telephone.

Different modems provide different data transmission rates, measured in bits per second (bps or BAUD). Acoustic-coupler modems only allow a baud rate of about 300 bps. The transmission rate is also dependent on the type of line used.

Types of Telecommunications Lines

Dedicated lines. These can be leased from British Telecom and provide a permanent connection for devices in a network. They provide high transmission rates and are relatively error free. They are only cost-effective for high volume data transmission, or when a permanent link is vital to the users. Charging is by a flat rate rather than when calls are made.

Dial-up or switched lines. These are cheaper, but support lower transmission rates than leased lines. They are cheaper than leased lines for low-volume work and allow the operator to choose the destination of transmissions.

Communication Standards

Parallel and Serial Transmission

Devices differ in the ways they communicate or 'talk' with each other. One such difference is in the number of channels they use to transmit data.

Serial Transmission

With serial transmission, the binary signals representing the data are transmitted one after the other in a SERIAL fashion. This is necessary when there is only one channel available for transmission. Serial transmission is used in all network communications other than for short distances. Links between devices in a WAN thus use serial transmission. The technique is illustrated below.

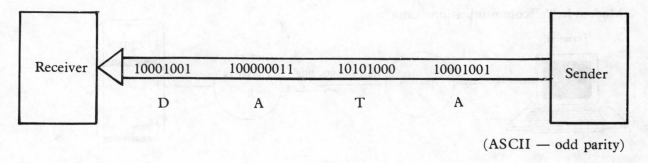

(ASCII — odd parity)

A standard device for serial communication between devices is the RS-232C interface.

Parallel Transmission

As the term suggests, data bits are transmitted as groups in PARALLEL, as is illustrated below.

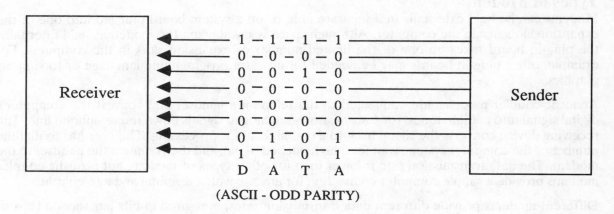

(ASCII - ODD PARITY)

This is obviously faster than sending them serially, but it is only practical over short distances. Communication between a computer and its nearby peripherals can be carried out using parallel transmission. This is particularly important where high-speed devices, such as disk or tape units, are concerned. Microcomputer systems often use parallel transmission to communicate with a nearby printer. An example of a popular standard device is the Centronics parallel interface.

Asynchronous and Synchronous Serial Transmission
Asynchronous Transmission

When a sending device transmits characters at irregular intervals, as does for example, a keyboard device, it is said to be transmitting ASYNCHRONOUSLY. Although the characters are not sent at regular intervals, the bits within each character must be sent in regular timing intervals. An asynchronous character generally has a format similar to that illustrated on the following page.

It can be seen from the diagram that the line has two electrical states, representing 1 and 0. Between characters, the line is in the 'idle' state, a 1 or MARK condition. To indicate the start of a character, the first or START bit is set to 0. A STOP bit follows each character. The machine at the receiver end 'listens' to the line for a start bit. When it senses this it counts off the regularly timed bits which form the character. When a stop bit is reached, the receiver switches to its 'listening' state. Because start and stop bits mark the beginning and end of each character, the time interval between characters can be irregular, or asynchronous.

Asynchronous Character Format

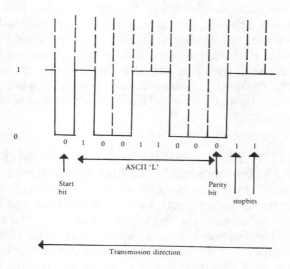

Synchronous Transmission

The start and stop bits used in asynchronous transmission are wasteful, in that they do not contain information. Where higher speed devices are involved, or where data can be buffered and transmitted in larger blocks, it is more efficient to send the data in timed or SYNCHRONOUS blocks. The following diagram illustrates the technique.

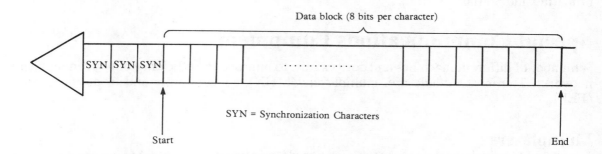

A variety of formats may be used, each having their own operating rules or PROTOCOL. Communications protocol is dealt with later in this chapter.

In synchronous transmission a data stream may be very long, so it is vital that the timing between transmitter and receiver is synchronized and that the individual characters are separated out. This is done by using a clock lead from the transmitter. Synchronization (SYN) characters are placed at the beginning of each data block and, in case timing is lost by line disturbance, several SYN characters may be situated at intervals within the data block. Thus if timing is lost, the receiver can re-time its bit groupings from the last SYN character. Like the start and stop bits used in asynchronous transmission, SYN characters are not part of the data and as such, have to be 'stripped' out by the receiver. Synchronous transmission is generally used for data speeds of 2400 bps and more.

Some VDU terminals are designed for high speed data transmission and use synchronous transmission. Many others use asynchronous transmission.

Communication Protocols

In the past networks were designed to work with particular types of workstation and were known as 'closed networks'. Unfortunately, users of such systems were unable to take advantage of improved hardware produced by other manufacturers. Neither were they able to attach any of their existing stand-alone systems to the network, unless they were compatible with it. The trend more recently has been towards 'open' systems, so that workstations from different manufacturers could be attached to the same network. For example, non-IBM workstations can be attached to IBM's Token Ring network. To achieve such openness requires the setting of standards relating to both hardware and software, which may be used in a network. Strong standards encourage manufacturers to make products which conform to those standards. This in turn, creates a wide range of compatible products, from which users can choose.

The OSI (Open Systems Interconnection) Reference Model

The OSI model (developed by the International Standards Organization) has been used to some extent by manufacturers in a move to more open network systems, although some of the standards have initially been set through commercial products, such as the Ethernet and Token Ring Networks and then adopted as part of the OSI model. The model identifies seven hierarchical layers, each of which has a specific function within a network. For example, Layer 1, the lowest in the hierarchy, is the Physical Layer and defines aspects of the hardware, such as the network connection. This may relate, for example, to the number of pins used in a network connector and the function each pin should have. It also defines standards for the electrical transmission of binary data (protocols). Layer 7, the highest in the hierarchy, defines standards, for example, concerning the transfer of information between end-users (electronic mail), applications programs and graphical data exchange. There is still much work to be done regarding the formation and acceptance of standards, particularly at the upper levels, although some LAN and communications equipment suppliers have specified their own protocols within the guidelines of the model and these have been established in many widely accepted LAN products. For example, three major standards for hardware have been established and accepted by another international standards body, the Institute of Electrical and Electronics Engineers (IEEE). They are Token Ring (IBM being the main proponent), Ethernet (DEC primarily) and Starlan (AT&T).

Special Communications Equipment

A number of different machines and devices exist to improve the efficiency of telecommunications networks. The most notable are, multiplexers (MUX), concentrators and front-end-processors (FEP).

Multiplexers

Low speed terminals, such as those with keyboards, transmit at about 300 bps, whereas voice-grade telephone lines can support transmission speeds of up to 9600 bps. A MULTIPLEXER allows a number of low-speed devices to share a high-speed line. The messages from several low-speed lines are combined into one high-speed channel and then separated out at the other end by a demultiplexor. In two-way transmissions, both these functions are carried out in one unit at each end of the higher speed channel. The operation of a multiplexer linking several remote terminals to a host computer is illustrated on the following page.

Multiplexers use different methods to combine signals and separate them out.

Frequency Division Multiplexing (FDM) differentiates between the signals from different devices by using a different frequency range for each. Allowing for spacing between the different ranges, a 2400 bps circuit can handle twelve 110 bps terminals.

Time Division Multiplexing (TDM) provides a time slice on the higher-speed line for each terminal. The multiplexer has a number of registers, one per low-speed channel. Each register can store one character. The multiplexer scans each register in sequence, emptying the contents into a continuous stream of data to be transmitted. A multiplexer will send a null character whenever it finds an empty slot. Concentrators aim to overcome this wastage.

Multiplexers to Connect Low-speed Devices to a Host Computer

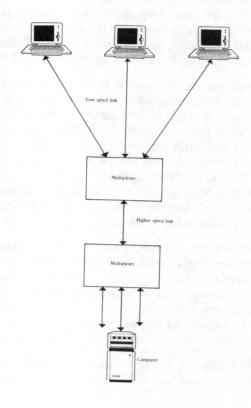

Concentrators

A concentrator greatly increases data throughput by increasing the number of low-speed channels and instead of transmitting a null character, empties the contents of the next full register. The data from each low-speed device is identified by extra identification bits and this constitutes an overhead.

Front-End-Processors (FEP)

A FRONT-END-PROCESSOR is the most sophisticated type of device for communications control and is usually a minicomputer held at the site of a mainframe host computer. Its main task is to handle all the communications traffic, leaving the mainframe free to concentrate on processing tasks. Its main tasks include:

- parity checking;

- 'stripping' of overhead characters from serial transmission, start/stop
  bits and SYN characters;

- conversion from serial to parallel transmission and vice versa;

- network control;

- network accounting;

- character conversion.

Linking Microcomputers to Mainframes

In organizations with mainframe computers, it is often desirable for staff with microcomputers on their desks to be able to communicate with the mainframe via those systems. With non-IBM systems, where the host computer uses asynchronous transmission, the connection can be made via the

RS232C (this refers to a standard used in most serial communications) serial transmission port, located at the back of the microcomputer's system casing. However, the most common mainframe systems, IBM and ICL in particular, use synchronous communications, so special 'terminal emulation' cards are required. IBM systems usually make use of additional expensive hardware, namely, a specialized coaxial cable to make the link, together with a terminal cluster controller. This latter device provides for the connection of a number of terminals to an IBM mainframe.

Thus, microcomputer workstations can be converted to mainframe terminals using a technique called EMULATION. Terminal emulation requires a terminal emulation card to be fitted into one of the expansion slots in the microcomputer's system casing. If there are a number of terminals to be connected, the microcomputer is then connected, via a coaxial cable, to a terminal cluster controller. The controller is linked to a front-end processor (usually a minicomputer, dedicated to handling incoming and outgoing communications for the mainframe), which is itself connected to the mainframe computer. In this way, a microcomputer can, for example, be converted into an emulation of an IBM 3270 terminal. The majority of terminal emulation cards are designed for the IBM 3270 market, a well-known one being the Irma card from DCA. Emulation products are primarily, though not exclusively, available for IBM 'compatible' microcomputers.

The advantage of using a microcomputer as a mainframe terminal, is that it can also be used on a stand-alone basis for local processing tasks, such as word processing or spreadsheet work. The terminal emulation package ensures that the mainframe responds in the same way as it would to a dedicated terminal. Security mechanisms, such as passwords, prevent users of emulated terminals from carrying out processes which are forbidden to users of dedicated terminals. However, the microcomputer's facility for local storage and processing can present serious security problems for the mainframe's data and various mechanisms have to be included to prevent unauthorized updates.

Where emulated terminals are to be linked to a mainframe via a wide area network, adaptor cards are available which combine the terminal emulation with the gateway software, to access the intervening network.

Assignment   Booking for Sunshine

Sunshine Holidays Limited is a medium-sized company which operates a chain of travel agencies throughout the North of England. The company's Head Office is in the centre of Nottingham. A minicomputer system at Head Office is used for all the company's main information processing activities. At present there are no computer facilities at the individual travel agencies, although each agency does have a Prestel unit for checking on travel and holiday vacancies. A travel industry database called Travicom would be a useful service for the company in that the database specializes in travel and holiday information. Although Prestel provides relevant information, it also deals with many other subjects as well. The company's Managing Director, Bill Sissons is convinced that their future survival in the industry depends on the quality of the service they provide to their customers and that the latter can only be improved if communications between the agencies are enhanced. The most effective mechanism for this communication would seem to be through the establishment of computer links between the various agenices and Head Office. A link into Travicom is also seen as being an important contributor to improvement of services and this may be effected with the use of a Gateway from the existing Prestel connection. The company's competitors already make extensive use of the Travicom facility.

Sunshine Holidays Limited have approached Inter-net Limited, a company specializing in computer networks. You are employed by Inter-net Limited as a Sales Representative and the Sales Manager, Michael Turnpenny, has asked you to visit the offices of Sunshine Holidays to give a presentation on the systems available for Local and Wide Area Networks, which may fill their requirements. The company is interested in the idea of a Local Area Network at their Head Office, linked into a Wide Area Network to connect the agencies to the Head Office computer and to Travicom. It is likely that microcomputer systems with local storage and printing facilities would be used as terminals linking into the Wide Area Network.

Task

1. As a sales representative for Inter-net Limited, prepare a talk for presentation to the management of Sunshine Holidays Limited. Make use of diagrams to illustrate your talk. Your talk should introduce the concepts of Local and Wide Area Networks and describe in a non-technical way, the various configurations which may be used. Identify any hardware requirements. Suggest how the networks may be used to improve the communication and information processing systems within the company.

Assignment   **A Database for Power**

Power Tools Limited is a small company with three DIY shops in Bradford and Leeds. The business was established by ex-joiner Harry Turner in 1968 with a single shop in Leeds. He joined forces with Geoff Baker, an accountant, to form the present company in 1982 and the two additional shops were opened in 1985. A new shop may be opened in Halifax in the near future. At present, you are employed as manager of one of the shops in Leeds. The directors are considering the use of microcomputer systems for the accounting tasks in the business. This follows their recent attendance at a one-day seminar entitled 'Small Business Systems'. Mr. Baker has asked you to investigate the benefits which may be gained from using a database system with all the shops connected to it via a computer network.

Task

Prepare an informal report for the directors, in which you explain the concept of a database system and the benefits it may provide in combination with a computer network. Give examples of the kind of information such a system may provide, which would not be readily available if the shops maintained separate systems.

Developmental Task

Use a database package to set up some simple files and use the query language to extract information according to various criteria.

Chapter 11

□ SOFTWARE

Introduction

Software is the generic term which is used to describe the complete range of computer 'programs' which will convert a general-purpose digital computer system into one capable of performing a multitude of specific functions. The term 'software' implies its flexible, changeable nature, in contrast to the more permanent characteristics of the hardware or equipment which it controls.

The particular type, or types, of software controlling the computer system at any particular moment will determine the manner in which the system functions. For example, a certain type of software might cause the computer to behave like a wordprocessor; another might turn it into an accounting machine; another may allow it to perform a stock control function. In other words the behaviour of the computer is entirely determined by the item of software currently controlling it.

Computer programs

The terms 'software' and 'program' tend to be used synonymously, so what precisely is meant by the term 'computer program'?

At the level at which the computer operates, a program is simply a sequence of numeric codes. Each of these codes can be directly converted by the hardware into some simple operation. Built into the central processing unit (CPU - the heart of the computer) is a set of these 'simple operations', combinations of which are capable of directing the computer to perform complex tasks. Computer programs, in this fundamental form, are termed 'machine code' that is code which is directly 'understandable' by the machine.

The numeric codes of the program are in binary form, or at least the electrical equivalent of this numbering system, and are stored in the immediate access store (the 'memory') of the computer. Because this memory is volatile (its contents can be changed), it is possible to exchange the program currently held in the memory for another when the computer is required to perform a different function. For this reason the term 'stored program' is often used to describe this fundamental characteristic of the modern digital computer.

Instruction sets

The collection of numeric codes which directs the computer to perform such simple operations as those mentioned above is called the 'instruction set'. A typical computer would have some or all of the following types of instructions and, in addition, other more specialised instructions:

(a) **Data transfer.** This allows data to be moved within the CPU, between the CPU and the memory of the computer system or between the CPU and external devices such as printers, VDUs and keyboards;

(b) **Arithmetic operations.** Such instructions direct the computer to perform arithmetic functions such as addition, subtraction, multiplication, division, increment, decrement, comparison and logical operations such as AND, OR and NOT;

(c) **Shift operations.** These move data to the left or right within a 'register' or memory location;

(d) **Transfer of control.** This directs the machine to skip one or more instructions or repeat previously encountered instructions.

The Fetch-Execute Cycle

A program, consisting of a combination of the instructions outlined above is run or 'executed' by retrieving or 'fetching' each instruction in turn from the memory store of the computer, decoding the operation required and then performing this operation under the direction of the CPU. This sequence of events is termed the 'fetch-execute' cycle.

On completion of each current instruction, the next instruction in the program's logical sequence of execution will be 'fetched' from store automatically. This process ends or 'terminates', under normal circumstances, when a halt instruction in the program is recognised by the computer. The term 'automatic sequence control' is often used to describe this characteristic of most current digital computers.

An Example of A Machine Code Program

The following example illustrates some of the concepts outlined above. Suppose that a computer has currently in its main store memory a simple machine code program to add two numbers together and store the result in memory. It could be shown as follows:

Address	Operation	Memory
Binary Code representing a location in the memory	Contents of each Location represented in Binary Code	
1000	1010010100010100	Load the number specified in the instruction into an internal register
1001	1110100010101110	Add the number specified here to the contents of the internal register
1002	1000100011101011	Transfer the result to the specified area of memory.
1003	1111111111111111	Halt

Each instruction in turn, starting with that resident in memory location 1000, would be fetched from memory, decoded and executed. This process would continue until the halt instruction in location 1003 was decoded.

The particular binary code or combination of binary digits (0s or 1s) in the instruction, causes the decoding circuitry of the CPU to transmit to other components of the hardware, the sequence of control signals which is necessary to perform the required operation.

Programming Languages

When it is considered that a typical program might contain tens of thousands of machine code instructions it might seem that programming is a formidable task, well beyond the capabilities of all but the most determined and meticulous of computer professionals. Indeed, if machine code were the only computer language in use, it is extremely unlikely that society would today be experiencing such a widespread presence of computers in almost every aspect of industrial, commercial, domestic and social life.

Fortunately for the computer industry, programming techniques have evolved along with advances in hardware. There is now a proliferation of programming languages designed to allow the programmer to concentrate most of his attention on solving the problem, rather than on the tedious task of converting the solution to machine code form.

In the history of programming languages, one of the first significant innovations was the development of assembly languages. A program written in an assembly language is much more readable and understandable than its equivalent in machine code; the problem arises, however, that it is no longer directly executable by the computer.

For example, a program, in some typical assembly language, equivalent to that given earlier in the chapter for the addition of two numbers, might take the following form:

LD	R,N1	LoaD register, R, with contents of location N1
ADD	R,N2	ADD contents of location N2 to contents of R
ST	R,N3	STore the result in location N3
HLT		HaLT

Notice that the operation codes LD, ADD, ST and HLT (representing LOAD, ADD, STORE and HALT respectively) are now easily recognisable and easy to remember; such mnemonics, or 'memory aids', are chosen for these reasons. The references, N1,N2 and N3, relate to memory locations and are called 'symbolic addresses' and in many assembly languages it is possible to use meaningful names such as HRS or RATE to indicate the type of data stored there. The internal register, R, may be one of several available within the computer for use by the programmer.

The CPU is unable to decode instructions in this form; they must first be converted into the equivalent machine code. An 'ASSEMBLER' is a machine code program which performs this function. It accepts an assembly language program as data, converts mnemonic operation codes to their numeric equivalents, assigns symbolic addresses to memory locations and produces as output the required machine code program. (This is represented in the diagram below).

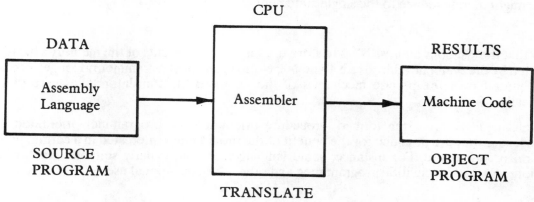

The assembly language program is termed the 'source program' and the final machine code program is the 'object program'.

Having an assembler means, of course, that it can be used to produce an improved version of itself! (This is illustrated in the following figure).

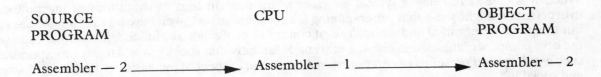

SOURCE PROGRAM	CPU	OBJECT PROGRAM
Assembler — 2 ────────▶	Assembler — 1 ────────▶	Assembler — 2

Thus there is no need to write any machine code programs at all and a considerable burden has been removed from the programming task; the computer itself now does much of the work required to produce the object program.

Though assembly languages aid the programmer considerably, they are still closely related to machine code; there is a 1:1 correspondence between a machine code instruction and one in assembly language. In other words each machine code instruction must have a matching assembly language instruction. This fundamental correspondence has led to the term 'low-level' being applied to this type of programming language as they are not sufficiently sophisticated to allow one assembly language instruction to represent several instructions in machine code.

Computer scientists recognised, however, that most programs could be broken down into a collection of smaller identifiable tasks and that no matter what the program, such tasks were present in all, in some recognisable form, though probably occurring in different logical sequences.

For instance, the majority of programs require the evaluation of arithmetic expressions such as

$$X + Y \times Z - P/Q$$

in other words expressions involving combinations of the four arithmetic operators

$$+, -, \times \text{ and } /.$$

Most programs will produce some form of visible output, whether printed on paper or displayed on a screen; most programs require data to be input for processing.

All of these tasks require lengthy, complicated sequences of instructions, but significantly, they can all be stated in a generalised form, and can therefore be implemented using generalised machine code programs. 'High-level' languages make extensive use of this characteristic. A high-level language is almost entirely constructed of these generalised sets of instructions or 'statements'. A single statement, for instance, in a high-level language can specify the evaluation of a complex arithmetic expression requiring many machine code instructions. The translator required for such a source language is therefore much more complex than an assembler, since each source language statement will generally generate many machine code instructions.

Taking the simple addition program introduced earlier to its conclusion, the program in a high-level language might merely reduce to the single statement

$$N3 = N1 + N2$$

meaning that the symbolic address N3 is to store the sum of the contents of the memory's locations represented by the symbolic addresses N1 and N2. Notice that the programmer no longer needs to concern himself over the precise mechanics of the addition: the translator takes care of that automatically.

High-level languages are often termed 'procedure orientated' or 'programmer orientated' languages, because they are designed for the benefit of the programmer interested in a certain type of application or procedure. For instance, some languages are particularly suitable for business applications, others for scientific programming and others for educational use.

Translators

It has already been noted that assemblers translate assembly language programs into machine code and that translators for high-level languages must perform a similar function. However, the precise mechanism by which this is accomplished for high-level languages varies considerably from language to language.

There are two main types of high-level language translators (or language processors as they are often known):

    (a) compilers;

    (b) interpreters.

It is important from a programming point of view to be quite clear about the difference between the two.

a. Compilers

The following figure illustrates the way in which a compiler is used to produce an executable program.

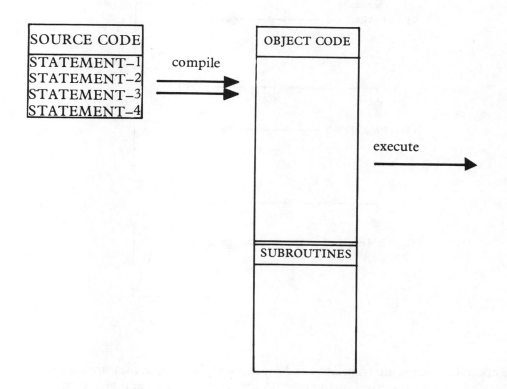

A compiler is essentially a sophisticated assembler, taking the source program and processing it to produce an independent object program in machine code. In addition, a compiler will often have access to a library of standard routines and special routines appropriate to the application area for which the language was designed; this collection of subroutines is called the 'run-time library'. Included in this library of machine code subprograms will be routines for performing arithmetic operations, input-output operations, backing-storage data transfers and other commonly used functions. Whenever the source code refers to one of these routines specifically, or needs one to perform the operation specified, the compiler will ensure that the routine is added to the object program.

Note that the final object code is independent of both the source code and the compiler itself, that is neither of these two programs needs to be resident in main store when the object code is being executed. However, any alterations to the program necessitates modification and re-compilation of the source code prior to executing the program again.

Examples of compiled languages are FORTRAN, COBOL and PASCAL.

b. Interpreters

The procedure used by interpreters is entirely different from that of compilers. The figure below illustrates this fundamental difference.

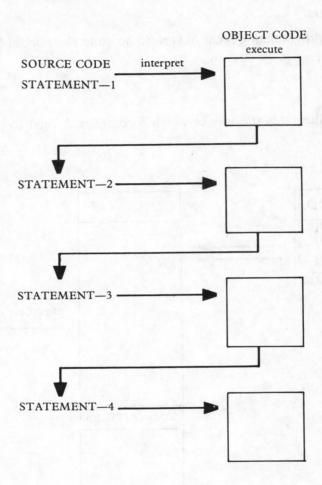

The source code statements are translated and executed separately, as they are encountered, while the source code is being processed by the interpreter. The object code that is actually executed is held within the interpreter; the latter merely identifies from the source statement which piece of machine code is relevant and causes it to be executed. On completion of a statement, control returns to the interpreter which then processes the next logical statement in the program sequence.

It might, therefore, seem that an interpreter is faster, more efficient and generally far superior to a compiler, but in fact the converse is almost invariably true. An interpreter must do a considerable amount of work before it can even begin to cause a source statement to be executed; on the other hand, a compiler has already done this work during compilation. Moreover, should a section of source code be repeated one or more times, an interpreter must re-interpret the section each time. Consequently interpreted programs tend to run significantly slower than equivalent compiled programs.

Because the translation and execution phases are interwoven, the interpreter must be resident in memory at the same time as the source code. If memory space is at a premium, this can be a severe limitation of an interpreted language.

On the credit side, interpreted languages generally allow program changes to be made more easily; it is merely necessary to make the modifications to the source code which is then immediately ready for execution.

Interpreted languages include BASIC and LISP.

Categories of Software

The tree diagram in the figure below illustrates the different categories of software and, to some extent, their relationships to each other. This chapter begins by examining the distinction between systems and applications software.

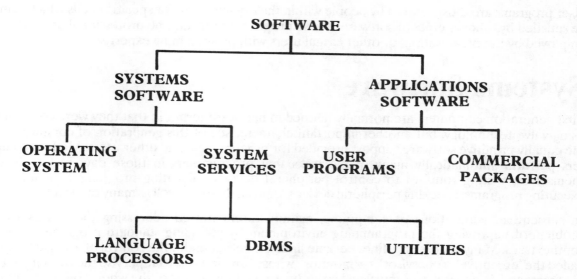

The term 'systems software' covers the collection of programs usually supplied by the manufacturer of the computer. These programs protect the user from the enormous complexity of the computer system, and enable the computer to be used to maximum effect. Without systems software a modern digital computer would be virtually impossible to use; as computer hardware has evolved, so systems software has been forced to become more and more complex in order to make effective use of it. The relationship between a user program and the systems software invisibly allowing its operation, was once amusingly compared to an elephant riding on the back of a mouse, such is the size and complexity of systems software compared to the individual programs it supports.

Broadly speaking, systems software consists of two elements:

(i) those programs concerned with the control and co-ordination of all aspects of the computer system, namely the 'Operating System';

(ii) a number of other programs providing various services to users. These services include compilers and interpreters for any languages supported by the system, database management systems (DBMS) for the manipulation of large volumes of data, and utility programs such as program editors and other aids to programming.

Applications software refers to programs which have some direct value to the organisation, and will normally include those programs for which the computer system was specifically purchased. For example, a mail order company might acquire a computer system initially for stock control and accounting purposes, when its volume of business begins to make these functions too difficult to cope with by manual means. Applications programs would be required to record and process customers' orders, update the stock file according to goods sent or received, make appropriate entries in the various accounts ledgers, etc.

Commercial packages come in two main categories:

>   (i) special-purpose packages;

>   (ii) general-purpose packages.

A package consists of one or more programs on some form of file medium (such as magnetic disc). It will be accompanied by documentation explaining in detail how the programs function and how they are used. An example of a special-purpose package is a payroll program which is used to store employee details and generate details of pay for each individual employee.

An example of a general-purpose package is a wordprocessor, a program which allows the computer to be used somewhat like an electronic typewriter and is therefore useful in a wide variety of ways.

User programs are those written by people within the organisation for specific needs which cannot be satisfied by other sources of software. These program writers may be professional programmers employed by the organisation, or other casual users with programming expertise.

Systems Software

First generation computers are normally defined in hardware terms, in that they were constructed using valve technology, but another important characteristic of this generation of computers was the equally primitive software support provided for programmers and other users. Modern computers perform automatically many of the tasks that programmers in those days had to handle themselves; writing routines to control peripheral devices, allocating programs to main store, executing programs, checking peripheral devices for availability, as well as many other routine tasks.

In subsequent generations of computers, manufacturers started addressing themselves to the problem of improving the programming environment by providing standard programs for many routine tasks. Many of these routines became linked together under the control of a single program called the 'executive', 'supervisor', or 'monitor', whose function was to supervise the running of user programs and, in general, to control and co-ordinate the functioning of the whole computer system, both hardware and software. Early programs of this type have evolved into the sophisticated programs collectively known as 'Operating Systems'.

Systems software has three important functions:

>   (i)   to facilitate the running of user programs;

>   (ii) to optimise the performance of the computer system;

>   (iii) to provide assistance with program development.

The operating system takes care of the former two requirements and language processors (such as assemblers and compilers), editors, diagnostic routines and other utility programs aid the third requirement.

a. Operating Systems

If a computer system is viewed as a set of resources, comprising elements of both hardware and software, then it is the job of the collection of programs known as the Operating System to manage these resources as efficiently as possible. In so doing , the operating system acts as a buffer between the user and the complexities of the computer itself. One way of regarding the Operating System is to think of it as a program which allows the user to deal with a simplified computer, but without losing any of the computational power of the machine. In this way the computer system becomes a virtual system, its enormous complexity hidden and controlled by the Operating System and through which the user communicates with the real system.

The Main Functions of Operating Systems

Earlier it was stated that the function of an operating system is to manage the resources of the computer system. These resources generally fall into the following categories:

Central Processing Unit (CPU). Since only one program can be executed at any one time, if the computer system is such that several users are allowed access to the system simultaneously, in other words a 'multi-user' system, then access to the CPU must be carefully controlled and monitored. In a 'timesharing' multi-user system each user is given a small 'time-slice' of processor time before passing on to the next user in a continuously repeating sequence. Another common scheme is to assign priorities to users so that the system is able to determine which user should have control of the CPU next.

Memory. Programs (or parts of programs) must be loaded into the memory before they can be executed, and moved out of the memory when no longer required there. Storage space must be provided for data generated by programs, and provision must be made for the temporary storage of data, caused by data transfer operations involving devices such as printers and disk drives.

Input/Output (I/O) Devices. Programs will request the use of these devices during the course of their execution and in a multi-user system conflicts are bound to arise, when a device being utilised by one program is requested by another. The Operating System will control allocation of I/O devices and attempt to resolve any conflicts which arise. It will also monitor the state of each I/O device and signal any faults detected.

Backing Store. Programs and data files will usually be held on mass storage devices such as magnetic disk and tape drives. The Operating System will supervise data transfers to and from these devices and memory and deal with requests from programs for space on them.

Files. These may be regarded as a limited resource in the sense that several users may wish to share the same data file at the same time in multi-user systems. The Operating System facilitates access to files and ensures restricted access to one program at any one time for those files which are to be written to.

Resource allocation is closely linked to one part of the Operating System called the 'scheduler'. The term 'scheduling' refers to the question of when, in a multi-user system, should a new process be introduced into the system and in which order the processes should be run.

The above is by no means an exhaustive list of the functions of an Operating System. Other functions include:

- interpretation of the command language by which operators can communicate with it;

- error handling. For example, detecting and reporting inoperative or malfunctioning peripherals;

- protection of data files and programs from corruption by other users;

- protection of data files and programs from unauthorised use;

- accounting and logging of the use of the computer resources.

b. System Services

Often a manufacturer will provide a number of programs designed specifically for program or application development. Three such aids are:

    (i)   Language Processors;

    (ii) Database Management Systems;

    (iii) Utility Programs.

Language Processors

Translators such as assemblers, compilers and interpreters fall into this category. The characteristics of these types of programs have been explored earlier in this chapter, though it is worth noting here, that in terms of program development they generally offer a valuable service in addition to those previously described. During the program development process it is very easy for programmers to write program instructions in violation of the rules for their formation. These are called 'syntax errors' and will normally be detected by a compiler. This may occur, for instance, as it scans the instruction and attempts to parse it (that is split it into recognisable chunks prior to converting it into machine code). The compiler will report all such errors that it is capable of detecting, by terminating the attempted compilation, specifying the nature of the errors, and indicating at which source statements they occurred. This report, usually called an 'error listing', is an invaluable aid to producing an executable (though not necessarily correct) program.

Database Management System (DBMS)

The term 'database' is used to describe a form of mass storage file organisation where the user is not directly concerned with layout, structure, or location of files; he or she only defines the information that is to be stored, and the form in which any reports derived from the data are to be presented. For this method of processing to be possible, a great deal of generalised software must be provided and, since such software must be closely related to many of the routines within the Operating System, manufacturers will often provide such a DBMS either with the rest of the computer system when purchased, or offer it as an additional piece of software to be purchased as and when required.

Utility Programs

As part of the systems software provided with a computer system there are a number of utility programs specifically designed to aid program development and testing. These include:

Editors. These permit the creation and modification of source programs and data files. The facilities offered by these programs usually include such things as character, word and line insertion and deletion, automatic line numbering, line tabulation for languages which require program instructions to be spaced in a specific manner, the storage and retrieval of files from backing storage, and the printing of programs or other files.

Diagnostic and Trace Routines. Programs in which the appropriate translator can find no fault will often contain errors in logic, known as 'bugs', which only become apparent when the program is run and produces results which are contrary to expectations. These 'run-time' errors are often very difficult to detect and may lead to long delays in the implementation of the program. Certain types of run-time errors will produce diagnostic messages to be produced by the operating system, but errors in the logic of a program must be isolated by the programmer himself.

A Trace routine will allow the user to follow the path taken through the program so that it may be compared with the expected route; thus the point at which any deviation occurred can be detected. Breakpoints may be inserted at strategic points in the program, such that when they are encountered, program execution is halted temporarily to allow the current state of the program variables to be examined and displayed in order to check their validity. Other similar facilities can be called on from these packages to speed the 'debugging' process.

File Managers. These simplify and facilitate a number of operations connected with program development and maintenance such as:

       (i) keeping backup copies of important files;

      (ii) deleting files and creating space for new ones;

     (iii) merging files;

     (iv) listing details of current files held on backing storage;

      (v) sorting file names into specified orders.

Without the help of such dedicated programs, operations such as these could be extremely time-consuming and consequently expensive.

Case Study - The MS/DOS Operating System

This case study examines Microsoft's single stream Disk Operating System (MS/DOS) which has become the industry standard for business software running on microcomputer systems. Its widespread acceptance stems largely from its adoption by IBM (as PC/DOS) and other manufacturers producing 'compatible' machines.

a. File Management Facilities

Each filename is held in a DIRECTORY, together with its size (expressed in bytes) and the date it was created or last accessed. For this reason it is important to ensure that the system date is always correct (date and time prompts are given at system start-up). Directories can be used to divide disk space into a number of user or application areas. A floppy disk with 360kb (kilobytes) capacity may contain, say, 30 or 40 files at most, so that it is fairly easy for a user to scan a single directory in the search for a particular file name. Hard disks, on the other hand, with capacities of 20 mb (megabytes) to 50 mb and more may contain hundreds or even thousands of files, which makes management in a single directory extremely difficult. For this reason, all operating systems which support hard disk-based machines allow the creation of sub-directories to which groups of files can be assigned. When the operating system's attention is directed to a particular directory, it is known as the current or working directory.

b. File Commands

All MS-DOS commands are entered at the operating system drive prompt, for example, drive A is displayed as A> and drive C (usually the hard disk) as C>. Whichever is displayed indicates the currently active drive to which the operating system is directed, unless otherwise instructed. A Command Line Interpreter allows the user to communicate with the operating system through a wide range of commands, some of the most frequently used being described later. Some commands are 'memory resident' or 'internal' and are always available once MS/DOS has been loaded. Other, less frequently used commands, are called from disk as required. Thus, if MS/DOS is called from a diskette, the relevant disk has to be in the drive at the time the command is entered.

The DIR (directory) Command

This command allows the user to display all the file names recorded in the working directory on a particular disk (referenced by the drive number, for example, A, B or C). For example, the command

> dir A:

displays the names of all files held in the working directory on the disk in drive A. The figure on the following page illustrates such a directory listing.

Note that the columns from left to right contain, filename, filename extension, size of file in bytes, date and then time last accessed, respectively. The file extension indicates the file type, for example, BAS indicates a BASIC program file and EXE an executable machine code program. Applications packages add their own file extension to any file created with the package. For example, if a user creates a spreadsheet with the Framework II package and names it 'BUDGET', the file will appear in the directory as BUDGET.FW2. The details of a named file can also be viewed by the command

> dir a:budget.fw2

Wild Card (*)

A wild card allows the user to broaden the scope of a command. For example, to display details of files on drive B and which begin with the filename 'TEST' could be entered as

> dir b:test*

The wild card can be used with some other commands, including the COPY command, which is explained in the next section.

File Listing from Dir Command

```
C>dir
Volume in drive C is TANDON
Directory of C:\PASCAL
.                       <DIR>           23-06-89        9:27
..                      <DIR>           23-06-89        9:27
PAS             EXE     12800           4-07-89        15:03
PROPAS1         EXE     79104          30-09-89        12:59
PROPAS2         EXE     86016          30-09-89        20:32
PROPAS          ERR      5248          13-09-89        16:20
PASLIBS         OBJ     71168          30-09-89        10:57
PROLINK         EXE     54016          15-08-89        13:16
PROG1           BAK      1324          12-10-89        14:15
PROG1           PAS      1324          12-10-89        14:13
PRINT           COM      4608          30-09-89         9:30

        11 File(s)         16279552   bytes free
```

c. Other File and Disk Commands

Each of the following commands is followed by an example command list, assuming a twin floppy disk drive system and direction of the operating system's attention to the A drive.

ERASE - to remove a named file (or, using the wild card, group of files) from disk. DEL has the same effect.

                    erase b:stock.dat

removes the named file from the disk in the B drive.

COPY - to a named file or group of files to another disk and/or directory.

                    copy test.bas b:

copies the named file from the source disk in the A drive to the target disk in the B drive.

ATTRIB - protects a file by setting it to 'read only'. The command

                    attrib +r budget.fw2

prevents any write operation of the named file. Similarly, for example,

                    attrib -r budget.fw2

removes the protection.

COMP - compares the contents of two files or two groups of files. For example,

                    comp a:wages1.dat b:wages2.dat

compares the named file on the disk in drive A with the named file on the disk in drive B.

DISKCOMP - compares the contents of two disks on a track-by-track basis, rather than by reference to particular files. The command

                    diskcomp a: b:

compares the disk in drive A with the disk in drive B.

DISKCOPY - allows the copying of one complete disk onto another. It is generally used to carry out security backups. The command

                    diskcopy a: b:

copies the entire contents of the disk in drive A to that in drive B. The DISKCOMP command would normally be used after this process to ensure that the two disks are identical.

FORMAT - formats the disk in the specified drive. All new disks must be formatted to accept MS/DOS files before use (a similar command exists in all operating systems). The command initializes the directory and file allocation tables on disk. It completely destroys any existing files as the complete disk contents are wiped. File protection attributes provide no protection. The only protection against accidental formatting of diskettes is to use the appropriate write protection mechanism (Chapter 5 Peripherals). Hard disks cannot be write-protected but more recent versions of MS/DOS provide more user warnings if the specified drive contains the hard disk. The accidental wiping of a 50mb hard disk could be catastrophic. The command

> format b:

formats the disk in drive B.

PRINT - initiates a primitive form of 'spooling' and prints a named text file on the attached printer while other commands are processed. Thus,

> print b:sales.lst

prints the named file from the disk in drive B. MS/DOS first responds with:

> name of list device [prn]:

Pressing the RETURN key sends the output to the printer.

RECOVER - recovers a file or entire disk containing some 'bad' or corrupted sectors. The command causes MS/DOS to read the file sector by sector and skips the bad sectors, marking them to ensure that they are not used again. Thus, the uncorrupted parts of a file can be recovered. The command

> recover b:wages.cob

recovers the named file from the disk in drive B, skipping the bad sectors.

TYPE - displays the contents of a file on screen. Thus, for example,

> type a:test.dat

displays the contents of the named file stored on drive A. A wild card cannot be used with the TYPE command.

Applications Software

An analysis of the uses to which companies and individuals put computers would reveal that the same types of tasks appear time and time again. Many organizations use computers to facilitate payroll calculations, others to perform stock control functions, accounting procedures, management information tasks and numerous other common functions.

These types of programs are classed as 'applications software', software which is applied to practical tasks in order to make them more efficient or useful in other ways. Systems software is merely there to support the running, development and maintenance of applications software.

An organisation wishing to implement one of these tasks (or any other vital to its efficient operation) on a computer has several alternatives:

(i) Ask a software house to take on the task of writing a specific program for the organisation's needs;

(ii) Use its own programming staff and produce the software 'in house';

(iii) Buy a commercially available program 'off the shelf' and hope that it already fulfils, or can be modified to fulfil, the organisation's requirements;

(iv) Buy a general purpose program, such as a database or spreadsheet package, that has the potential to perform the required functions.

The final choice will depend on such factors as the urgency of the requirements, financial constraints, size of the company and the equipment available.

It is beyond the scope of this book to enter into a discussion regarding either the strategy for making such a decision or to investigate specific items of software available for specific applications; but, with the immense and growing, popularity of general purpose packages, particularly for personal-business microcomputers, it is worth looking in more detail at this category of software.

General Purpose Packages for Microcomputers

Discussion of this class of software will be restricted here to the following headings , though they are not intended to represent an exhaustive list of all the categories of general purpose packages which are available:

(a) Wordprocessors

(b) Ideas or Thought Processors

(c) Spreadsheets

(d) Databases

(e) Graphics packages

(f) Expert System Shells

(g) Integrated packages

What characterises these software types as belonging to the category of general-purpose packages is that they have been designed to be very flexible and applicable to a wide range of different applications. For instance, a spreadsheet can be used as easily for simple accountancy procedures as for stock control; a database can be used with equal facility to store information on technical papers from journals, stock item details and personnel details for payroll purposes.

The suitability of a particular general-purpose package for a specific application will be largely dependent on the characteristics of the package. Though the general facilities afforded by different database packages may be roughly equivalent (for instance every package performs basically the same functions), each manufacturer will adopt its own style of presentation and will provide certain services not offered by its competitors. A prospective buyer should have a clear idea of the main uses for which the package is to be purchased right at the outset, because some packages may be much more suitable than others.

Advantages of general-purpose software compared to other forms of applications software are as follow:

(i) Because large numbers of the package are sold prices are relatively low;

(ii) They are appropriate to a wide variety of applications;

(iii) As they are already perfected they allow a great reduction in the time and costs necessary for development and testing;

(iv) They prove suitable for people with little or no computing experience;

(v) They are very easy to use;

(vi) They have been thoroughly tried and tested;

(vii) Most such packages are provided with extensive documentation.

Some of the disadvantages are as follow:

(i) Sometimes the package will allow only a clumsy solution to the application;

(ii) The user must still develop the application. This requires a thorough knowledge of the capabilities of the package, and how to make the best use of them;

(iii) The user will need to provide his own documentation for the particular application for which the package has been tailored;

(iv) Unless the software is used regularly, it is easy to forget the correct command sequences to operate the package, particularly for people inexperienced in the use of computer software of this type;

(v) The user must take responsibility for his own security measures to ensure that vital data is not lost, or to prevent unauthorised personnel gaining access to the data.

a. Wordprocessors

The wordprocessor performs much the same function as a typewriter, but it offers a large number of very useful additional features. Basically a wordprocessor is a computer with a keyboard for entering text, a monitor for display purposes, and a printer to provide the permanent output on paper. A wordprocessor is really nothing more than a computer system with a special piece of software to make it perform the required functions; some such systems have hardware configurations specifically for the purpose (such as special keyboards and letter-quality printers) but the majority are merely the result of obtaining an appropriate wordprocessor application package.

Wordprocessors are used for such purposes as producing

- letters

- legal documents

- books

- articles

- mailing lists

and in fact any type of textual material.

Some of the advantages they have over ordinary typewriters are as follow:

- typing errors can be corrected before printing the final version;

- the availability of such automatic features as page numbering, the placing of page headers and footers and word-line counting;

- whole document editing such as replacing every incidence of a certain combination of characters with another set of characters. For instance, replacing each occurrence of the name 'Mr. Smith' by 'Mrs. Jones';

- printing multiple copies all to the same high quality;

- documents can be saved and printed out at some later date without any additional effort.

However, wordprocessors do have some drawbacks. For instance, prolonged viewing of display monitors can produce eyestrain. They are generally considerably more expensive than good typewriters, and to be used properly, a certain amount of special training is required.

On the whole, wordprocessors are now firmly established in the so-called 'electronic office' and there is no reason to suppose that their use will not continue to expand.

A typical word processing package may provide the following facilities:

Word Wrap. As text is typed, words move automatically to the start of a new line if there is insufficient room for them at the right hand margin. With this facility, the only time that the RETURN key needs to be pressed is at the end of paragraphs or to insert blank lines;

Scrolling. Once the bottom of the screen is reached during text entry, the top of the text moves, line by line, up out of view as each new line of text is entered. This ensures that the line being entered is always visible on screen. The directional arrow keys allow scrolling to be carried out at will to view various parts of the document;

Deletion. This facility allows the deletion of characters, words or complete blocks of text;

Insertion. This is concerned with the insertion of single letters or continuous text within an existing block of text;

Block Marking. Usually, a special function key allows the marking or highlighting of text to be dealt with separately from the rest of the document. The marked text may be moved, deleted, copied or displayed with a different character font, for example, italics or bold print;

Text Movement or Copying. The user may need to move a marked block of text or repeat it by copying the same piece of text to different parts of the document;

Tabulation. Tabulation markers can be set to allow the cursor to be moved directly to column positions with the use of the TAB key. This is useful when text or figures are to be presented in columns;

Formatting. Text can aligned to a particular format, for example, with a straight (justified) or ragged (unjustified) right hand margin, or different margin settings (left, right, top and bottom);

Printing Styles. Text can be printed in a variety of styles, including bold, condensed, italic or underlined. Some word processors allow these styles to be displayed on the screen as well as on the printer and are known as WYSIWYG (What You See Is What You Get) packages;

Mailing List. This allows a user to personalise standard letters. The mailing list is, in effect, a file of names and addresses, details from which can be inserted into marked points in a standard letter. The word processor prints multiple copies of the standard letter selected by the user and personalises each with data extracted from the mailing list.

Additional Features. These include facilities for the checking of spelling in a document by reference to a dictionary held on disk, the import of text and figures from other packages such as spreadsheets, the export of text to other packages and the electronic transmission of text to other computers.

Hardware Constraints on Word Processors

The term WYSIWYG (What You See Is What You Get) describes word processing packages which allow text to be displayed on screen exactly as it is to be printed. Most packages have some WYSIWYG features but sometimes lack of an appropriate screen display, for example, one without high resolution graphics (Chapter 5 on Peripherals) can prevent their use. Typical WYSIWYG features include the ability to display characters in italic or boldface and words or phrases underlined or centred. Most dot matrix printers allow a full range of printing styles, so the main restriction on WYSIWYG features tends to be the screen display. On the other hand, most small business computer systems now include, as a minimum, a high resolution monochrome graphics screen display. Packages with very few WYSIWYG features rely on embedded commands and control characters within the text to indicate the beginning and end of specially selected printing requirements such as centring or boldface printing.

b. Ideas Processors

As the name suggests, software of this type enables users to process ideas or thoughts. Ideas, opinions and thoughts are generally unstructured and cannot, therefore, be processed in any useful way by a word processor or organized into files in a database. Ideas processors allow the user to organize and analyse unstructured information of a variety of different types, such as, for example, notes, memos, concepts, which are stored in a variety of different forms, for example, diaries, reference books, reports, files etc. A well known package is Agenda from Lotus. The package allows the user to enter random, spontaneous information in the same way as it would be jotted down on a notepad; such 'jottings' are known as Items. These items can then be placed in Categories; in other words the items can be indexed with any key required by the user, for example, name, date, place, product, area and town. Items can then be re-categorized at will and the user can then view them by category.

c. Spreadsheets

Just as wordprocessors are designed to manipulate text, spreadsheets are designed to do the equivalent with numerical information. A spreadsheet program presents the user with a blank grid of 'cells' each of which is capable of containing one of three types of information:

> - a label consisting of alphanumeric characters;
>
> - a number;
>
> - a formula, which may make reference to other cells.

These are sufficient to allow a wide range of applications to be implemented in a very convenient and easily understandable way. For example, suppose that a small business dealing in the sale of personal computer systems wishes to use such a program to record on a monthly basis, the sales values attributable to each of its four salespersons. The spreadsheet might be set up as follows:

	A	B	C	D	E	F	G
1	ITEM	SALE		COMMISSION			
2		VALUE					
3				John	Jim	Joan	Janet
4	IBM PC	2000			100		
5	Amstrad 1512	670				33.50	
6	IBM XT	3200					160
7	Compaq	1800			90		
8	Olivetti	1900	95				
	....	etc					....
50	TOTAL SALES	88860.00	265.50	468.30	922.80	565.90	
51							
52	TOTAL COMMISSION	2221.50					

Column A contains labels describing the systems purchased. Column B the sales value of the item, and the remaining four columns contain the calculated commissions for the salespersons. The actual sales data in columns A and B, and the commissions, are typed in at the appropriate places according to who made the sales. The totals, however are calculated by the program through formulae installed in the cells B50 to F50. Such a formula might be written as

$$@SUM(B4..B49)$$

and it would automatically calculate the sum of the contents of cells B4 to B49. Installed in cell B50, it would produce the figure '88860.00'; any empty cells, or those containing !abels, would be treated as having a value of zero. Any change in the data on the spreadsheet would cause all the calculations to be repeated.

This automatic calculation facility gave rise to the expression 'what if' which is often used to describe an important capability of spreadsheets. It is possible to set up complex combinations of inter-dependent factors and see 'what' happens to the final result 'if' one or more of the factors is changed. The spreadsheet, once set up, takes care of all the recalculations necessary for this type of exercise.

The earliest program of this form was called 'Visicalc' and it ran on an Apple Microcomputer. Many such programs now exist, having capabilities far exceeding those of Visicalc, but they still closely resemble the original concept in appearance and operation.

Spreadsheet Size

A typical spreadsheet, for example, that available in the Lotus 123 integrated package, provides 256 columns and over 8000 rows. The problem is that the user can only view about 20 rows and 8 columns on the screen at any one time and applications taking up more than, say 60 rows and 30 columns can become unmanageable. Another restriction on the amount of spreadsheet which can be used is the amount of RAM available to the user. The more sophisticated the package, the more RAM it tends to take, so a user should check that the system on which the spreadsheet program is to be used has sufficient RAM to accommodate the package itself and any data to be stored on the spreadsheet. There are packages which hold the current worksheet on disk and though this may allow the construction of larger worksheets, data retrieval and manipulation is inevitably slowed by the need for frequent disk accesses.

Typical Spreadsheet Facilities

Apart from the entry of labels, numbers and formulae, a spreadsheet package normally allows the user to use various facilities from a menu to handle the data stored on the worksheet. Some packages allow the experienced user to automate spreadsheet operations through the use of macros. Macros are user-defined groups of individual instructions which can be executed by single key strokes combined with the ALT key (see Chapter 5 on Peripherals). In addition, some spreadsheets can be programmed using basic programming constructs such as IF...THEN...ELSE. This somewhat de-feats the object of spreadsheets, which is to provide the business user with an easy-to-learn decision tool. Typically, spreadsheets offer the following facilities:

Copying. This allows the copying of fixed values or labels, or formulae which are logically the same in another part of the worksheet. Thus, for example, in the earlier worksheet sample, the formula @SUM(C4..C49) which totalled a group of values for John could be copied to succeeding columns to the right for Jim as @SUM(D4..D49), for Joan as @SUM(E4..E49)and for Janet as @SUM(F4..F49) and so on. The formula is logically the same but the column references change, according to the position of the formula. Where part of a formula is to remain absolute during copying, the relevant reference is pre-fixed with, for example, a $ sign. Thus, for example, the formula (B3+C3)*A6 would add the contents of B3 and C3 and then multiply the resulting sum by the contents of A6. The $ prefixes will ensure that when the formula is copied, the reference to A6 remains constant. Thus when copied to, for example, rows 4 and 5 the formula becomes (B4+C4)*A6 and (B5+C5)*A6 respectively;

Formatting. A label can be centred, or left or right justified within a cell. Values are invariably right justified but can be displayed in a variety of formats including fixed decimal, integer, percent and scientific or as money values prefixed by a $ or £ sign to 2 decimal places. Individual formats can be selected 'globally', that is throughout a worksheet or for selected ranges of cells;

Functions. These include SUM (adds the contents of a specified range of cells), AVG (calculates the average value in a specified range of cells), MIN (extracts the minimum value held in a specified range of cells) and SQRT (returns the square root of a value in a specified cell). The full range of functions usually include those used in mathematics, trigonometry, finance and statistics;

Macros. Groups of regularly used key sequences can be executed by one key press in combination with the Alt key, for example, Alt C. These can be useful when the spreadsheet has been tailored for a particular application which may be used by inexperienced users. The application may be menu driven as the example figure shows.

A Menu Display for a Sales Figure Analysis Application on a Spreadsheet.

	A	B	C	D	E	F	G	H
1			Sales Analysis System					
2			Menu					
3								
4	Alt	A...	Enter Figures for New Analysis Period					
5	Alt	B...	Enter Figures for Existing Analysis Period					
6	Alt	C...	Save Latest Entries					
7	Alt	D...	Print Analysis Figures					
8	Alt	E...	Draw Graph of Sales Figures					
9	Alt	F...	P rint Graph of Sales Figures					
10	Alt	Q...	Quit System					

Without macros, each user would have to be completely familiar with the spreadsheet commands needed. With macros, one experienced user can tailor the spreadsheet so that training time for other staff is minimized. Unfortunately, the macros are defined on the worksheet along with the data and they may be accidentally or deliberately erased by a user. Cell protection facilities can help prevent this, although there is nothing to stop a user from removing such protection with a few simple keystrokes;

Windows. A user may wish to keep one area of the worksheet in view whilst looking at another. Horizontal or vertical windows allow the screen to be split accordingly. The user can 'toggle' between the windows which can be scrolled synchronously or independently of one another;

Sideways Printing. Where the number of columns used cannot be accommodated in one print line on a printer, the package turns the worksheet sideways and prints column by column, rather than row by row. This facility is integral to some packages but can be bought as an add-on for others;

Graphs. Numerical data can be displayed in a variety of graphical forms, including bar charts, line graphs, scatter diagrams and pie charts. Lotus 123 provides graphical output directly but others allow numerical data to be exported to another package for graph production. The range and quality of graphs vary greatly from one package to another. With the use of a colour printer, very attractive and presentable graphs can be produced to illustrate business reports;

Consolidation. This feature allows the merging of several worksheets into a summary sheet, whilst keeping the original worksheets intact. Consolidation adds together cells with the same co-ordinates in the various worksheets;

Other Facilities. These include, amongst others, cell protection facilities to prevent alteration of certain entries, the alteration of individual column widths and the display of cell contents as formulae instead of the results of their calculation.

Spreadsheets have a number of attractive features compared to traditional programming solutions to processing needs:

- designed for laymen;

- easy to learn and use;

- wide range of uses;

- relatively cheap;

- easily modified;

- well tried and tested;

- provide quick development time.

On the debit side, they tend to be:

- too general purpose and therefore provide satisfactory rather than ideal solutions;

- the problem must still be analysed and a solution method identified.

d. Database

At one time database programs, or Database Management Systems (DBMS) as they are often called, were restricted to mainframe computers because of the large memory requirements demanded of such applications. Currently, however, even personal business microcomputers have sufficient internal memory (1 megabyte - roughly 1 million characters of storage - is quite common) to make such applications not only feasible but also extremely powerful.

These programs allow files, comprising collections of records, to be created, modified, searched and printed. A good database program will offer, as a minimum, the following facilities:

- user-definable record format allowing the user to specify the fields within the record;

- user-definable input format to allow the user to define the way the data is to be entered into the computer;

- file searching capabilities for extracting records satisfying certain criteria from a file;

- file sorting capabilities so that records can be ordered according to the contents of a certain field;

- calculations on fields within records for inclusion in reports;

- user-definable report formats, so that different types of reports containing different combinations of record fields may be produced.

Recently, an innovative feature has begun to appear with database programs. Some software houses are adding 'natural language' interfaces to their programs to allow users to state their requirements in (almost) ordinary English. This is a very attractive feature to inexperienced users of computers. For instance, if the system has been set up for a personnel file of employees of a business, the enquirer might want to know how many of the employees are earning less than a certain salary. The question to the program could be phrased:

"Print the names and departments of employees whose salaries are less than '£6000'"

and the program would search the file and print the required details for all those records satisfying the stated criterion.

The main value of such a facility is the brevity with which quite complicated requirements may be stated; English is a very expressive and concise language compared to formal query languages or menu-driven strategies for information retrieval programs. However, natural language processing is still in its infancy and programs offering this facility generally are able only to cope with a very limited form of English. The user, to get the most benefit from the free-form style of input, must be very much aware of the nature of these restrictions, otherwise a great deal of time will be wasted in phrasing questions in a form that the system is unable to 'understand'.

Database Packages for Microcomputers

These packages fall broadly into two groups, CARD INDEX and RELATIONAL. The relational type is described in Chapter 6. Generally, card index systems are simpler to set up and operate but they provide less sophisticated data manipulation and search facilities than do the relational type. Further, the relational type provide a programming language which allows the development of 'user friendly', tailored applications. Thus, a user can be protected from the complexities of package operation by being presented with, for example, a menu-driven system with options for record insertion, modification, deletion and retrieval and perhaps the production of summary reports. The card index type cannot be programmed in this way, so the user must have a more detailed knowledge of package operation. On the other hand, card index packages tend to be easier to use. The superior data management facilities provided by the relational type tend to be under-used unless professional database designers and programmers are involved in the development of the database. The business executive who plans to use the database as a personal tool without such professional help, will probably be well advised to purchase a card index package rather than a relational database package.

Another factor to be considered when choosing a database, is disk space and access speed. In contrast with spreadsheet packages, database packages require frequent disk accesses when carrying out sorting and retrieval operations. Floppy disk access times tend to be too slow and their storage capacity inadequate for anything but the simplest application. A package should also allow sorting with the use of indexes, so that files do not have to be physically sorted. Indexed sorts are much quicker and a number of different indexes can be set up so that the database can be displayed in a variety of logical orders without re-organizing the data on disk.

e. Graphics Packages

These generally fall into three categories according to their main area of use:

- Business graphics;

- Graphic design;

- Desktop publishing.

Business graphics packages allow the production of such things as Bar Charts, Line Graphs and Pie Diagrams; diagrams of a statistical nature likely to be included in business reports.

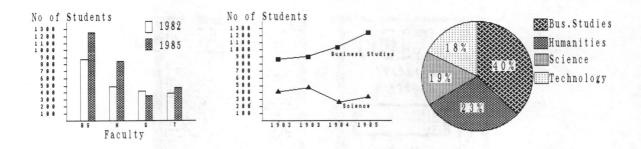

Packages for graphic design consist of a collection of special functions aimed at aiding the graphic designer. The artist uses the screen as his canvas and a light-pen (or equivalent device) as his brush. They generally allow work of professional quality to be produced in a relatively short amount of time, and include such facilities as

- large colour palette

- geometric figure drawing, e.g. lines, rectangles, circles

- filling areas with colour or patterns

- undoing mistakes

- moving/copying/deleting/saving areas of the screen display

- choice of a variety of character fonts

- printing the finished design.

Desktop publishing programs are designed to facilitate the production of documents such as posters, illustrated articles and production of documents such as posters, illustrated articles and other documents which combine large amounts of text with illustrations, the type of thing we frequently see in newspapers. As such they tend to contain a number of facilities in common with graphic design packages, but emphasise the printing aspect much more and generally just work in black and white. These packages place a lot of emphasis on being able to experiment with arranging sections of the document and seeing its overall appearance. Text is also given more importance; a rudimentary wordprocessor may be provided, or text may be 'imported' from a prepared file, and the user is generally able to experiment with different type fonts on text already displayed on the screen.

f. Expert System Shells

Pure research in the field of artificial intelligence has had a number of practical spin-offs. One such spin-off has been the development of programs known as 'Expert Systems'. These are programs designed to be able to give the same sort of help or advice, or make decisions, as a human expert in some narrow field of expertise. For instance, a program called PROSPECTOR is capable of predicting the existence of mineral ores given various pieces of information gathered from physical locations. In the same way that, given certain evidence, an expert might say that a particular site looked favourable for containing ore, PROSPECTOR indicates the probability of the existence of the ore. PROSPECTOR is in fact attributed with the discovery of an extremely valuable quantity of molybdenum which had previously been overlooked by human experts.

Expert systems have been developed in all kinds of areas which have traditionally been the responsibility of human experts, including medical diagnosis; decisions in areas such as this are so important, however, that it would be foolish to blindly accept the pronouncement of a computer. For this reason, expert systems have built-in the ability to 'explain' the reasoning behind any conclusion so that this chain of reasoning can be checked and verified (or rejected) by a human.

A typical expert system has three main components:

(i) a knowledge base consisting of facts and rules by which facts can lead to conclusions. For example, the rule

IF (1) STEM is woody

AND (2) POSITION is upright

AND (3) ONE MAIN TRUNK is NO

THEN TYPE is SHRUB

could be one of many in an expert system knowledge base for botanical classification;

(ii) an 'inference engine' which processes the knowledge base;

(iii) a user interface to facilitate communication with the user.

The term 'Shell' is given to expert systems which have been given no specific knowledge base, only the inference engine and user interface; the knowledge base has to be provided by the user. An expert system shell can thus be used to provide advice or help in a number of areas of expertise, providing it is given the appropriate knowledge base for each area.

For example, an expert system shell could be used to give advice on the legal procedures and sequence of steps necessary for selling a house (what solicitors call 'conveyancing'), or to give advice about possible causes and cures of diseases in houseplants, or diagnosing faults in cars. Not only could these applications be of practical use, but they could also be instructive, because the user could ask for and obtain the reasons behind any conclusions.

One of the problems of using such shells, is the determination of the rules which represent the wisdom of a human expert; many experts are not consciously aware of the precise reasoning processes they themselves use in order to come to some conclusion, yet in order to produce an expert program, these processes must be defined in a form that is usable. The process of determining the knowledge base rules is known as 'knowledge elicitation' or 'knowledge acquisition' and is performed by 'knowledge engineers'.

g. Integrated Packages

Once it became evident that packages such as those described above were going to become more and more in demand, software houses started producing packages which offered integrated combinations of wordprocessors, databases, spreadsheets, graphics and more recently, expert system shells. In fact one integrated package called Lotus 123, offering spreadsheet, database and business-type graphics, became the most successful ever general purpose applications package for microcomputers. Its huge success can be attributed to several important factors typifying the many variations of the program which have since appeared on the market:

(i) The extremely 'user-friendly' presentation - facilities are selected by choosing options from menus, which call up further menus until the actual operation required is displayed and performed. There are on-line help facilities which the user can have displayed at any time;

(ii)   The same data can be used for each of the three main applications: for calculations, information retrieval or to provide data for the production of diagrams such as bar charts or pie diagrams;

(iii)   The large number of special functions by which almost every need can be met;

(iv)   The same command sequence and menu structures are used for each of the three functions, making the package very easy to learn;

(v)   Relatively cheap considering the number of functions supplied in the one package.

Integrated packages offering even more functions are now on the market. Many now offer wordprocessing in addition to the three original functions. A recent development combines these four with an expert system shell and a natural language interface to the database. One reviewer of this package noted that, although the program could do just about everything, it was so complicated that it was difficult to get it to do anything! Fortunately this is not generally true of integrated packages which are what can be considered (at least for the moment) the ultimate in general purpose applications programs.

Assignment   Williamson's Operating System

R. & G.H. Williamson Limited is a small building company based in Kendal. The high quality of their work has led to the rapid expansion of the business, which now employs over thirty full-time workers who are skilled in various aspects of building work. The company is owned by Gareth and Robert Williamson who carry out initial job estimates on site. The two directors plan to buy a computer system, primarily to carry out their general accounting procedures. They have already approached Sys-Time Ltd, a software house, but were disappointed with the advice which they received, partly because they themselves were a little vague about their requirements and partly because Sys-Time 'blinded them with science'.

You are employed as a trainee office manager and Gareth Williamson, being aware of your knowledge of computing, has asked you to explain to him the significance of a few of the terms that the Sys-Time consultant threw at him. He wants you to brief him so that he is better prepared when he meets the representative of another software house.

Task

Gareth Williamson wants to understand the meaning and significance to him of the terms:

(a) operating systems;

(b) integrated package;

(c) spreadsheet;

(d) wordprocessor;

(e) database;

(f) WIMPs.

Prepare notes explaining all these terms and suggesting the relevance and potential usefulness of each to his company.

Developmental Task

Identify particular commercial packages/versions belonging to each of the software categories listed above.

Assignment   Turbo Cars

Turbo Cars is a small car repair business operating from a back street garage in South Shields. The owner, Ray Pitts, has bought himself a second-hand Apple microcomputer, equipped with twin disk drives, a printer and a version of the C/PM operating system. He plans to keep computer records of his stocks of spares. A friend of his, Tom Finney, who runs a small motorist's discount shop, has an IBM system which supports the MS/DOS operating system; he uses the system for his business accounting applications. Tom is a computer enthusiast and has already written his own stock control program, using the COBOL programming language. He has given Ray Pitts a copy of the program listing which will require some modification for the Apple system.

Unfortunately, Tom Finney has moved out of the area and cannot be contacted. Ray Pitts knows that you have some knowledge of computing and asks you why the COBOL coding needs to be changed and why Tom Finney told him that he would need a COBOL compiler.

Task

You are going to visit Ray Pitts at his home to explain matters to him. Prepare some notes for him, explaining why the source code needs to be changed and the role that the compiler plays in providing an executable program.

In a role play exercise with other members of your group, give your explanations and tactfully offer some advice on alternative actions he may take.

Developmental Task

Research some different programming language dialects. BASIC will probably be the most familiar to you and it should be possible to identify a number of variations in the range and format of instructions available, for different versions of the language. Use any examples you find to illustrate your explanations to Ray Pitts.

Assignment   A Soft Option

Powerdrive Ltd is a wholesale supplier of DIY and gardening power tools, such as drills, routers, lawn mowers and hedge trimmers. The main data processing applications for general accounting, order processing, stock control and so on, are already computerized. The company uses a local area network formed from IBM PS/2s, so all departments have access to and can share corporate information. There are two specialist computing staff, including yourself, employed by the company. One, the network manager, is responsible for hardware purchase and management. Your main responsibility is for applications development. All applications computerized to date make use of special-purpose packaged software, so the company is well aware of their benefits in terms of cheapness and reliability. The managing director has expressed interest in the idea of task automation, using general-purpose packages such as spreadsheets and databases. The secretarial staff already make use of word processors, but they are not used by other members of staff. The Financial Director is keen to make use of computer facilities because the preparation of, for example, financial reports and cash budgets can be extremely tedious and time-consuming. The Sales Manager has identified some tasks which may be eased with the use of a database package.

In order that management can make a better assessment of the potential uses of these general-purpose packages, you have been asked to prepare a series of talks and presentations to deliver to certain key staff.

Task

1. **Prepare suitable notes and materials for a talk and presentation on ONE general-purpose package. Your support materials may include OHP slides, wall charts, handouts etc. In order to provide a context for your audience, the presentation should make use of a particular application of your own choice and design. Present the talk.**

2. **Prepare a brief informal report, pointing out the main advantages and disadvantages inherent in using such a package. These will tend to relate to, for example, user friendliness, documentation, the problems of user training and the tailoring of the package.**

Chapter 12

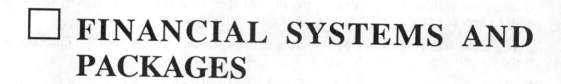

☐ FINANCIAL SYSTEMS AND PACKAGES

Introduction

This chapter describes the various financial systems of a typical business and the packaged software available to support them. Financial systems primarily support the accounting functions of a business. Two types of accounting are briefly explained below.

Financial Accounting

Financial systems exist to control the accounting functions of a business. Financial accounting or 'bookkeeping' is the process of recording the financial transactions of a business which result from the day-to-day operation of the business, for example, the sale of goods to a customer and the subsequent settlement of the debt. Apart from their function as a control mechanism over the financial transactions of a business, accounting records can be analysed to provide information on the performance of a business over a period. Typically, such information is extracted annually or every six months in the form of a balance sheet and trading and profit and loss account. These financial statements will also be required by external agencies, for example, the Inland Revenue (for tax assessment) and the bank, if loan facilities are required.

Cost and Management Accounting

Financial accounting is largely concerned with past events and cost and management accounting aims to provide management with information to support their decisions on the planning of future business activity. The information should enable management to:

(a) establish and monitor the financial targets of the business, which may be, for example, to increase sales of a particular product by 10 per cent in the next six months and at the same time to cut the cost of producing each unit of the product by 5 per cent. Targets are usually fairly specific so that their achievement or otherwise can be determined.

(b) control income and expenditure within the business. Financial accounting is concerned with the whole of the business whereas cost accounting identifies cost 'centres' (for different parts of the business) and provides for the preparation of budgets for each part of the business and the costing of its operations.

Financial system packages are available for both these areas of accounting but the remainder of this chapter concentrates on financial accounting systems and related applications. The chapter is divided into two main sections. The first section briefly describes the function and operation of the main accounting ledgers in which transactions are recorded. The second section looks at other business applications, specifically, stock control, sales order processing and invoicing. Immediately following the description of each ledger and application there is a description of the main data requirements of an appropriate software package and the facilities it offers.

The Ledgers

Business accounts are needed to record:

- transactions with debtors; these are people or organizations who owe money to the business for goods or services provided (Sales) as part of its normal trading;

- transactions with creditors; these are people or organizations to whom the business owes money for the supply of goods (Purchases).

These transactions are recorded in the Sales Ledger and the Purchases Ledger respectively. A third ledger, the Nominal Ledger is used to record the overall income and expenditure of the business, with each transaction classified according to its purpose.

a. Sales Ledger

General Description

The purpose of the sales ledger is to keep a record of amounts owed to a business by its trading customers or clients. It contains a record for each customer with a credit arrangement. Most businesses permit their customers to purchase goods on credit. The goods are usually supplied on the understanding that, once payment has been requested, the debt will be paid for within a specified period of, for example, 14 or 30 days. Payment is requested with the use of an invoice addressed to the customer and containing details of goods supplied, the amount owing and credit days given. Once a customer order has been accepted and processed, the total amount due for the order is recorded in the relevant customer's account in the sales ledger and the balance owing is increased accordingly. When a payment is received from the customer, the amount is entered to the customer's account and the balance owing is decreased by the appropriate amount. There are two main approaches to sales ledger maintenance, balance forward and open item.

Balance forward. This method provides an opening balance (the amount owing at the beginning of the month), the transactions for that month giving the date, type (for example, goods sold or payment received) and amount of each transaction and a closing balance. The closing balance at the end of the month is carried forward as the opening balance for the next month. A statement of account detailing all the transactions for the month will normally be sent to the customer and a copy filed away for business records. The customer's account in the sales ledger will not then contain details of the previous month's transactions so any query will require reference to the filed statements of account.

Open item. The open item method is more complicated in that each invoice is identified by a code and requires payments from customers to be matched against the relevant invoices. All payments received and relating to a particular invoice are recorded against it until it is completely paid off. This method can make control difficult as some customers may make part payments which cannot be tied to a particular invoice. If a customer does not specify to which invoice a particular payment relates it is normally assigned to the oldest invoice(s). Once an invoice has been completely settled it is cleared from the ledger and any subsequent statements of account.

A typical statement of account from an open item ledger is shown on the following page.

Statement of Account from Open Item Ledger

```
From:  J.WILSON LTD              To:  P.Downes
       12 WATLING ST.,               14 Main St.,
       YORK                          York

                 STATEMENT  at 31.7.89
   Account 36147
```

Date	Invoice Ref.	Description	Transactions dr	cr
13.6.89	1715	Invoice	350.00	
16.6.89	1365	Invoice	100.00	
7.7.89	1715	Cash		350.00
14.7.89	1217	Invoice	150.00	
21.7.89	1378	Invoice	125.00	
23.7.89	1365	Cheque		100.00
30.7.89	1217	Cash		150.00
		Balance due	125.00	

Sales Ledger - Typical Package Requirements and Facilities

Customer Master File

When setting up the Sales Ledger system, one of the first tasks is to set up the customers' (debtors) accounts. This file will be a master file which is updated by sales and account settlement transactions. A typical package should provide as a minimum, the following data item types for each customer record:

Account Number - used to uniquely identify a customer record;

Name and Address - this will normally be the customer's address to which statements of account and invoices are sent;

Credit Limit - the maximum amount of credit to be allowed to the customer at any one time. This will be referred to by sales staff before an order is authorized for processing;

Balance - this is the balance of the customer's account at any one time.

A choice will usually be provided to select the form of sales ledger required, either open item or balance forward (see previous section). Normally, when the file is first created, a zero balance will be recorded and outstanding transactions entered to produce a current balance.

An open item system should allow for the storage of information on invoices relating to each customer's account and the facility for payments to be tied to referenced invoices. A balance brought forward system should provide a statement file with records related to each customer account to allow the production of monthly statements.

Transaction Inputs

Transactions may update the customer accounts in the sales ledger directly (transaction processing) or they may be initially stored as a transaction file for a later updating run. Whichever method the package uses, it should allow for the entry of the following transaction types:

Invoice - this is sent to the customer requesting payment in respect of a particular order. The amount of the invoice is debited to the customer's account in the sales ledger, thus increasing the amount owing;

Credit Note - if, for example, goods are returned by a customer or there is a dispute concerning the goods, a credit note is issued by the business to the customer. The amount of the credit note will be credited to the customer's account in the sales ledger, thus reducing the balance owing. Credit notes are often printed in red to distinguish them from invoices.

Receipt - this is any payment or remittance received from a customer in whole or partial settlement of an invoice. Such an entry will be credited to the customer's account and reduce the balance owing accordingly.

The following data may be entered with each type of transaction:

Account Number - essential to identify the computer record. Although some packages allow for the entry of a shortened customer name and subsequent search if the account number has been forgotten, the account number is still necessary to uniquely identify a record;

Date of Transaction;

Amount of Transaction;

Transaction Reference - normally this is the invoice number to which the transaction relates.

Outputs

The following facilities may be expected:

Single Account Enquiry - details of individual customer accounts to be displayed on screen. Retrieval may be via an account number or a search facility using a shortened version of the customer name, for example, the first 15 characters, excluding spaces and punctuation. If more than one record is retrieved by this method they may be scanned through on screen until the required details are displayed;

Customer Statement Printing - it is essential that the system can produce monthly statements for sending to customers;

Management Information Summary Reports, for example:

Debtors' Age Analysis - this provides a schedule of the total amounts owing by customers, categorized according to the time various portions of the total debt have been outstanding (unpaid). It is important for a business to make financial provision for the possibility of 'bad debts'. These are debts which are unlikely to be settled and have to be taken out of business profits. The figure below illustrates an aged analysis report.

Period debt has been owing	Amount
	£
Less than 1 month	10,000
1 month to 2 months	4,000
2 months to 3 months	2,000
3 months to 6 months	1,000
Over 6 months	500

From their own experience of the trade, a business's management should be able to estimate the percentage of each amount that is likely to become bad debt. Generally, the longer the debt has been outstanding, the greater the likelihood that it will turn out to be bad.

Customers Over Credit Limit - this may form the basis of a 'black list' of customers whose further orders require special authorization by management. Of course, some may warrant an increase in their credit limit.

Dormant Account List - if there has been no activity on an account for some time, it may warrant removal from the file or perhaps a contact to see if further business may be forthcoming.

Validation and Control

The package should provide for careful validation of entry details and the protection of records from unauthorized access or amendment. Generally, for example, a customer record cannot be removed from the Sales Ledger while the account is still 'live', that is, there is a balance outstanding. More details of validation and control are given in Chapter 7.

b. Purchase Ledger

General Description

The purchase ledger mirrors the sales ledger, except that it contains an account for each supplier from whom the business buys goods. When the business buys goods from a supplier it is usually on similar credit arrangements to those provided by the business for its own customers. Thus, the business will receive an invoice requesting payment within a certain period for goods purchased. The amount of the invoice will be credited to the supplier's account and the balance owing to the supplier is increased accordingly. When payment is made to a supplier in full or part settlement of an invoice, the supplier's account is debited by the appropriate amount and the balance decreased.

Most purchase ledger systems operate on an open item basis so incoming invoices are given reference numbers so that payments to suppliers can be tied to particular invoices.

Purchase Ledger- Typical Package Requirements and Facilities
Supplier Master File

The supplier master file contains the suppliers' (creditors) accounts. It will be updated by supplier invoices and payments to suppliers. A typical package should provide, as a minimum, the following data item types for each supplier record:

Account Number - used to uniquely identify a supplier record;

Name and Address - the name and address of the supplier business;

Credit Limit - the maximum amount of credit allowed to the business by the supplier at any one time. A check should be kept on this to avoid rejection of orders;

Settlement Discount - this is the amount of discount given by a supplier if an invoice is settled within a specified discount period;

Due Date - the system may issue a reminder when payment is due; a report may be output on request listing all invoice amounts due for payment within, say 7 days;

Balance - the current balance on the account.

A choice will usually be provided to select the form of purchase ledger required, either open item or balance forward.

Transaction Inputs

Transactions may update the supplier accounts directly (transaction processing) or they may be initially stored as a transaction file for a later updating run. A purchase ledger package should allow for the following transaction inputs:

Supplier Invoices - before entry, each invoice must be checked against the appropriate order to ensure that they have been ordered and then checked against the relevant delivery note for actual receipt of goods. The balance on a supplier's account and thus the amount owing to the supplier, will be increased by an invoice entry. Some packages allow unsatisfactory invoices to be held in abeyance until cleared;

Approved Payments - once an invoice has been cleared for payment, a voucher may be raised to ensure payment on or before a due date to ensure discount is obtained for prompt payment. The entry of the payment value will decrease the balance of a supplier's account and thus the amount owed by the business to the supplier. Cheques may be produced automatically on the due date, but there should be some checking procedure to ensure payments are properly authorized;

Adjustments - to reverse entries made in error.

Outputs

The following output facilities may be expected:

Single Account Enquiries - details of individual supplier accounts to be displayed on screen. Retrieval may be via a supplier code;

Payment Advice Slips - these may be produced to accompany a payment to a supplier and detail the invoice reference, the amount due and the value of the payment remitted. Payment advice slips help the supplier who may be using the open item system for their own sales ledger system.

Automatic Cheques - the package may, with the use of pre-printed stationery produce cheques for payment to suppliers as and when invoices fall due. There must be a careful checking and authorization procedure to prevent incorrect payments being made.

Management Information Summary Reports may provide, for example:

Unpaid Invoices - a list of all outstanding invoices, together with details of supplier, amount owing and due date;

Creditors' Age Analysis - this is the supplier equivalent of debtors' age analysis. The report provides a schedule of total balances owing to suppliers and analysed according to the length of time the debt has been outstanding. The report may be used to determine the payments which should be given priority.

c. Nominal Ledger

General Description

The nominal ledger is used for the recording of a business's income and expenditure classified according to purpose. Thus, for example, it contains an account for Sales to which totals are entered according to the day on which they were made. The sales ledger analyses sales by customer, whereas the Sales Account provides a cumulative total for sales as the accounting year progresses. The Purchases Account in the nominal ledger fulfils a similar purpose for purchases by the business. Other income and expenditure accounts recorded in the nominal ledger may include, for example, Rent, Heating and Wages. If some items of income and expenditure are too small to warrant separate analysis, there may also be Sundry Income and Sundry Expenditure accounts. The information held in the nominal ledger accounts is used to draw up a Profit and Loss Account which provides information on the trading performance of the business over the year and a Balance Sheet which gives a 'snapshot' view of the business's assets and liabilities at a particular point in time.

Nominal Ledger -Typical Package Requirements and Facilities
Nominal Accounts Master File

When an account is opened in the nominal ledger, the following data item types should be available:

Account Code - each account is given a code to allow the allocation of transactions, for example, an entry for a gas bill payment may be directed to the Heating account by the code 012;

Account Name - for example, Sales, Heating, Rent;

Balance

Associated with each account will be a number of transactions processed during the current accounting period.

Transaction Inputs

Sales and Purchases - these may be entered periodically as accumulated totals or, in an integrated accounts system, values may be posted automatically at the same time as they update customer and supplier accounts in the sales ledger and purchase ledger;

Other Income and Expenditure - entries concerning, for example, wages, rent, rates or heating.

Outputs

Typical output facilities include:

Trial Balance - this is a list of debits and credit balances categorized by account. The balances are taken from the nominal ledger and the total of debit balances should agree with the total of credit balances. The nominal ledger makes use of the double entry bookkeeping principle which requires that each transaction results in a debit to one account and a corresponding credit to another. Double entry bookkeeping practice is beyond the scope of this book but is described in numerous textbooks on the subject;

Transaction Report - a full list of transactions which may be used for error checking purposes or as an audit trail to allow the validity of transactions to be checked by an external auditor. The topic of auditing is described in more detail in Chapter 7;

Trading and Profit and Loss Account - a statement of the trading performance of the business over a given period;

Balance Sheet - a statement of the business's assets and liabilities at a particular point in time.

The major benefit of the computerized nominal ledger is that such reports can be produced easily and upon request. The manual production of a trial balance, trading and profit and loss statement and balance sheet is comparatively laborious and means that they tend only to be produced when needed for tax assessment or when loan facilities are required from the bank.

Other Business Applications

Apart from the basic ledgers described in the previous section, there are other applications which can benefit from computerization. They include:

    (a)   Stock Control;

    (b)   Sales Order Processing and Invoicing.

a. Stock Control

General Description

Different businesses hold different kinds of stock, for example, a grocer holds some perishable and some non-perishable stocks of food and a clothing manufacturer holds stocks of materials and finished articles of clothing. Whatever the nature of the stock, it needs to be controlled, although the reasons for control may vary from one business to another. Using the earlier examples, the grocer wants to ensure that the shop has the full range and quantities of food items expected by customers but does not want to be left with stocks of unwanted items, especially if they are perishable. The clothing manufacturer's stocks will not perish if they are unsold, but space occupied by unwanted goods could be occupied by more popular items. On the other hand, if the manufacturer runs out of raw materials the production process can be slowed or even halted. Apart from such differences, there are some common reasons for wanting efficient stock control:

- excessive stock levels tie up valuable cash resources and increase business costs. The cash could be used to finance further business;

- being unable to satisfy customer orders promptly because of insufficient stocks can often lead to loss of customers to competitors.

It is possible to identify some typical objectives of a stock control system and these can be used to measure the usefulness of facilities commonly offered by computer packages:

- to maintain levels of stock which will be sufficient to meet customer demand promptly;

- to provide a mechanism which removes the need for excessively high safety margins of stock to cover customer demand. This is usually effected by setting minimum stock levels which the computer can use to report variations outside these levels;

- to provide automatic re-ordering of stock items which fall below minimum levels;

- to provide management with up-to-date information on stock levels and values of stock held. Stock valuation is also needed for accounting purposes.

Stock control requires that individual records for each type of stock item held are maintained. Apart from details concerning the description and price of the stock item, each record should have a balance indicating the number of units held. A unit may be, for example, box, carton, tonne, pack of 100 etc. The balance will be adjusted, for example, whenever units of that particular stock item are sold or purchased. Manual or computerized stock records can only record what should be in stock. Physical stock checks need to be carried out to determine their actual levels. For example, there may have been losses through pilferage or damage.

Stock Control - Typical Package Requirements and Facilities
Stock Master File

The stock master file contains records for each item of stock and each record may usefully contain the following data item types:

Stock Code or Reference - each stock item type should have a unique reference, for example, A0035. The code should be designed so that it is useful to the user, for example, an initial alphabetic character may be used to differentiate between raw materials (R) and finished goods (F) and the remaining digits may have ranges which indicate particular product groupings. The stock file may also be used to record any consumable items used by a business, for example, stationery and printer ribbons. The initial character of the stock code could be used to identify such a grouping. The number and type of characters in a code, as well as its format, are usually limited by the package because the code will also be used by the software to determine a record's location within the file;

Description - although users may become used to referring to individual products by their codes or references, a description is needed for the production of, for example, purchase orders or customer invoices;

Analysis Code - this may be used in conjunction with sales orders so that they can be analysed by product group. If, for example, a clothing manufacturer produces different types of anorak, it is important for production planning purposes to know the relative popularity of each type;

Unit Size - for example, box, metre, tonne, kilo;

Re-order Level - this is the stock level at which an item is to be re-ordered, for example, 30 boxes. Reaching this level may trigger an automatic re-order when the appropriate program option is run or it may be necessary to request a summary report which highlights all items at or below their re-order level. The decision on what the re-order level should be for any particular item will depend on the sales turnover (the number of units sold per day or week) and the lead time (the time taken for delivery after a purchase order is placed with a supplier). Seasonal changes in sales figures will necessitate changing re-order levels for individual items from time to time;

Re-order Quantity - this is the number of item units to be re-ordered from a supplier when new stock is required;

Bin Reference - this may be used to indicate the physical location of stock items within, for example, a warehouse;

Minimum Stock Level - when an item falls to this level, a warning is given that the stock level of the item is dangerously low. As with the re-order level, the warning may be produced by a request for a special summary report which highlights such items. Even though the re-order level warning may have already been given, it is possible that no new stocks were ordered or that the supplier was unusually slow with deliveries;

Cost Price - the price paid by the business for the stock item;

Sale Price - the price charged to the customer. The package may allow the storage of more than one sale price to differentiate between, for example, retail and wholesale customers;

VAT Code - different items may attract different rates of Value Added Tax (VAT);

Supplier Code - if orders can be produced automatically, then the supplier code may be used to access a supplier file for the address and other details needed to produce an order;

Quantity Issued - generally, several values may be entered, so that the turnover of an item can be viewed for different periods, for example, from 3 months ago to date, the preceding 3 month period and so on;

Stock Allocated - a quantity may not have been issued but may have been allocated to a customer order or factory requisition;

Quantity in Stock - the current recorded level of stock. This will change whenever an issue, receipt or adjustment transaction is entered.

Transaction Inputs

Goods Received - stock received from a supplier;

Goods Returned - for example, stock returned by a customer or unused raw materials returned from the factory;

Goods Issued - this may result from a customer order or if the business has a manufacturing process, from a factory requisition;

Stock Allocated - this will not reduce the quantity in stock figure but the amount allocated should be used to offset the quantity in stock when judging what is available;

Amendments - for, example, there may be amendments to price, re-order level or supplier code.

The method used to update the stock master file will depend on how up-to-date the figures need to be (this will depend on how 'tight' stock levels are) and how often the data entry operator can get at the computer. To keep the file up-to-date throughout the day, physical stock changes have to be notified immediately to stock control and the transactions have to be entered as they occur. Unfortunately, this means that a single-user system would be unavailable to any other users such as sales staff who needed to know quantities in stock. A networked or centralized system (see Chapter 10) with central file storage would allow continual updating and enquiry access. If the stock levels are sufficiently high to allow differences to arise between physical and 'book' totals without risking shortages, then batch update at the end of the day may be sufficient. In such a situation, an enquiry on a stock item may reveal, for example, a 'book' stock of 200 units when in fact the physical stock is only 120 units, 80 having been issued since the last update at the end of the preceding day.

Outputs

Typical outputs from a stock control package include:

Stock Enquiry - details concerning a stock item may be displayed on screen, or output to a printer;

Various Management Information Reports including:

Stock Out Report - a list of stock items which have reached a level of zero;

Re-order Report - a list of stock items which have fallen to their re-order level, together with supplier details and recommended re-order quantities;

Stock List - a full or defined limit (for example, within a certain stock code range) list of stock items giving details of quantities held and their value. The value may be calculated using the cost or sale price depending on the costing method used by the business;

Outstanding Order Report - a list of all purchase orders not yet fulfilled and the dates ordered. This may be used to 'chase up' orders where stocks are falling dangerously low;

This is not an exhaustive list and some packages offer many other analytical reports which can help a business to maintain an efficient customer service and plan future production and purchasing more effectively.

b. Sales Order Processing and Invoicing

General Description

Sales Order Processing

Sales order processing is concerned with the handling of customers' sales orders. It has three main functions:

- the validation of orders. This means checking, for example, that the goods ordered are supplied by the business or that the customer's credit status warrants the order's completion;

- to identify quantities of individual items ordered. A customer may request several different items on the same order form. An item will probably appear on many different order forms and the quantities for each need to be totalled to provide lists (picking lists) for warehouse staff to retrieve the goods;

- to monitor back orders. If an order cannot be fulfilled it may be held in abeyance until new stocks arrive. The system should be able to report all outstanding back orders on request.

The efficient processing of customer orders is of obvious importance to the success of a business and in whatever form an order is received, the details should be immediately recorded. Preferably, the details should be recorded on a pre-designed order form which ensures that all relevant details are taken. The order details should include:

      (i) the date the order is received;

      (ii) the customer's order number;

      (iii) a description of each item required including any necessary stock references or codes;

      (iv) the quantity of each item ordered;

      (v) the price per item excluding VAT;

      (vi) the total order value excluding VAT;

      (vii) any discount which is offered to the customer;

      (viii) the VAT amount which is to be added to the total price;

      (ix) the total order value including VAT;

      (x) the delivery date required.

Invoicing

The invoice is the bill to the customer requesting payment for goods or services supplied by the business. The following section describes typical package facilities which allow the integration of the sales order processing and invoicing systems.

Sales Order Processing and Invoicing-
Typical Package Requirements and Facilities

To be effective, the sales order processing system needs to have access to the customer file (sales ledger) for customer details and to the stock file, so that prices can be extracted according to stock item codes entered with the order. This latter facility means that the system may also be integrated with invoicing.

Files

Customer File - when a customer account number or name is keyed in with an order, the package usually accesses the customer file and displays the address details so that the operator can confirm the delivery address or type in an alternative address if this is required. The process also ensures that all orders are processed for registered customers;

Stock File - as stock item codes are entered from an order form, the system accesses the price and displays it on the screen for confirmation by the operator. Access to the stock file also ensures that only valid stock codes are used;

Completed Order File - this is used for the generation of invoices after an order's completion;

Back Order File - this is needed to ensure that orders which cannot be fulfilled immediately are kept on file and processed as soon as goods become available.

Transaction Inputs

Sales Order - details concerning an individual order, including customer number, items required (by item code), quantity of each item, delivery date, discount allowed and the date of the order;

Outputs

Invoice - an invoice can be generated by using the details of customer number, stock codes and quantities from the order, together with information retrieved from the customer and stock files;

Back Order Report - a report can be requested detailing all unsatisfied orders. This is useful for planning production schedules or generating special purchase orders;

Picking List - a summary of the quantities required of each item ordered. These are used by warehouse staff to extract the goods needed to make up orders for delivery;

Sales Data - details of each customer's order need to be passed to accounts for updating the sales ledger and sales account in the nominal ledger.

Many popular packages, such as Pegasus, which is designed for microcomputer systems, allow the integration described for the sales order processing and invoicing system to be extended to include the financial ledgers (sales, purchase and nominal ledger). Such integration should not usually be attempted all at once but full integration does reduce the number of inputs necessary and automates many of the updating procedures described in this chapter.

Assignment

Accounting for Taste

Haute Couture specializes in ladies' individually designed formal evening wear. The use of costly materials and the labour intensive nature of the production methods mean that a single evening gown can cost well over a thousand pounds. Many of the materials are bought from the Far East and lengthy delivery times are often experienced. Nothing is supplied ready made or 'off the peg' and clothes are only made on customer request. Not all customers are particularly prompt in settling their accounts and a close watch needs to be kept on lengthy outstanding debts. The firm's proprietors are two young designers, Catherine Parker and Nigel Kingsley, whose designs have come to the notice of some of the most famous London and Paris fashion houses. They have refused a number of employment offers, because they want to retain their independence in clothing design. The firm employs five production staff and one to take care of the business accounts. The firm also employs the services of an accountant for the auditing of the business accounts. The preparation of the final accounts each year often causes a bit of a panic and the accountant has suggested that the process could be improved.

The main information processing tasks are those common to most businesses:

* *Stock control - although clothes are made on request, the firm does keep stocks of materials which the designers anticipate customers will want. There are also stocks of standard consumables such as sewing cottons, binding and so on;*

* *Accounting - sales, purchases etc;*

* *Order processing and invoicing;*

* *Payroll - this takes one person about half-an-hour each week.*

Until recently, one person (yourself) has been able to cope with all these tasks, but the business is expanding rapidly and more production staff are to be employed. Before your employment with the firm, you followed a vocational computing course and have convinced your employers of the benefits of using a computer for the routine accounting tasks. They already use computers in their design work, but they are not available for other applications. You have been asked to outline the details of your requirements and the ways in which they will be met.

Task

1. Prepare notes advising your employers of the applications which may benefit from computerization and the particular benefits to be gained for each application.

2. In order that you can make a proper choice of software, detail the system requirements of TWO applications, in terms of:

(a) the required contents of the master file;

(b) the data input requirements for updating the master file;

(c) how validation is to be performed and on what data;

(d) the contents and forms of output, including any management information requirements.

Your answer should provide illustrative data related to the business outlined in the assignment. In order to help you in this activity, make a study of the documentation for a real package and identify in your answer, any features relevant to Task 2.

Developmental Task

As a group of, say three students, use a package to set up one application, for example, Sales Ledger or Stock Control and give a demonstration and talk on its practical operation. The demonstration could given to other students or staff and may form part of a College Open Day.

Chapter 13

□ PROGRAMMING

Program Development

Introduction

Program development constitutes an important part of the process of systems development, which is described in Chapter 14. The System Specifications produced by the systems analyst at the design stage include a specification relating to the applications software. If the specification involves the writing of new programs, as opposed to the purchase of 'off-the-shelf' packaged software, then applications programmers are needed to carry out the task of program writing. The programmers may be employed on a permanent basis by the organization which is to use the system, or the organization may buy in expertise from outside agencies, such as software houses or computer bureaux. In either case, the task of program development requires a disciplined approach, similar to that required for the development of the system as a whole. There are a number of stages to follow and standards to be maintained. Although such programming standards may vary from one organization to another, it is important that programs are written in such a way that, for example, programmers can understand each other's work and thus work as a team.

Program development is a labour-intensive task, so the major portion of development costs is tied to the salaries of programmers. Such labour costs have increased steadily and because programs need to be maintained throughout their life, software costs do not end after a program's initial development and implementation. For many large organizations, it is estimated that 80 per cent of the software costs relate to program maintenance. Considerable efforts have been and are being made, to improve the efficiency of program development and a variety of techniques and 'tools' are used to achieve this aim. One technique is to make programs 'structured'. This chapter outlines the stages involved in program development and examines some of the design and development tools used by programmers.

Stages in Program Development

The following stages can be identified:

- (a) Problem analysis by the systems analyst;
- (b) Understanding of the problem by the programmer;
- (c) Designing a solution to the problem;
- (d) Coding the program in the chosen language;
- (e) Debugging - finding and removing errors in the program;

(f) Testing;

(g) Preparing documentation for users and for programmers who will maintain the program.

a. Problem Analysis

As Chapter 8 explains, the task of program development involves both systems analysts and programmers. The initial stage of problem analysis is primarily the responsibility of the systems analyst, although programmers may be involved. Having analysed the problem in consultation with potential users, the systems analyst specifies the requirements, which each application program must fulfil, in a Program Specification. The content of the specification can be itemized as follows:

Output Definition
The output is defined in terms of:

Content. The sort of information to be produced, for example, that required to produce a customer invoice;

Format. The layout and presentation of the output, as it appears, for example, on a screen or printout. Sometimes, the output may have to conform to pre-printed stationery;

Timing. The response time must be specified, for example, weekly, monthly, or if an interactive system is required, a maximum response time of, say, 2 seconds;

Flexibility to changing user requirements. It is important that the program is written in such a way that it is reasonably easy to modify, as and when users' requirements change.

Input Definition
The input necessary to produce the defined output is specified in the following ways:

Data requirements. For example, the data needed to produce an invoice generally includes customer details, item codes, descriptions, quantities and prices;

Data sources. The data may need to be collected or it may already exist on another computer file. The files that a program requires, the size and nature of records and fields within them are detailed;

Data entry procedures. The programmer needs to know the device through which data is to be entered.

Processing Requirements
This section is concerned with the processing work to be carried out by the computer, in other words, the processes required to transform the input into the required output. For example, the production of payslips requires a number of calculations on input data, such as the hourly rate of pay and the number of hours worked by an employee. Similarly, for example, a stock report may require a program to analyse stock records according to criteria, such as price and quantity.

Processing Controls
These include, for example, validation controls on input and are aimed at ensuring accuracy of processing. Controls may also be required to ensure security of data from unauthorized persons or to prevent loss of data.

Program Testing Plan
It is important that a program functions as expected, so a comprehensive test plan is designed to test, as far as is possible, all conditions. This usually takes the form of data designed to test the various 'paths' a program may follow during execution. For example, if in the production of a customer invoice, a discount is calculated according to the total value of the invoice, except when it is less than £100, the test data must include values which are less than, equal to or greater than £100.

Program testing is dealt with in more detail later in this chapter.

b. Understanding the Problem

The programmer needs to understand the program requirements and will normally work from the Program Specification described above.

c. Designing a Solution

A program design or plan should detail all the tasks required of the program, as well as how they are to be sequenced and organized. Without proper design, 'spaghetti' programs often result, which are extremely difficult to correct or maintain, even if they happen to work properly in the first place. One consequence of an undisciplined approach is that, having produced a substantial part of a program, the programmer may discover that a vital processing routine has been left out. If the logic behind the program is rather obscure, then insertion of the routine may be impossible without completely rewriting the program from the beginning. Even if a program 'works', in the sense that it produces the required output, without structure it may be extremely difficult for anyone other than the original programmer to understand. A systematic approach is therefore desirable and a number of design approaches and design tools exist to help the programmer in this regard. These are dealt with later in this chapter.

d. Coding the Program

Following completion of the program design, the programmer must express it in a programming language. This is called program coding and is the exclusive job of the programmer. Each programming language has its own conventions regarding the layout of the coding, so the coding process is often carried out on CODING SHEETS specifically designed for the chosen language. Labelled columns ensure that the conventions are adhered to. In many large computer installations, the actual keying-in of the code is carried out by a keyboard operator and the coding sheets help to ensure that the program is entered according to the specific language requirements.

Coding Standards

To ensure readability, many computer installations enforce certain common standards for coding. For example, standards may be set regarding:

Data Names. When referring to data used by a program, the programmer can use symbolic names to reflect the type of data to which each relates. Standards may be set regarding prefixes which indicate the source of the data. For example, data input from disk files may have to be prefixed with "D-IN", as in "D-IN-ITEMCODE" or "D-IN-PRICE";

Program Structures. These generally refer to the use of CONTROL CONSTRUCTS, which are described later in this chapter.

Although the 'creative' programmer may find such standards restricting, they are essential for efficient program development and maintenance.

e. Program Debugging

Debugging is the task of finding and removing errors or 'bugs' from the program.

Syntax Errors

The first type of error a programmer is likely to encounter is the SYNTAX error, that is, an error caused by the incorrect use of rules of the syntax of the programming language. Such errors are usually discovered at the translation stage.

In Chapter 11, it is explained that the program instructions coded in the programming language constitute SOURCE CODE. A translator program, called a compiler, is needed to convert the source code into the MACHINE or OBJECT code, which forms an executable program. The compiler attempts to translate the source code and produces DIAGNOSTIC ERROR messages when it discovers syntax errors. Errors discovered at this stage are know as 'compile-time' errors.

Programs are rarely error-free at the first translation attempt, although careful 'desk checking' beforehand can avoid the most obvious errors. After a failed compilation, the programmer checks the source listing and accompanying error messages to see what is wrong, makes the necessary corrections and attempts a further compilation. This compilation/check/correct routine may be repeated several times during the development of the program. Generally, compilation errors terminate the translation process, so all such errors must be removed before any attempt can be made to 'run' the program and test for 'run-time' errors.

Run-time Errors
Run-time errors occur, for example, when a program statement attempts to divide a number by zero or when a memory variable designated for numeric data receives a non-numeric value.

Logic Errors
As soon as the program is executable, it has to be checked to ensure that it is functioning as expected.

Logic errors may be obvious at first. For example, a program designed to print a Stock File report may fail to print out the headings at the top of each page. Initially, limited test data may suffice to check that the program appears to be generally correct, but before the program can be used in a real situation, it must be thoroughly tested.

f. Program Testing

Program testing should be carried out according to the Test Plan described in the program specification. Good test data will subject the program to all the conditions it might conceivably encounter when put into use. This topic is dealt with in more detail at the end of this chapter.

Program Design

Introduction

One of the major problems which confronts the beginner faced with the task of writing a computer program, is where to start. How is it possible to organise program instructions to perform the required task, and how can the programmer be sure that the finished program will always perform as desired? The aim of this chapter is to answer these questions by introducing a program design technique which replaces inspiration with a simple logical sequence of steps which are easy to learn, understand and apply.

The technique is called 'Jackson Structured Programming', or 'JSP', and is fully described by Michael A. Jackson in his book 'Principles of Program Design'. The method has the following characteristics:

(i)   it depends on the application of a small number of simple, clearly defined steps;

(ii) it can be taught because of (i);

(iii) it is practical, resulting in programs which are easy to write, understand, test and maintain.

JSP is a "Top-down" programming technique in which the programmer, starting from the premise that the complete program will be too difficult to comprehend in its entirety, breaks the problem down into a sequence of manageable components. Each such component is then broken down into smaller parts, and so on until a level is reached which cannot easily be further simplified. Without this technique, a programming problem can be too large and complex in its complete form. This process produces a program structure resembling a tree diagram as shown below:

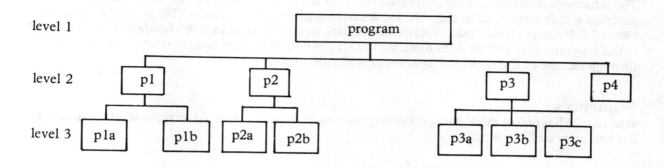

Each level lists the procedures (p1, p2 etc.) which provide a complete description of the program. The amount of detail increases with the level number. Thus the program can be considered equally to consist of the sequence

p1..p2..p3..p4 or

p1a..p1b..p2a..p2b..p3a..p3b..p3c..p4.

p1a and p1b, for example, provide a more detailed picture of p1.

Basic Components of JSP Design

There are only four basic components:

(i)   ELEMENTARY COMPONENTS which are not further sub-divided into constituent parts;

(ii) a SEQUENCE of two or more parts occurring in order;

(iii) a SELECTION of one part from a number of alternatives;

(iv) an ITERATION in which a single part is repeated zero or more times.

Each separate part of a sequence, selection or iteration may be a sequence, a selection or an iteration, so there is no limit to the complexity of structure which can be formed. For example, a sequence of three parts may be:

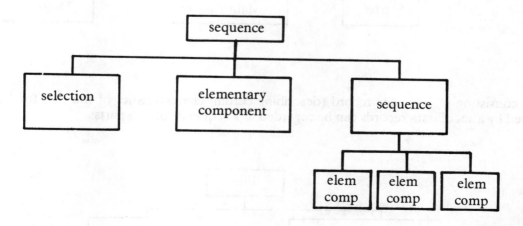

The structures developed using combinations of these four component types are equally useful for describing data structures as they are for describing program structures. This property forms the basis of JSP design, which uses descriptions of data structures to define the fundamental structure of the program. The next sections illustrate the idea of data structures and how they can be described through the use of the four basic components identified above.

Sequences

A sequence has two or more parts, occurring once each, in order. It would be represented as follows, for a sequence of three parts:

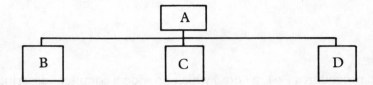

If we wish to describe a pack of cards which has been sorted into suits, we might consider it as being a sequence of four suits:

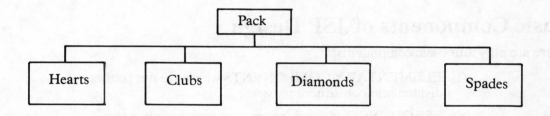

A meal might be considered to be a sequence of starter, main course and dessert:

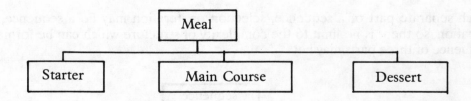

A file consisting of a header record (describing certain characteristics of the file, for instance) followed by a set of data records can be regarded as a sequence of two parts:

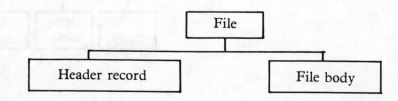

A computer-generated report of a sales file might consist of a list of transaction details giving item description, number sold and total selling price, followed by a grand total of the sales value:

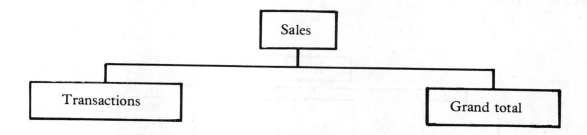

Each transaction could itself be regarded as a sequence of three parts: item description, number sold, and sales value. In fact the item description might also be recognised as a sequence of code number and name.

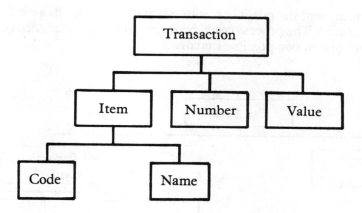

In this instance, the elementary components of the transaction would be code number, name, number, and value, since none of these is further defined. This hierarchical type of description illustrates the way in which a simple concept such as a sequence can give rise to quite complicated structures.

As a final example of a sequence, a COBOL program which consists of four divisions could be represented as the sequence

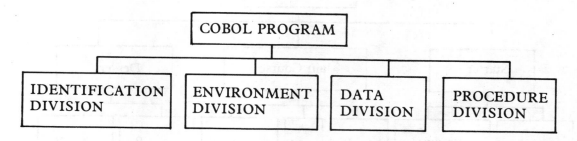

The examples illustrate that it is just as easy to describe a data structure as it is to describe a sequence of processes.

Selections

The selection component indicates what choices are available when a choice is to be made of one single part from several alternatives:

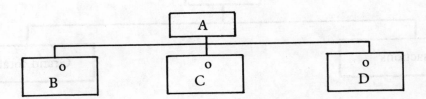

The small circles in the three boxes show that A is a selection and that only one of the three items is to be selected.

Suppose it is wished to represent the possible results when two people cut a pack of cards in order to see who has the higher card. The process could be represented as a sequence of two actions, the second of which can have one of two possible outcomes:

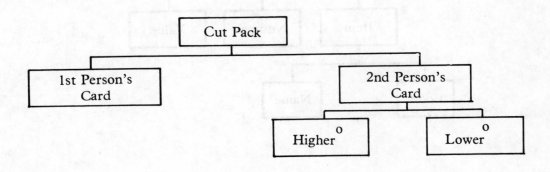

We could use this notation to describe a menu having a number of alternatives for each course:

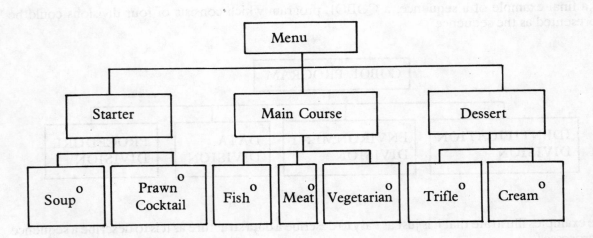

Similarly, in the sales file report described earlier, we might wish to differentiate between cash sales and credit sales for each transaction:

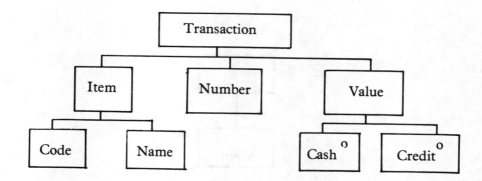

Sometimes a selection will consist of only one part which will be of interest while any other possibility is of no interest. For example, if we wished to count the number of times that three shows when a dice is thrown, it could be represented as follows:

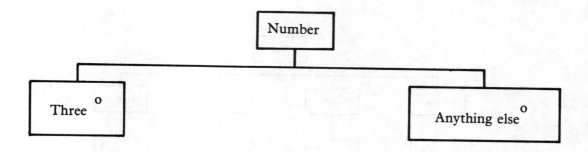

But as anything other than three is of no interest, it is allowable to show it as:

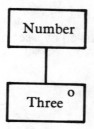

Iterations

An iteration consists of one part which is repeated zero or more times. Diagrammatically, an iteration A with iterated part B, could be shown as:

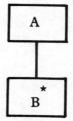

The asterisk indicates that B is repeated zero or more times, and A represents the complete process. A shuffled pack of cards can be represented as:

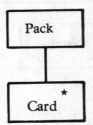

and the pack organised into suits would be:

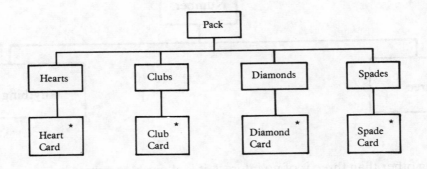

A file consisting of a header record followed by a set of data records becomes:

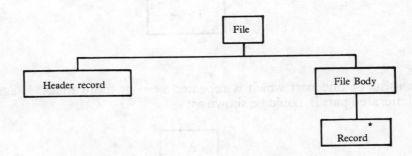

and our sales report can now show that the report consists of a number of lines, each showing the details of one transaction:

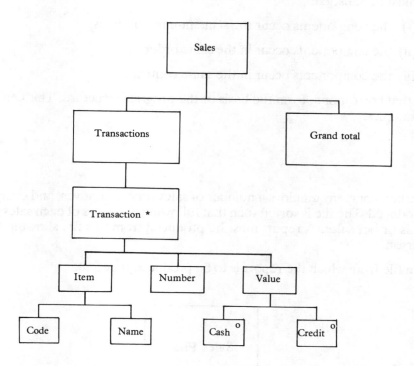

The iterated part of a process continues until some terminating condition is encountered, or only while some condition holds true. For example, the condition to terminate the processing of a file could be the physical end of the file, that is the process continues UNTIL the end of file is encountered; alternatively, this could be regarded as the continuance of processing WHILE the end of file has NOT been detected. Both conditions amount to the same thing. However, there are occasions when one form of the conditions may be more suitable than the other. The conditions for terminating iterations or for making choices, are specified as part of the design process after the various structure diagrams have been created and this aspect of program design is dealt with in more detail in a later section.

The Principal Stages of JSP Design

The basic design technique is a three-step procedure:

(i) define the structure of the data to be processed;

(ii) determine the program structure from the data structures. This, in effect, identifies the main processing tasks needed to process the data. The program structure thus formed will generally need filling out when step (iii) is performed;

(iii) define the tasks to be performed in more detail by allocating elementary operations available to appropriate components of the program structure. Such elementary operations represent single (or at least small numbers) of programming statements.

Definition of Data and Program Structures

The first step is to define the data structures. The form in which the data is to be supplied to the program must be clearly stated, and the form of the data to be output from the program must also be defined. In addition, it is necessary to identify CORRESPONDENCES between all the data structures in order to combine them to form the program structure. For a correspondence to exist, three conditions must be satisfied:

> (i)   the components occur the same number of times;
>
> (ii) the components occur in the same order;
>
> (iii) the components occur in the same context.

The components that correspond, form the basis of the program structure. This can be illustrated by a number of examples.

Example 1

Suppose that a certain company employs a number of sales representatives, and every month a file of their sales is produced. The file is sorted such that following the name of each salesperson in turn there is a list of his or her sales. A report must be produced from this file showing the total sales value for each person.

To begin, the data file from which the report is to be produced is defined:

This indicates that the sales file is an iteration of salesperson (there are a number of salespersons records), and salesperson is an iteration of sale (each salesperson has a number of sales figures).

The summary report that is required looks like this:

MicroPhile Computers		
Sales Summary Dec 1987		
Salesperson	Total Sales (£)	Commission (£)
J. Smith	3275.62	263.56
H. Morgan	4456.40	345.22
P. Sheridan	3986.80	286.45
....	....	....
....	....	....
A. Morrow	2269.50	200.34
TOTALS	52986.28	5032.66

The data structure would have the following representation:

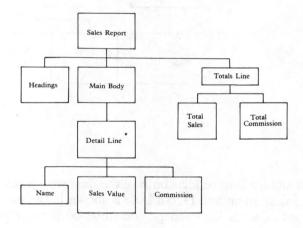

The Sales Report is a sequence of Headings, Main Body and Totals Line. The Main Body is an iteration of Detail Line which is to contain three items of information: Name, Sales Value and Commission. The Totals Line is a sequence of Total Sales and Total Commission.

The correspondences are

Sales File ⟷ Sales Report

Salesperson ⟷ Detail Line

The first correspondence is quite obvious since it is the sales file which is used to produce the sales report.

The second correspondence results from the fact that for each salesperson a single line is required which is the sales summary for that person.

It is usual to draw the data structures side-by-side with arrowed lines indicating the correspondence.(This is shown in the previous figure).

The two structures are now combined into a program structure in which the components represent processing operations:

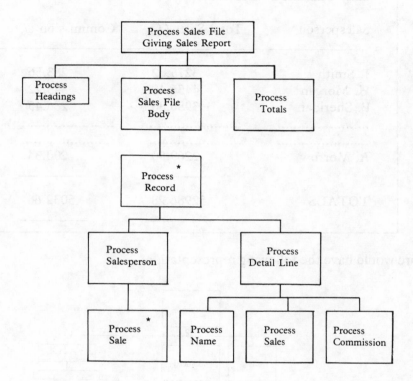

The program structure thus reflects both of the data structures used in its design. The correspondence between Salesperson and Detail Line is shown in the program structure as a sequence since the complete set of sales for each person must be processed before the summary line can be produced.

Example 2
A sequential file consists of records containing details of magazine articles about computer-related subjects, such as hardware, software and programming. A program is required to print out the titles and authors of all articles about programming. Titles and authors relating to other subjects are to be ignored.

(i) Consider first the case where the articles are in random order of subject. The data structure is shown below.

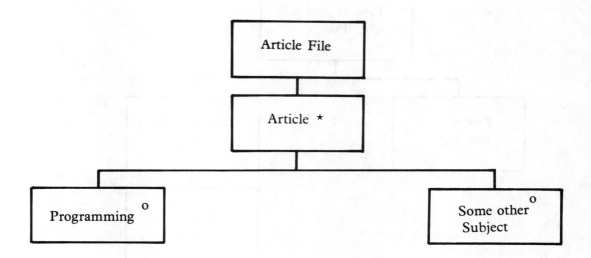

The output structure is of the form:

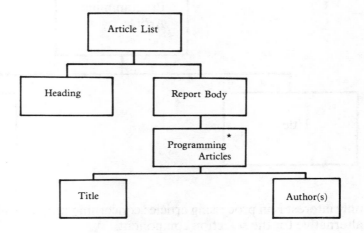

The correspondences in this case are:

The second correspondence is between the Programming component of Articles in the Article File and the Programming Articles component of the selection in the Article List report. Because the file is not sequenced according to subject, it is necessary for the whole Article File to be processed to allow the extraction of Programming articles as and when they are reached.

The program structure is then

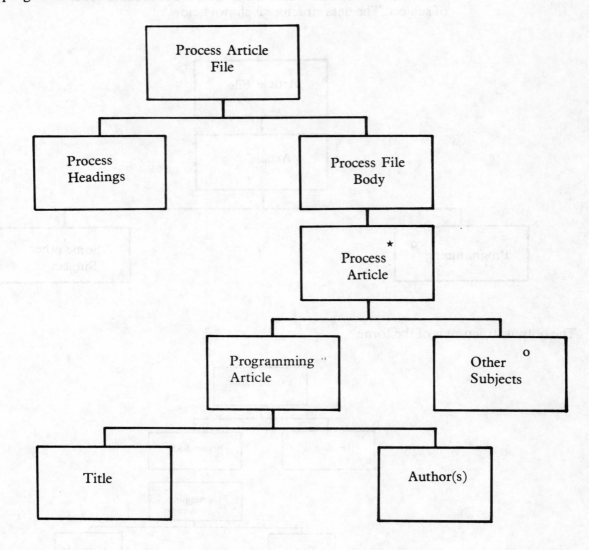

Since the only interest is in processing articles concerning programming, it is not necessary to show the other alternative for the selection component.

(ii) Suppose now that the file has been sorted into subject order, so that all articles on software are grouped together, all articles on operating systems are together, all articles on programming are together and so on. The data structure for the input file is now as follows:

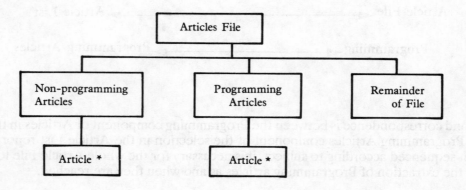

where the file now may be considered to consist of three parts:

(i) a number of articles not relating to programming;

(ii) a number of articles on programming;

(iii) the rest of the file, which is of no interest.

Notice that in this instance the selection component is missing, and it is replaced by two iterations, one of unwanted records and the other of records of interest. The report structure is still the same, but the correspondence is now between Programming Articles in the Articles File and Report Body in the report file. The sorting of the file into subject order means that the records on programming are grouped together and therefore correspond directly to the data required in the report.

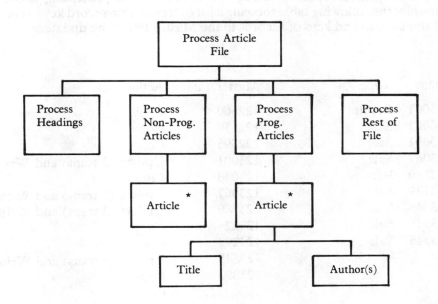

Notice that the final procedure, Process Rest of File, does not involve an iteration; once the subject changes from programming to something else, the processing is finished and the program in effect stops.

Example 3
The examples above deal with the process of combining a single input file with a single output file to produce a program structure. However there are an important class of processing problems which involve two input files whose records need to be 'matched' or 'collated'.

The process might, for example, require the matching of a Master File of items of stock and a Transaction File containing details of items received from suppliers or sold to customers. If both of these files are in some particular order (for instance in ascending order of stock reference number) then updating the Master File involves reading a transaction record and then attempting to find a stock record in the Master File with the same key value (in this case, the stock reference number). If it is assumed that there should be a stock record for every transaction then, in the process of comparing a transaction record key value with a stock record key value, a number of situations can arise:

(i)   The transaction record key has a value which is greater than the stock record key. In this instance the stock record does not have a matching transaction and does not require updating. The stock record merely needs to be copied to the file holding the updated stock records. We will call this new file the Updated Master File;

(ii)   The transaction record key is the same value as the stock record key. Here it is necessary to determine the nature of the transaction, whether it is a sale or receipt, before processing the stock record. The updated record will then be written to the Updated Master File;

(iii)   The transaction record key has a value which is less than the stock record key. This situation should not arise in this example and therefore indicates that an error has occurred, possibly as a result of the transaction file being out of sequence. To help clarify the nature of the processing tasks, consider the following table showing a list of transaction record keys, type of transaction and keys of records in the Master File to be updated:

Trans	Type	Master File	Action
123001	Receipt	122500	Copy
123001	Sale	122570	Copy
123001	Sale	122595	Copy
123067	Sale	123001	Update (3 trans) and Write
123189	Receipt	123048	Copy
123189	Sale	123067	Update (1 trans) and Write
123345	Sale	123189	Update (2 trans) and Write
123345	Sale	123224	Copy
123345	Sale	123297	Copy
		123345	Update (3 trans) and Write
		123890	Copy
		....	Copy
		etc	....
		....	Copy
		134347	Copy

Notice that it is possible to have several transactions for the same stock record in the Master File. The first three records of the Master File do not have any matching transaction records and therefore are copied to the Updated Master File without modification. All stock records occurring after the end of the Transaction File are also written to the new Updated Master File.

The data structures and correspondences for this example are therefore

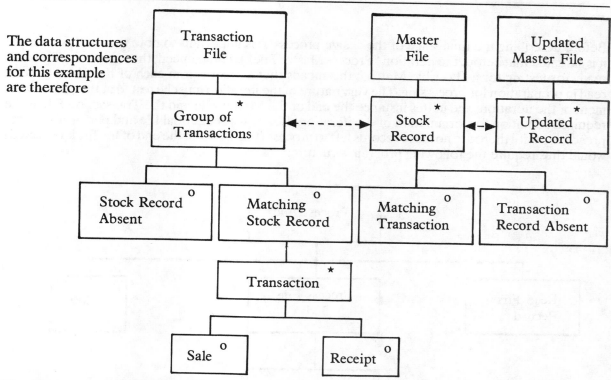

The Transaction File is considered to contain a number of groups of transactions, each group containing records with the same key value (stock reference number); each record in the group is used to update a single stock record from the Master File. In the table described earlier, the stock item with key value 123001 has a group of three transactions comprising a receipt and two sales transactions, whereas stock item 122570 has no transactions associated with it (that is, the transaction record is absent).

The outline program structure is

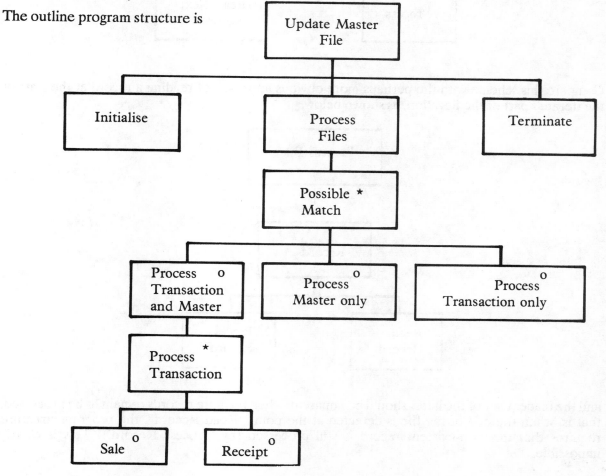

Before describing the final stage of the design process, it is important to note that in this example it is assumed that before the iteration "Process Master File" is commenced, there is a pair of records ready for testing for a "Possible Match"; this means that a record from each of the files has been read in preparation for processing. The very nature of the iteration must be tested at the commencement of the iteration, and in this instance the end of the Master File and the Transaction File is the required condition for termination of the iteration. Reading a sequential file and performing some processing until there are no more records left to process (that is, when the end of the file is detected) would thus require the following program structure:

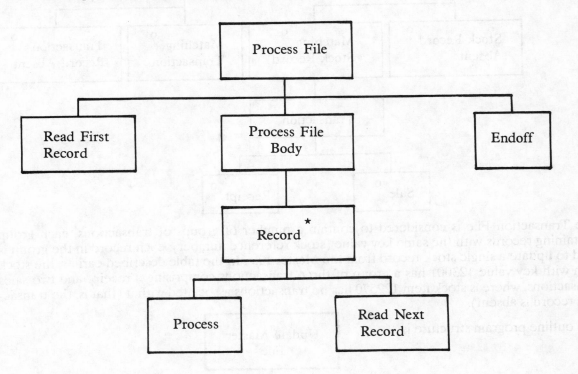

Compare this scheme with the perhaps more obvious approach of reading a record at the start of the iterated part of the iteration, as shown below,

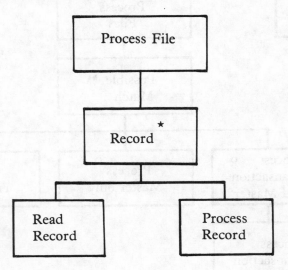

and the inadequacy of the latter should be apparent: when no more records remain to be processed, that is, when the end of the file is detected at the point "Read Record", the program structure requires that this non-existent record is still processed (by 'Process Record')! This is clearly impossible.

The technique, illustrated in the first example above, of reading the first record as soon as possible and subsequently reading at the completion of the processing of a record, is called "reading ahead". It is important to note that the processing of each record CONCLUDES with reading another record, so that there is always a record ready for processing, and the end of the file can be detected at the end of each iteration.

Allocation of Elementary Operations

The final stage in the design technique is to allocate elementary operations to the program structure. The elementary operations include the following types :

> Opening files ready for reading or writing;
>
> Closing files after processing;
>
> Reading records;
>
> Writing records;
>
> Displaying information;
>
> Printing information;
>
> Incrementing counts;
>
> Making calculations;
>
> Specifying conditions for the termination (or continuance) of iterations;
>
> Specifying criteria for selections.

To illustrate the process we will list and allocate the elementary operations required for Example 3.

Initialisation operations:

> 1. Open Master File for Input
> 2. Open Updated Stock File for Output
> 3. Open Transaction File for Input

Program Termination operations:

> 4. Close Master File
> 5. Close Updated Stock File
> 6. Close Transaction File
> 7. Stop

Input/Output operations:

> 8. Read Master File
> 9. Read Transaction File
> 10. Write Updated Stock Record

Processing operations:

> 11. Subtract number of sales from stock level
> 12. Add receipts to stock level
> 13. Display error message: "No stock record for this transaction"
> 14. Store transaction record key

Iteration conditions:

C1. Until End of Master File and Transaction File

C2. Until change of transaction record key

Selection conditions:

C3. Transaction record key matches stock record key

C4. Transaction record key >stock record key

C5. Transaction record key <stock record key

C6. Transaction type = Sale

C7. Transaction type = Receipt.

It is now possible to add
some detail to the
program structure diagram:

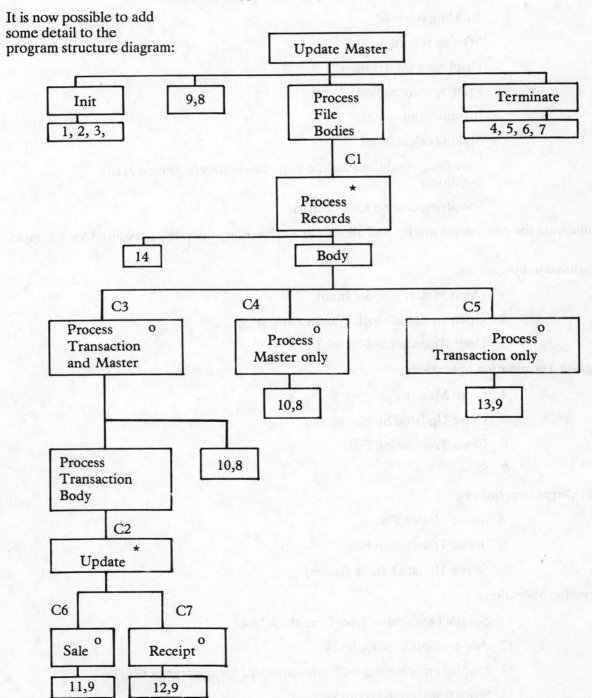

Examination of the program structure above might suggest the possibility of 'improving' its efficiency by combining such operations as "9. Read Transaction File" or "8. Read Master File", both of which appear to be repeated unnecessarily. For example, operation 9 could be extracted from the Sale and Receipt operations and it could become a separate operation following the selection:

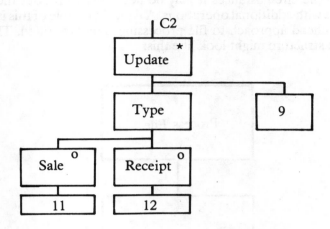

Though this simplified program structure would still be correct, the danger is that should it be necessary to modify the program at some later date, unnecessary complications might result. In his book "Principles of Program Design", M.A. Jackson, talking about this process of program optimisation, provides two rules:

> Rule 1: Don't do it

> Rule 2: Don't do it yet

meaning that it is best, in the interests of program clarity, not to optimise the structure at all, but if you must do it, first begin within an unoptimised structure and then optimise it later.

To summarise, the steps by which the final program structure is defined are as follow:

1. Define the structure of the data to be processed. In many data processing applications these will be files.

2. Define the structure of the desired result of the processing. This output could be in the form of files or printed reports for instance.

3. Identify the correspondences between the data structures in order to help to clarify the program structure.

4. Define the outline program structure by combining the data structures and utilising the correspondences identified.

5. List the elementary operations, grouped under the headings:

   Initialisation

   Program termination

   Input/Output

   Processing

   Iteration conditions

   Selection conditions.

6. Assign these elementary operations to each part of the outline program

structure. These elementary operations should be capable of being easily converted into one or more instructions in the target language. If the program structure has been defined well, the elementary operations should be easy to identify.

7.   Under some circumstances it may be necessary to fill out the program structure with additional operations. A typical example of this is when the reading ahead approach to file processing is incorporated. The outline program structure might look like this:

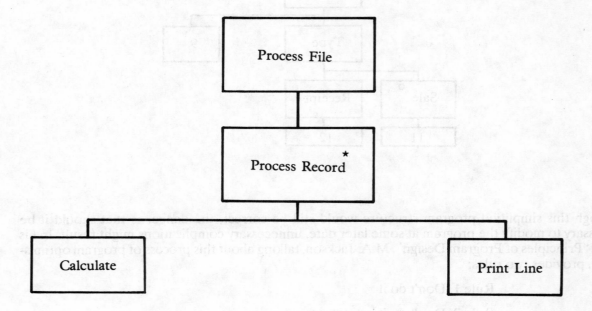

When more detail is added, it might then become

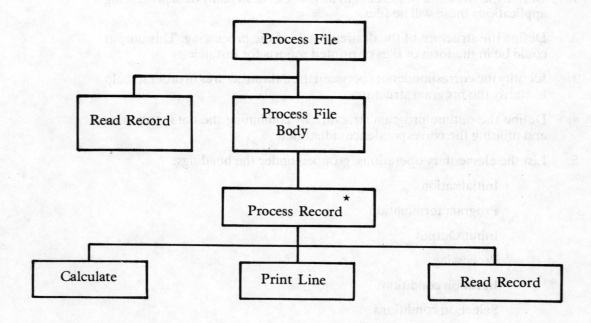

Program Debugging and Testing

This part of the chapter examines the processes used to debug and test a program. Once the program has been written, it must go through two stages in order to remove errors which almost inevitably will be present. No matter how much care has been taken in the design and coding of a program,it is very likely to contain errors in syntax, that is incorrectly formed statements, and almost as likely to also contain errors in logic. 'Debugging' is the term given to the process of detecting and correcting these errors or 'bugs'.

The first stage in the removal of errors is the correction of syntax errors and obvious errors in logic. Fortunately for the programmer, modern interpreters and compilers provide considerable assistance in the detection of syntax errors in the source code. Malformed statements will be reported by a compiler after it has attempted to compile the source code; an interpreter will report illegal statements as it attempts to execute them. Logic errors, however, are largely undetectable by the translating program. These are errors which cause the program to behave in a manner contrary to expectations. The individual statements in the program are correctly formed and it runs, but the program as a whole does not work as it should; it may give incorrect answers, or terminate prematurely, or not terminate at all.

Hopefully, even the most puzzling logic errors, once detected, can eventually be removed. But how can the programmer be confident that the program will continue to behave properly when it is in use? The answer is that the programmer can never be absolutely certain that the program will not fail, but by the careful choice of test data in the second stage of the debugging process, the programmer can test the program under the sort of conditions that are most likely to occur in practice. Test data is designed to determine the robustness of the program, in other words, how well it can cope with unexpected or spurious inputs as well as those for which it has been designed specifically to process.

Syntax and Logic Errors

Because translation programs such as compilers must contain detailed rules concerning the allowable structures of statements in the language, they are generally able to provide the programmer with quite detailed information on the cause and location of syntax infringements. A COBOL compiler for example, having attempted to compile a source program, might produce an error report of the following form:

```
64 E - Syntax error (resumption at next PARAGRAPH/VERB): DIASPLAY
65 E - Syntax error (resumption at next PARAGRAPH/VERB): LOOP3
70 E - Bad nesting of DO/END-DO.
84 E - Procedure-name is unresolvable: AMEFND-ALLOW

--- End of compilation ----------
Number of errors found:      4
Number of warnings given:    0
Number of source lines:    354
----------------------------------------
```

Each line of the report gives the following information:

    (a)   the line in the source code at which the error was located;

    (b)   the degree of severity of the error, that is to what extent it has prevented the production of the object code;

    (c)   a description of the error;

    (d)   the offending part of the statement if this can be isolated.

After correcting the source code, the program must be recompiled. Further errors may then be revealed and the process repeated. Only after the program has been compiled successfully, with no errors reported, should the object code be run. At this stage the operating system may report difficulties in attempting to execute the object code. For instance, if the program attempts to read a file which has not been opened prior to the read instruction, the operating system might halt execution of the program and report the detection of this 'run-time' error. This constitutes an error in logic which the compiler is unable to detect; the error only becomes apparent when the program is run. Generally, the nature of the run-time error and perhaps its location in the source code will be reported, again with an error code through which further information might be obtained.

With a compiled programming language the programmer can be confident that all syntax errors have been removed from the program; the compiler itself will report this fact. However, since an interpreter only processes instructions as they are encountered, a syntax error in a statement will only be detected if that statement is executed. As a result, a complex program written in BASIC for instance, might hide a number of syntax errors which may only reveal themselves after the program has been run several times. For example, the following program statement contains a syntax error which might not reveal itself immediately:

. . . .

. . . .

100 IF code   = 89 THEN GOTO SUB 2000

. . . .

The fact that the instruction should have read

100 IF code = 89 THEN GOSUB 2000

would only become apparent when the variable 'code' actually had the value 89. Any other value would cause the coding following the condition in the statement to be ignored and allow the syntax error to remain hidden.

This same instruction could also hide a logic error. If line 2000 did not exist then it would be impossible to execute the subroutine starting at this point. Again the error might not become apparent immediately.

These examples illustrate the importance of testing a program thoroughly using data which will exercise every part of the program.

Detecting Logic Errors

Frequently logic errors do not prevent the program from executing, rather they cause some sort of processing error. The symptoms of the error may be obvious, but the cause might not be so apparent. Every programmer comes up against the logic error which 'cannot' exist; the coding appears to be perfectly correct and yet the program behaves incorrectly. No matter how many times the coding is scrutinised, there seems to be no reason for the problem. The mistake that many beginners at programming make is to spend an inordinate amount of time looking at program listings in order to find the error; though intuitively this seems to be the obvious approach, in practice it is a sort of 'gumption trap' which can waste a great deal of time and result in a great deal of frustration. It seems easier to stare at a listing in the belief that the error must eventually reveal itself rather than having the gumption to adopt some positive and systematic approach which might appear to involve more unnecessary work.

If, after examining a program listing for a reasonable amount of time, the cause of the error remains elusive, there are a number of courses of action which will probably be much more productive than continuing to pore over the listing:

> (i) Ask a fellow programmer to listen critically while you explain
> the operation of the program and the way it is behaving. Quite
> often you will see the cause of the error as you are making the

explanation. Alternatively, your helper might recognise the type of error and its probable cause from his/her own experience, or might ask a question which makes you reconsider some aspect of the program which you have assumed to be correct or had no direct bearing on the problem. It is surprising how often this technique works.

(ii) Examine the values of key variables while the program is running. Install temporary lines of coding throughout the program to display the value of variables and to pause until you press a key. For example, in COBOL you might insert the statements

DISPLAY "AT PARAGRAPH/PROC-REC/", inrec.

ACCEPT dummy.

The DISPLAY statement indicates the current position in the program, and the contents of the variable "inrec". The ACCEPT statement causes the program to wait until "dummy" (defined in the WORKING-STORAGE SECTION as PIC X) is given a value (pressing the RETURN /ENTER key is sufficient). In BASIC, PRINT and INPUT instructions can be used to perform the equivalent operations.

Comparison of the values actually displayed with expected values will normally indicate the likely source of the error.

(iii) Use debugging utilities provided in the language itself or separately in the system software. Several versions of BASIC have a trace facility which, when turned on, displays the line number of statements prior to their execution. Sometimes a particular implementation of a language will provide more sophisticated debugging facilities which will display the values of particular variables as they are encountered during program execution. Minicomputer systems and mainframes will usually have special debugging software which can be used with any of the languages supported by the system. It is up to the programmer to investigate the debugging aids available and make good use of them.

Test Data

When the programmer feels that the most obvious program errors have been detected and removed, the next stage is to test the program using carefully selected data. The nature of the test data should be such that:

(i) every statement in the program is executed at least once;

(ii) the effectiveness of every section of coding devoted to detecting erroneous input is verified;

(iii) every route through the program is tried;

(iv) the accuracy of the processing is verified;

(v) the program operates according to its original design specification.

In order to achieve these aims, the programmer must be inventive in the design of the test data. Each test case must check something not tested by previous runs; there is no point in proving that a program which can add successfully a certain set of numbers can also add another similar set of numbers. The goal is to strain the program to its limit, and this is particularly important when the program is to be used frequently by a number of different people.

There are three general categories of test data:

Normal data. This includes the most general data which the program was designed to handle.

Extreme values. These test the behaviour of the program when valid data at the upper and lower limits of acceptability are used. The process of using extreme values is called 'boundary testing' and is often a fruitful place to look for errors. For numeric data this could be the use of very large or very small values. Text could be the shortest or longest sequence of characters permitted. A program for file processing could be tested with a file containing no records, or just a single record. The cases where zero or null values are used are very important test cases, frequently highlighting programming oversights.

Exceptional data. Programs are usually designed to accept a certain range or class of inputs. If 'illegal' data are used, (that is data which the program is not designed to handle), the program should be capable of rejecting it rather than attempting to process it. This is particularly important when the program is to be used by people other than the programmer, since they may be unaware of what constitutes illegal data. From the outset a programmer should assume that incorrect data will be used with the program; this may save a great deal of time looking for program errors which may actually be data errors.

Top-down Testing

Top-down program design techniques, such as those discussed earlier in this chapter lend themselves to methodical testing. In top-down design, the program is designed by defining the main sections of the program first. These sections are then defined in terms of sub-sections of procedures which themselves may be further defined. Top-down testing proceeds in a similar manner. As a level of the program is coded, it can be tested by using program 'stubs' for uncoded lower levels. Stubs are 'empty' sections of the program which do nothing when executed. For example, in COBOL a program stub could be a paragraph merely containing the word EXIT which does nothing when executed:

```
            . . . . . . . . . . . .
            . . . . . . . . . . . .
    PROC5.
                EXIT.
    PROC6.
        etc.
            . . . . . . . . . . . .
            . . . . . . . . . . . .
```

However, the paragraph PROC5 can still be PERFORMED from a higher level section of the program and thus allow the accuracy of the logic of this higher level to be investigated.

In this way the complete program need not exist in order for parts of it to be tested thoroughly. As the skeleton is fleshed out, more test data can be used. Thus the test data grows in parallel with the production of the program coding. Furthermore, the overall logic of the program can be tested right at the outset, and continues to be tested as more coding is added.

Validation

At some point the programmer must decide that the program has had sufficient testing. He or she will be confident that the program will operate according to specification and without 'crashing' or 'hanging up' under extreme or unexpected circumstances; the reputation of a professional programmer relies on this. Prior to release, the final testing is then performed by the user for whom the program was developed. The programmer may have overlooked areas of difficulty because it is often difficult to view a program objectively or entirely from the point of view of the user. If this is the case then the program will be modified and re-tested until all user requirements are met.

Program Documentation

The purpose of documentation is to provide the user with all the information necessary to fully understand the purpose of the program and how that purpose has been achieved. The precise form that the documentation takes will be determined by a number of factors:

(i) The type of program;

(ii) Who is likely to use the program;

(iii) Whether it will be necessary to modify the program coding after it has been finally tested and accepted.

This section will explore these factors and provide general guidelines for the contents of the documentation, but because of the wide variety of opinion regarding its format, no particular documentation standard will be advocated. The section concludes with an example of how a program might be documented.

Documentation Requirements

A program which validates a temporary file prior to creating it permanently will probably require a minimum of user interaction and only a small number of instructions for the benefit of the person who will run the program. However, at some later date, it might be necessary for the author of the program, or a different programmer, to modify it. This possibility means that the structure of the program will have to be explained in great detail, and test procedures to ensure its correct operation will have to be provided.

A general purpose program such as a spreadsheet, designed for naive users, will entail the provision of extremely detailed instructions regarding its function and use. Such programs are generally accompanied by extremely detailed user manuals and tutorials. On the other hand, users would not be expected (and definitely not encouraged) to modify the program coding; thus no details would be provided regarding the way the program has been written. This latter type of documentation would only be required by the people responsible for producing the program.

In addition to the documentation requirements of users and programmers, there is a third category of person to be catered for. These are people such as managers who are neither likely to use programs extensively nor want to attempt to modify them. They merely need to have an overview of the program - its function, capabilities, hardware requirements etc.

Thus there are many factors governing the coverage of documentation, and for this reason, in the next section, it is only possible to provide a checklist of items which might reasonably be included.

Documentation Checklist

The documentation for a simple program generally falls into four sections:

(i) Identification

(ii) General specification

(iii) User information

(iv) Program specification.

Most users will need access to the first three sections; in general the fourth section will only be needed if the program is to be modified. The amount of detail in each section will depend entirely on the particular application and, to some extent, the implementation language. COBOL, for example, is largely self-documenting: it contains an Identification Division containing all the information listed in the first section below. The Data Division of a COBOL program contains precise details regarding all of the files used by the program and which devices are required. The Procedure Division is written in 'English-like' sentences which are generally easy to understand, even by a non-programmer. Consequently, a program written in COBOL will generally require less documentation than one written in BASIC.

The following checklist is a guide to what might reasonably be included in the documentation for a program:

Identification

- title of program;

- short statement of its function;

- author;

- date written;

- language used and version if relevant;

- hardware requirements.

General specification

- description of the main action(s) of the program under normal circumstances;

- systems flowcharts;

- description of data structures, including data structure diagrams and file specifications;

- restrictions and/or limitations of the program;

- equations used or references to texts explaining any complex procedures/techniques involved;

User information

- format of input required, e.g. source document or screen mask;

- output produced, e.g. typical printout or screen display;

- detailed instructions for initially running the program;

- medium on which program located, e.g. floppy disc(s);

Program specification

- structure charts;

- pseudo-code;

- annotated listing;

- testing procedure including test data and expected output.

Example of Documentation

A simple stock file updating problem illustrating various aspects of program development is used to illustrate how a program might be documented. The implementation language is assumed to be BASIC since good documentation is particularly important for programs written in languages which, unlike COBOL, do not contain self-documentation characteristics.

Documentation Example

Identification

Program ID : STOCK-FILE UPDATE.

Author : Nick Waites.

Purpose : To update a master stock file with a transaction file containing details of sales and receipts of stock items.

Date written : March 1987.

Language: BBC BASIC II.

Hardware: BBC Model B, Single 40 track floppy disc drive.

General Specification

Operation of Program

The purpose of the program is to read a sequential transaction file held on floppy disc and use it to update a sequential file containing records of stock items. The transaction file comprises a set of records containing details of stock items received from suppliers, and records containing details of stock items sold. Each record in the transaction file will be used to modify a corresponding record on the master file. There may be several transaction records for each record on the master file. Where the transaction is a sale, the number sold will be subtracted from the current stock level; receipts will be added to the current stock level. The transaction file is assumed to have been pre-sorted such that all orders relating to a particular record are grouped together. Once all transactions for a record have been processed, the updated record is written to a new stock file, again sequentially organised.

Systems Flowchart

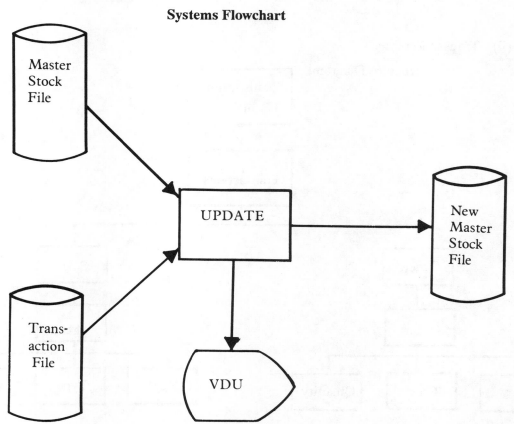

Data Structures

(i)   Master stock file.

(a)   Structure diagram:

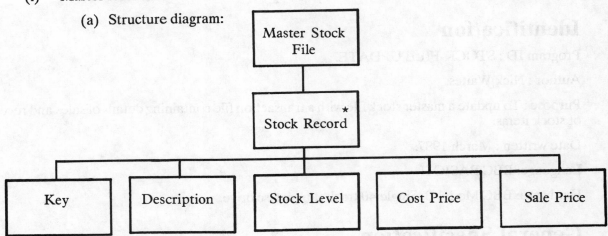

(b)   File Definition:

File Name: Masterfile

Field	Program name	Type	Size(char)
Key	mastkey	numeric integer	
Description	descrip$	alphabetic	30
Stock level	stock	numeric integer	
Cost Price	costprice	numeric real	
Sale Price	sellprice	numeric real	

(ii)   Transaction File.

(a)   Structure Diagram:

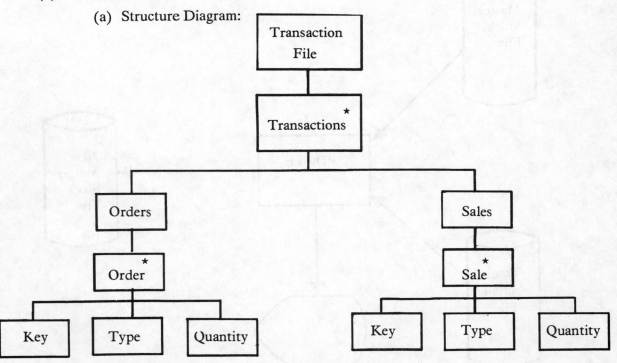

(b) File Definition:

File Name: Transfile.

Field	Program name	Type	Size(char)
Key	transkey	numeric integer	
Type	type$	"SALE" or "ORDR"	4
Quantity	quantity	numeric integer	

(iii) New stock file.

    (a) Structure diagram:

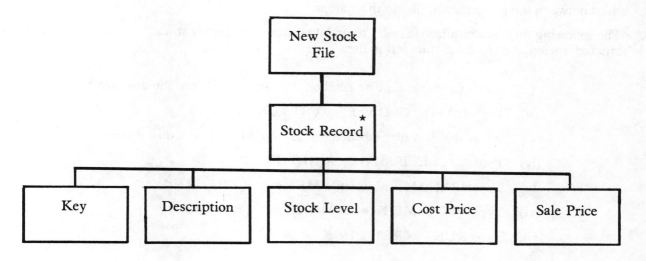

(b) File Definition:

File Name: Newfile

Field	Program name	Type	Size(char)
Key	mastkey	numeric integer	
Description	descrip$	alphabetic	30
Stock Level	stock	numeric integer	
Cost Price	costprice	numeric real	
Sale Price	sellprice	numeric real	

Restriction/limitations

The program operates under two important assumptions:

(i) The transaction file has been thoroughly validated.

(ii) The transaction file has been sorted into the same sequential order as the records in the master stock file, namely, ascending order of key field.

In addition, since the program creates a new master stock file (Newfile) whenever it processes the transaction file against the current master stock file (Masterfile), the new file must be renamed. This procedure is defined in the following section.

User Information

This program constitutes one element of a suite of programs forming a simple stock control system. The other processing tasks on which this program relies are defined and explained in companion documents. The complete system documentation, of which this is a part, defines the interrelationships between the program and files in the system.

The following steps are required in order to update the current master stock file using a previously created, sorted and validated transaction file:

(i) Insert the program disc labelled "SCSPROG1" into the disc drive.

(ii) Type LOAD "UPDATE" ⟨RETURN⟩ .

(iii) Insert the data disc labelled "SCSDATA1" into the disc drive.

(iv) Type *DELETE MFcopy ⟨RETURN⟩

(v) Type *RENAME Masterfile MFcopy ⟨RETURN⟩ .

(vi) Type *RENAME Newfile Masterfile ⟨RETURN⟩ .

(vii) Type RUN ⟨RETURN⟩ .

Program Specification

Program Structure Diagram
(see following diagram)

Operations
Initialisation operations:

1. Open Master File for Input

2. Open Updated Stock File for Output

3. Open Transaction File for input

Program Termination operations:

4. Close Master File

5. Close Updated Stock File

6. Close Transaction File

7. Stop

Input/Output operations:

8. Read Master File

9. Read Transaction File

10. Write Updated Stock Record

Processing operations:

11. Subtract number of sales from stock level

12. Add receipts to stock level

13. Display error message: "No stock record for this transaction"

14. Store transaction record key

Iteration conditions:

C1. Until End of Master File and Transaction File

C2. Until change of transaction record key

Selection conditions:

C3. Transaction record key matches stock record key

C4. Transaction record key >stock record key

C5. Transaction record key <stock record key

C6. Transaction type = Sale

C7. Transaction type = Receipt

Program Structure Diagram

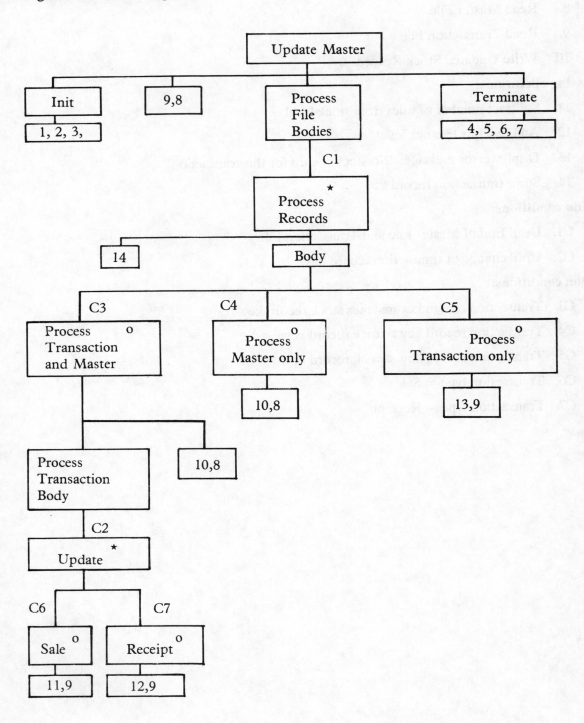

UPDATE
MASTER seq

Psuedo Code

    INIT seq

        Open Transaction File for Input;

        Open Master File for Input;

        Open Updated Stock File for Output;

    INIT endseq

        Read Transaction File;

        Read Master File;

PROCESS
FILE
BODIES iter until end of Transaction File and Master File

    PROCESS RECORDS seq

        Store transaction record key in Temp-key;

        BODY select transaction record key = Stock record key

            PROCESS
            TRANS
            BODY iter while transaction rec key = Temp-key

                UPDATE   select type = Sale

                        Subtract no. of sales from stock level;

                        Read Transaction File;

                UPDATE   or type = Receipt

                        Add receipts to stock level;

                        Read Transaction File;

                UPDATE   endselect

            PROCESS
            TRANS
            BODY enditer

            Write Updated Stock record;

            Read Master File;

        BODY or transaction record key > stock record key

            Write Updated Stock record;
            Read Master File;

        BODY or transaction record key < stock record key

            Display error message;

            Read Transaction File;

        BODY endselect

    PROCESS RECORDS endseq

PROCESS
FILE
BODIES enditer

    TERMINATE seq

        Close Transaction File;

        Close Master File;

        Close Updated Stock File;

    TERMINATE endseq

UPDATE
MASTER endseq

Program listing

```
 10   REM * UPDATE MASTER STOCK FILE sequence *

 20   REM * INIT seq *
 30        Transfile = OPENIN("transdata")
 40        Masterfile = OPENIN("mastdata")
 50        Newfile = OPENOUT("newdata")
 60   REM   * INIT endseq *

 80   INPUT # Transfile, transkey, type$, quantity
 90   INPUT # Masterfile,mastkey,descrip$,stock,costprice,sellprice

100   REM * PROCESS FILE BODIES iterate UNTIL end of Trans AND Mast *
110   IF EOF(Transfile) AND EOF(Masterfile) GOTO 530

115        REM * PROCESS RECORDS sequence *
120        LET tempkey = transkey
130        REM * BODY select transaction key = stock key *
135        IF transkey<> mastkey GOTO 340
140             REM * PROCESS TRANS BODY iterate WHILE transkey = tempkey
145             IF transkey <> tempkey GOTO 310

150             REM * UPDATE RECORDS type = Sale *

160                  IF type$ <> "SALE" GOTO 200
170                  LET stock = stock - quantity
180                  INPUT # Transfile, transkey, type$, quantity
190                  GOTO 300

200             REM * UPDATE RECORDS type = Receipt *
220                  LET stock = stock + quantity
230                  INPUT # Transfile, transkey, type$, quantity

300             REM * UPDATE RECORDS endselect *
305             GOTO 140
310             REM * PROCESS TRANS BODY end iteration *

320             PRINT # Newfile,mastkey,descrip$,stock,costprice,sellprice
330             INPUT # Masterfile,mastkey,descrip$,stock,costprice,sellprice
335             GOTO 500

340        REM * BODY or transkey > mastkey *
345        IF Transkey <  mastkey GOTO 380
350             PRINT # Newfile,mastkey,descrip$,stock,costprice,sellprice
360             INPUT # Masterfile,mastkey,descrip$,stock,costprice,sellprice
370             GOTO 500

380        REM * BODY or transkey < mastkey *
390             PRINT " Transactions out of order "; transkey, mastkey
400             INPUT # Transfile, transkey, type$, quantity

500        REM * BODY end selection *

510        REM * PROCESS RECORDS end sequence *

520        GOTO 100
530   REM * PROCESS FILE BODIES end iteration *

535   REM * TERMINATE sequence *
540        CLOSE # Masterfile
550        CLOSE # Transfile
560        CLOSE # Newfile

570   REM * UPDATE MASTER STOCK FILE end sequence *
575   REM * TERMINATE end sequence *
580   END
```

Testing Procedure

In order to facilitate the process of testing the program's operation, two special files have been prepared. The first file called 'MFtest' contains a small number (5) of stock records (see Table 1). The other file 'TRtest' contains a number of transactions (see Table2). When the program has been run using these special files, an updated master file called 'newfile' is created. The expected contents of this file are shown in Table 3.

The procedure required for testing the program is as follows:

    (i)   Insert the disc labelled "SCSPROG1" into the disc drive.

    (ii)   Type LOAD "UPDATE"   ⟨RETURN⟩ .

    (iii)   Insert the disc labelled "SCSTEST1" into the disc drive.

    (iv)   Type RUN   ⟨RETURN⟩ .

    (v)   Type CHAIN "REPORT1"   ⟨RETURN⟩ .

The contents of the newly created file will be displayed on the screen. (The contents of the file may be printed out by using the program REPORT2 instead of REPORT1).

The file displayed (or printed) should match that in Table 3.

Key Field	Description	Level	Cost	Sale
100011	Apple Juice	36	1.30	1.60
100027	Honey comb	20	0.35	0.50
100039	Long Grain Brown Rice (Organic)	44	0.32	0.41
100122	Sultanas (Australian)	22	0.55	0.69
100343	Shoyu (Japanese)	10	1.23	1.57

Table 1: Initial Contents of Master File

Key Field	Type	Quantity
100011	ORDR	12
100011	SALE	3
100011	SALE	5
100039	SALE	6
100039	SALE	2
100122	SALE	11
100122	ORDR	30
100122	SALE	5

Table 2: Transaction File

Key field	Description	Level	Cost	Sale
100011	Apple Juice	40	1.30	1.60
100027	Honey comb	20	0.35	0.50
100039	Long Grain Brown Rice (Organic)	36	0.32	0.41
100122	Sultanas (Australian)	41	0.55	0.69
100343	Shoyu (Japanese)	10	1.23	1.57

Table 3: Final Contents of Master File

Assignment   The Squash Club

The Arnside Squash Club in Guildford, Surrey, has a large and thriving membership, running about sixteen leagues held over six-week periods. Each league has five players and each member of a league must play at least three games during the six weeks, to stay in the league. At the end of six weeks, the points for each player are totalled and new leagues are drawn up according to the points placings. The club is run by a committee of six members, plus a chairperson and secretary.

The club has bought an Archimedes microcomputer system with twin disk drives, a monitor and a printer, which they intend to use for the membership records and league placings. A database package is to be used for the membership records, but the club's secretary, Bill Norris, has volunteered to write programs to set up and record the progress of the squash leagues. Although Bill has a good working knowledge of the BASIC language, he is unfamiliar with the techniques used by professional programmers to plan and develop their programs. You are a member of the club committee and as a trainee programmer with a local firm, you have gained some experience of program development techniques.

Task

1. Explain the need for programming standards;

2. Write a set of formal guidelines for Bill Norris, explaining the stages he should follow, from the initial consideration of the problem to the production of a fully operational program;

3. Suggest the techniques and programming aids he may use during each stage.

Assignment   Basic Steps

Task

1. Draw the data structures for the following input file and output report, identify the correspondences and derive a program structure. Fill out the program structure and draw up an elementary operation list and condition list. Use the format laid out in the Documentation Example in this chapter as a guide.

2. Use the program structure produced in Task 1 to code a BASIC program.

Program Requirements

(a) The input file (formed from DATA statements) contains book records with the following data items:

ISBN	(4 numeric characters);
Author	(max 15 characters);
Title	(max 15 characters);
Type	(fiction - F or non-fiction - N);
Status	(IN or OUT);

Date last issued (6 numeric characters of form DDMMYY).

(b) The input is to be validated as follows:

ISBN	- for fixed length of 4 characters;
Author	- for maximum length of 15 characters;
Title	- for maximum length of 15 characters;
Type	- for single character, which is either F or N;
Status	- for values IN or OUT only;
Date	- for fixed length of 6 characters.

Both valid and invalid records are to be printed in the report, but a final column headed 'Invalid' will contain an asterisk for any invalid records.

(c) The output report is to take a form similar to the following example.

Book File Validation Report

ISBN Author	Title	Type	Status	Last Issued	Invalid
1234 Higgins, J	Bomber	F	IN	230190	
1245 Braine, T	Firebug	F	OUT	250290	
1247 Graves, R	I, Claudius	F	IN	13068	*
1256 French, C	Computer Science	N	OUT	250290	*
1315 Knott, et al	Information Processing	N	IN	230190	*
1318 Kay, S	Legacy	N	ON	230290	*

In the above example, record 1247 is invalid because there are only 5 characters in the date; record 1256 is invalid because the title is 16 characters in length; similarly, record 1315 is invalid because the title has 22 characters; record 1318 has an invalid Status data item value.

(d) Test the program according to the recommendations given in the chapter. Record any adverse results and try to determine whether or not you can overcome them.

(e) Document the program according to the standards of the Documentation Example given in the chapter, but excluding the pseudo code. Record any limitations and restrictions of the program.

Chapter 14

☐ SYSTEMS DEVELOPMENT AND IMPLEMENTATION

Introduction

When a new computer system is introduced, or an existing computerized information system is to be changed or modified, then a process of development and implementation should be followed. This process is known as the 'System Life Cycle' and has a number of distinct stages.

An outline of this cycle can be illustrated as follows:

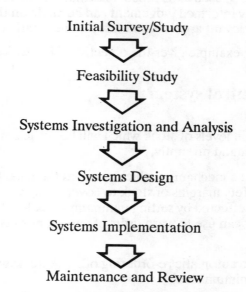

Initial Survey/Study

⇩

Feasibility Study

⇩

Systems Investigation and Analysis

⇩

Systems Design

⇩

Systems Implementation

⇩

Maintenance and Review

The need for an application to be computerized or for an existing computerized system to be changed is often identified by the users. Such an initiative is described as being from the 'bottom-up'. Alternatively if the initiative stems from management it is described as being 'top-down'. However it is initiated, innovation or change requires close consultation between users and management, to consider its consequences and benefits and to decide the way it is to be introduced.

The system life cycle begins when a need for change or innovation is identified. The cycle may of course, be stopped at any stage if it is found that the change is not after all desirable. The specialist responsible for each stage in the cycle is the Systems Analyst whose broad responsibilities are described in Chapter 8 on Management Information Services.

The activities within each stage of the system life cycle are described below:

a. Initial Survey/Study

Once a need for computerization has been identified, an initial survey is undertaken to decide whether or not such a need is justified. It is important that management establish what they are trying to achieve in terms of the overall objectives of the business and in the light of this, the objectives of the systems which contribute to their achievement. For example, two major business objectives may be to improve the delivery of customers' orders and to minimize the stock levels which tie up valuable cash resources. The achievement of these objectives may involve contributions from several different information processing systems and the list may include:

> (i) Stock Control - records stock movement and controls stock levels;
>
> (ii) Purchasing - responsible for the ordering of new supplies from suppliers;
>
> (iii) Sales Order Processing - receives customers' orders and initiates the process of order fulfilment;
>
> (iv) Purchase Ledger - the accounting record of amounts owed and paid to suppliers of stock;
>
> (v) Invoicing - the production of invoices requesting payment from customers for goods supplied;
>
> (vi) Sales Ledger - the accounting record of amounts owed by and received from customers for goods supplied.

Before any single application can be computerized, it is necessary to establish its objectives clearly because users may have become so used to its procedures that they no longer question their purpose. It is self-evident that before any informed judgement can be made on the design of a computerized system, the objectives of the relevant application must first be clearly understood.

To illustrate this, the following example gives the objectives of a stock control system:

Objectives of a stock control system

> (i) to maintain levels of stock which will be sufficient to meet customer demand promptly;
>
> (ii) to provide a mechanism which removes the need for excessively high safety margins of stock to cover customer demand. This is usually effected by setting minimum stock levels which the computer can use to warn users of variations outside these levels;
>
> (iii) to provide automatic re-ordering of stock items which fall below minimum levels;
>
> (iv) to provide management with up-to-date information on stock levels and values of stock held.

b. Feasibility Study

Having established that there exists the need for a new system, a feasibility study should provide sufficient information to either justify its computerization or make suggestions as to alternative methods for its operation. This is produced by a Study Team composed of systems analysts, users and management.

Such a study compares the costs and benefits of the existing system with the projected costs and benefits of a new system. Tangible savings , such as a reduction in staffing or, as is more likely, an increase in business without extra staffing, can be readily measured. The benefits of more accurate, up-to-date information and more management information however are less easy to quantify, yet they must nevertheless be taken into account when a comparison is made. Other tangible costs of the new system may include the costs of computer hardware, the costs of software which is either packaged or specially written, staff training and possibly specialist staff recruitment.

The social costs and benefits which relate to staff also have to be assessed. These may include training needs and changes in career prospects, salaries, job descriptions or job satisfaction. The feasibility study may well recommend that a particular manufacturer's computer system is purchased or that specific packaged software is employed.

The end product of this stage of the cycle is a FEASIBILITY REPORT for consideration by management. It should cover the following areas:

(i) A description of the application to be computerized, the overall business and individual system objectives which are to be satisfied and the position of the development in relation to the organization's overall computerization plans.

(ii) A description of the existing system, its good and bad features and the means by which the proposed system aims to improve on it. This area details the costs of the existing system to allow comparison with the proposed new system.

(iii) A description of the new system, its operation, costs and expected benefits. These can be difficult to quantify but may include, for example:

- estimated savings in capital expenditure on typewriters and photocopiers;

- more efficient stock management allowing customer service to be maintained whilst keeping stock levels lower. This releases valuable cash resources and reduces possible interest charges on borrowed capital;

- expansion in business turnover, without the need for extra staff or overtime working.

(iv) Possible alternatives and recommendations. This is an important area, for should the recommendation be against the proposed system, then alternatives need to be presented.

(v) Costs of development and the timescale for development and implementation (if the recommended system is to be adopted). These will include both CAPITAL and REVENUE or running costs. Capital costs are likely to be incurred for the following:

- computer hardware;

- systems software and software packages (either 'off-the-shelf' or 'tailor-made');

- installation charges for hardware and software;

- staff training.

Revenue costs may include those for the maintenance and insurance of the system. In addition, new specialist computer staff may need to be employed on annual salaries.

It must be remembered that an application will not necessarily benefit from computerization and the study team may well recommend changes in the system which do not involve a computer. Increasingly however, reduction in costs of computer hardware and advances in software development which cover most applications have lessened the likelihood of this happening in most cases.

c. Systems Investigation and Analysis

If the feasibility report is favourable then a more detailed investigation begins. The information obtained should be analysed in terms of its bearing on the design and implementation of the new system. The objective of this stage is to produce a 'Statement of User Requirements'. This is, in effect, a system proposal approved by the users. To design the most effective computerized system, the analyst needs first to gain a thorough knowledge of the operation of the existing system and then to analyse in detail the best solution for computerized working. This stage is a prerequisite of the detailed Systems Design stage.

The task of gathering such information may involve interviews with users, surveys by questionnaire, the examination of documents and procedure manuals and most importantly, the observation of users already operating the system. These various techniques are discussed later in this chapter.

The systems analyst should produce a report which covers the following areas.

The Objectives and Scope of the Existing System
The objectives of a system describe its main functions and what it seeks to achieve. By the scope, we mean the boundaries of the system to be investigated. In this way, the limits of the investigation are established.

Input
A number of details concerning the data inputs to a system need to be established:

- the source of the data. It may, for example, originate from a customer, a supplier, or another department in the business;

- the form of the data. The data may arrive, for example, by telephone, letter, or a by standard form such as an order form or supplier's invoice;

- the volume of the data and its frequency, for example, the number of orders received each day or week;

- the contents of the data, for example, the individual items of data which appear on a supplier's invoice.

Such information will allow the systems analyst to make recommendations on the most appropriate methods of computer input. Alternative methods may include, for example, direct keyboard entry, direct input with the use of bar code readers or optical character readers. The information on volumes and frequency of input data can also be used to determine the processing method which is most appropriate, for example, batch or real-time processing.

The Files Used
The storage of historic and current information is a vital part of any business system. For example, the computerized production of payslips requires not only transient input data concerning hours worked and sickness days, but also data on rate of pay, tax code, deductions of tax and superannuation to date etc., which are held in the payroll master file stored on magnetic tape or disk. Information on the contents of files can be gathered from existing manual files, together with responses from users regarding the output requirements of any new system. For example, each stock record in a master file may include:

> Stock Code
>
> Description
>
> Unit Price
>
> Minimum Stock Level
>
> Re-order Quantity

Quantity in Stock

Details of the master and transaction files to be used, the data items which will be included in each record, the sequence of organization and the frequency of updating or access, will assist the systems analyst in the choice of computer storage media and the most appropriate file organization and access methods. If packaged software is to be used then the contents of files and the file organization methods will be dictated by the package. In such cases, some data item types may be surplus to requirements, whilst others which would have been desirable may not be available.

Processing Tasks

All the clerical and machine-assisted procedures which are necessary to achieve the desired output from the given input need to be identified. This will allow the systems analyst to determine the role of the computer in the new system, the programs necessary to take over the processing stages and the changes needed to clerical procedures before and after computer processing. There are many instances when the processing requires not only the input data but also data retrieved from files. For example, to generate a customer invoice requires:

- input data concerning commodity codes and quantities ordered;

- data from the stock master file concerning prices of items ordered by reference to the input commodity codes;

- customer details from the customer master file.

The above processes can be completely computerized, but other processes may require human intervention. For example, before a customer order is processed, the customer's credit may need to be checked and referred to a supervisor before authorization.

Output

Information on the form and content of outputs produced by the system will give guidance to the systems analyst on the objectives of the new system. In addition, it may be found that a computerized system may also produce additional outputs which cannot be produced efficiently at present. The following need to be identified:

- the data items required as output. Some may be revealed in the existing system, whilst others may be requested by users as being desirable in any new system;

- the form of the output, for example, whether or not printed copy is required;

- the data volume of each output and the frequency with which output occurs. This information assists decisions on the types and number of output devices required.

Controls

The clerical procedures which control the accuracy and security of the data in the present system will provide a minimum standard for any new system. Of course, it would be hoped that a computerized system could improve such accuracy and security standards.

Management Information

The present system may already produce some management information, but generally, a computerized system can produce information which it is not practical to produce manually. Existing output should therefore be questioned. It may be that the management information currently produced is no longer necessary but continues to be produced through system inertia, in other words, because no one has realised that it is not really necessary or appropriate.

Problems and Difficulties

If the new system is to avoid the difficulties inherent in the existing system, then such difficulties must be clearly identified.

Methods of Gathering the Information

There are four main methods which a systems analyst can use to gather the information which has been discussed in the previous section. These are:

> (i) Interviewing;
>
> (ii) Questionnaires;
>
> (iii) Examination of records and procedure manuals;
>
> (iv) Observation.

The method or methods chosen will depend on the specific circumstances which relate to a system as each method has particular advantages and disadvantages.

Interviewing

This is probably the most commonly used method for collecting information even though the skills of interviewing are not easily acquired. The interviewer needs to know how to gain the confidence of the interviewee and ensure that the person feels that the information which is given will be of value in the design of the proposed new system. The questions need to be phrased unambiguously in order to obtain the desired information. Opinions, as well as facts, are valuable as they will tend to reveal the strengths and weaknesses of the present system.

It is important to ask the appropriate questions at the right level in the staff hierarchy within the organization. For example, the sales clerk would probably be the best person to ask about the completion of a customer order form.

For a check list of questions to be drawn up, the systems analyst needs to have prior knowledge of duties and responsibilities of staff who are to be interviewed.

Questionnaire

Questionnaires are useful when only a small amount of information is required from a large number of people. To provide accurate responses questions need to be unambiguous and precise. Questionnaires can be useful for gathering statistical information on, for example, volumes of sales transactions or customer enquiries at the different branches of a national organization.

Examination of Records and Procedure Manuals

If existing procedures are already well documented then the procedure manuals can provide a ready-made source of information on the way procedures should be carried out. However it is important to realise that the procedures detailed there may not accord with what actually happens. The examination of current records and the tracing of particular transactions from input to the production of the required output can be a method by which the systems analyst may discover how closely the set procedures are actually followed.

The use of special purpose records which may involve, for example, the ticking of a box when an activity has been completed, is another useful technique which does not significantly add to the work load of the staff involved.

Observation

It is most important to observe a procedure in action, so that irregularities and exceptional procedures are noticed. Observation should always be carried out with tact, and staff under observation should be made fully aware of its purpose to avoid suspicions of 'snooping'.

The following list details some of the features of office procedures and conditions which may be usefully observed by a trained person:

The Office Layout - This may determine whether the positioning of desks, filing cabinets and other office equipment is convenient for staff and conducive to efficient working;

The Work Load - This should indicate whether the volume of documents waiting to be processed is fairly constant or if there are peak periods during the week;

Delays - These could show that there are some procedures which are continually behind schedule;

Methods of Working - a trained observer can, through experience, recognize a slow, reasonable or quick pace of work and decide whether or not the method of working is efficient. It is important that such observations should be followed up by an interview to obtain the cooperation of the person under observation;

Office Conditions - These should be examined as poor ventilation, inadequate or excessive temperatures or poor lighting can adversely effect staff efficiency.

Recording the Facts

During the investigation stage, the systems analyst is likely to accumulate a large volume of notes on all areas of the system. It is good practice, therefore, to organize these notes into sections according to the department or procedure to which they relate. A continuous narrative may be difficult and laborious to read and so wherever possible, use should be made of diagrammatic representations such as:

Organization Charts

Organization charts provide an overview of an organizations's operations and show the relationships between people and the work for which they are responsible.

In attempting to discover how a current system functions, it is useful to know which individuals are responsible for each functional area. Organizations charts can be useful in this respect. An example is shown below.

A Formal Organization Chart

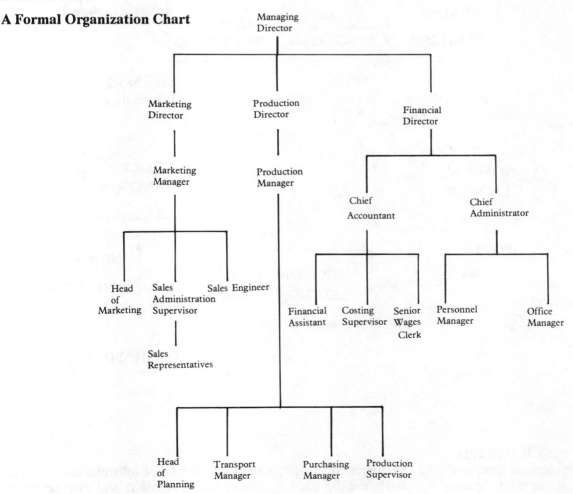

It should be borne in mind, however, that designated and actual job responsibilities can differ radically. For example, it may be that a junior sales clerk is carrying out the checking of orders, which should be the responsibility of the sales supervisor. Thus, it may be necessary for the analyst to draw an alternative informal organization chart to show the actual working relationships of staff.

Apart from identifying working relationships between staff, it is useful to draw up brief job descriptions, so that consultation on individual system procedures can take place with the appropriate staff. For example, a job description for a sales clerk may include the following activities:

- completion of standard order forms;

- checking stock availability;

- notification of orders to Accounts.

Therefore, although the sales departmental manager may have knowledge of such procedures, the sales clerk will have practical experience of their operation and should be consulted.

Information Interface or Flow Diagrams

Information interface diagrams provide a visual representation of information movement in an organization. They do not refer to specific hardware and are not, therefore, committing the systems analyst in this area. It is important that the systems analyst retains an 'open mind' in the early stages, so that improved hardware and software possibilities are not overlooked. The topic of information interface diagrams is introduced in Chapter 2. A further, simplified example is shown in the following figure.

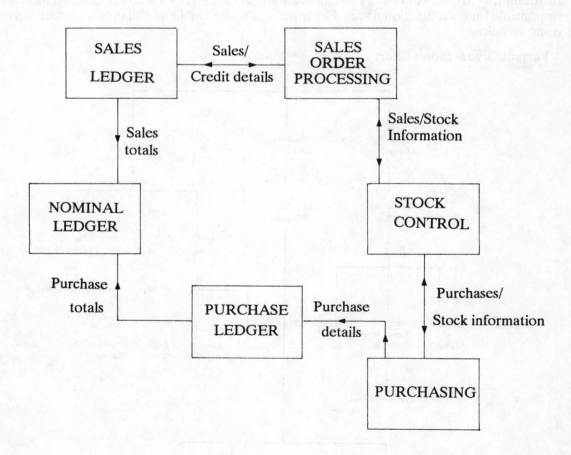

System Flowcharts

Most processes involve the use of documents to allow the transmission of information from one stage to another. System flowcharts can be used to model the movement and interaction of documents and the data they record, as well as the processes involved, as they pass from one functional area to another. System flowcharts can also allow the systems analyst to plan the selection of hardware for the proposed system. In such flowcharts, there is no detail of how processing is to be accomplished. A complete computer program to carry out the necessary computer processing, may be represented by one symbol in the flowchart. A number of standards exist for the drawing of system flowcharts and the range of symbols used depends on which stage of the investigation and design process has been reached. For example, in the early stages of investigation of an existing manual system, there will be no representation of computer methods of input, processing, output or storage. At a later stage, when computer methods are being considered, it will be necessary to use suitable symbols in the flowchart. The symbols are drawn using a flowchart template. A range of standard symbols is provided in the following figure.

Basic System flowchart symbols

a document, for example,
an order form or summary report

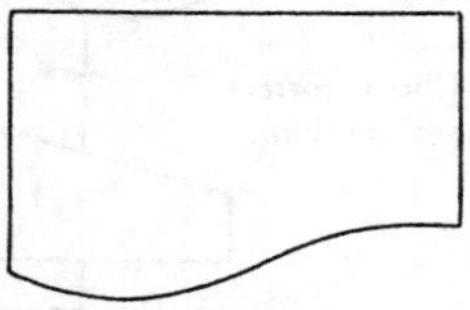

an on-line computer file

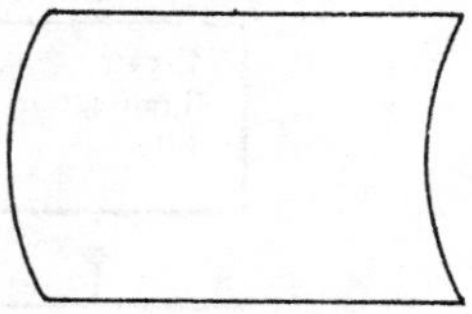

an off-line or manual file

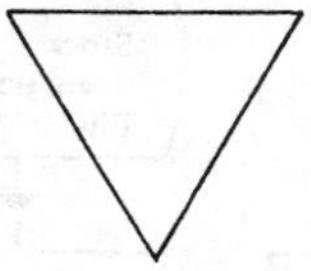

Keyboard entry

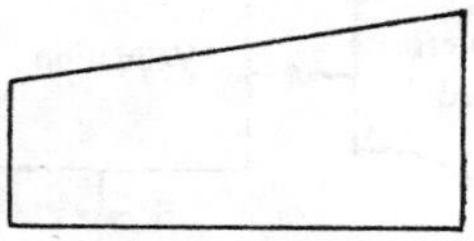

Screen display

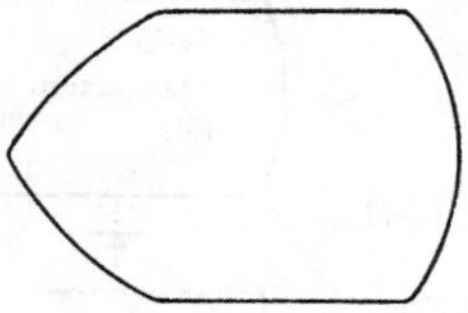

a decision

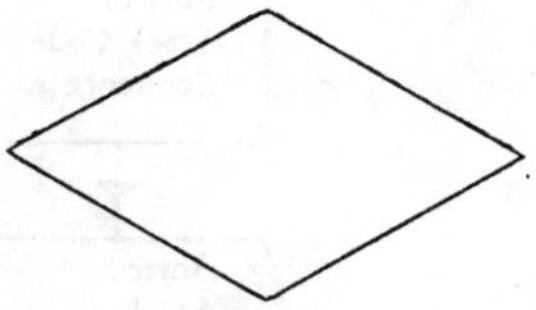

a manual process

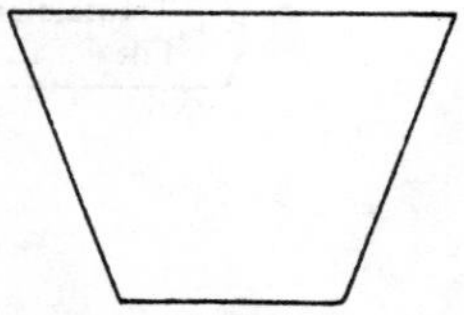

a computer process

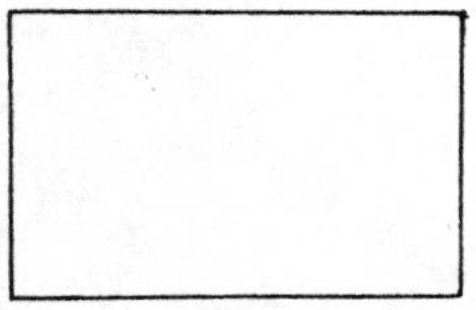

An example system flowchart without any specification of computer involvement is illustrated on the next page. In order that the involvement of each section, department or personnel grouping in the processes can be identified, the system flowchart is divided into columns representing these divisions of responsibility.

An example of a systems flowchart which is likely to be produced in the later stages of systems design and which identifies the role of computer hardware is shown below. A further example for a real-time system appears later in the chapter.

System Flowchart - Stock File Update Using Batch Processing

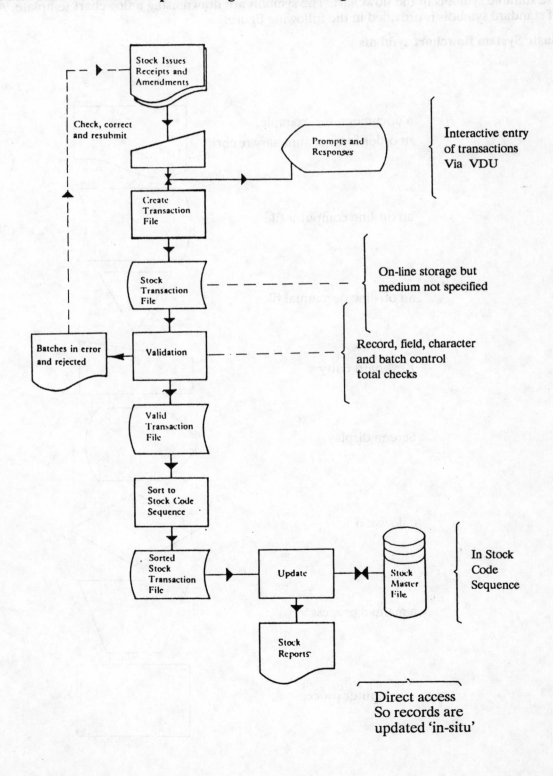

System Flowchart - without consideration of computer function

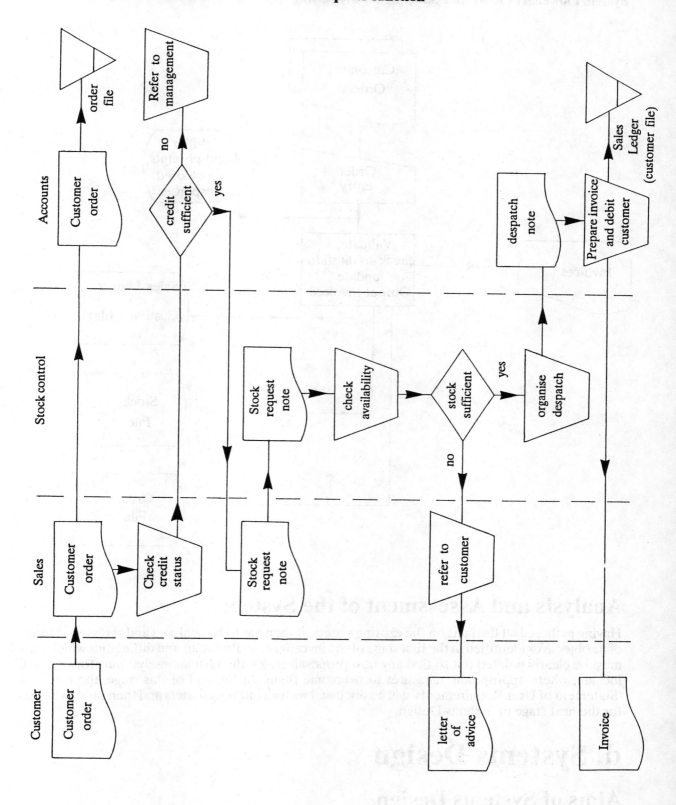

System Flowchart - Real-time Sales Order Processing

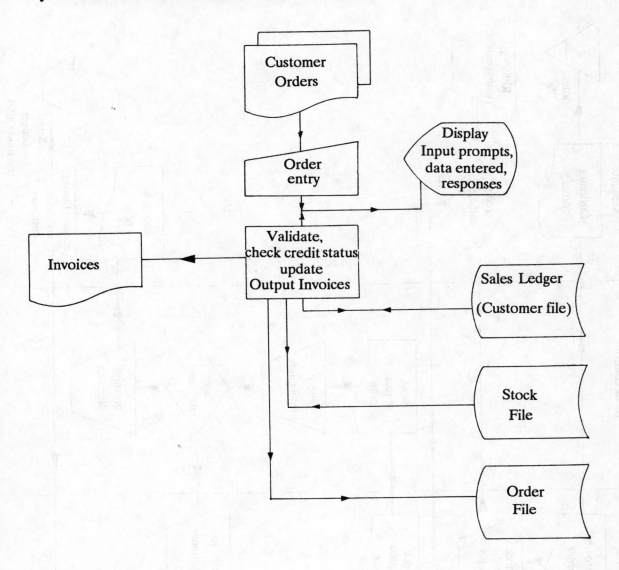

Analysis and Assessment of the System

Having gathered all the facts on the existing system, it then has to be analysed and assessed in terms of its objectives identified in the first stage of the investigation. Problems and difficulties which exist must be clearly pointed out so that any new proposals which the systems analyst puts forward will include, where appropriate, measures to overcome them. At the end of this stage, the resulting 'Statement of User Requirements' will be discussed with all interested users and then used as a basis for the next stage of Systems Design.

d. Systems Design

Aims of Systems Design

The aims are to design a system which:

(i)   satisfies the users' requirements as cost-effectively as possible;

(ii)   is as flexible as possible. The system must be adaptable to changes in the information needs of the user. Such changes will not necessarily be radical but for example may simply be changes in the volumes of transactions being processed. In other words, growth and change should have been anticipated at the design stage;

(iii) processes data accurately so that users can be confident that the information stored on the master files is both accurate and up-to-date;

(iv) has the necessary controls to prevent accidental or deliberate damage to the system. This means that it should be secure against unauthorized access and sufficiently fool-proof in its operation to prevent a person's careless mistakes disorganizing the system;

(v) is secure against loss of data. Security measures should prevent the loss of information from files by a user error or physical damage to storage media;

(vi) is easy to use;

(vii) falls within the limits set by legal and other constraints. An example of a legal constraint is the requirement by the Companies Acts that all limited companies produce annual accounts which must be sent to Companies House in Cardiff and are available for public inspection. Other constraints may be set simply by custom and practice or by agreements with Trades Unions. A constraint which applies to all organizations is the requirement that accounting systems must be capable of being audited, so the systems analyst must consult with the organization's auditors to ascertain their requirements.

Stages of Systems Design

Before identifying the stages in systems design it should be emphasized that analysis and design are not necessarily consecutive tasks in the sense that all the fact-finding is complete before the design stage begins. Continual reference back for further information may be necessary during the design of the new system.

Similarly, the steps involved in the design stage are not necessarily consecutive and may involve the systems analyst in going back over earlier steps to carry out more detailed design. Bearing this in mind, the stages of systems design can be carried out under the following headings:

The Nature of the System

This identifies the computer processing method(s) to be used in the system. The possible methods (which are described in Chapter 6) include batch, real-time and time-share processing, as well as systems controlled by database management systems. Of course, a system may use a combination of processing methods.

Output Specification

Logically, the systems analyst must decide what the system is required to output before deciding how to produce it.

It will be already be known, in some detail, what output is required of the system, as this is identified at the investigation stage. In considering the design of screen or printed output, the systems analyst will have to consider the following factors:

Content. One of a number of outputs from a stock control system, for example, could be a printed stock report of items whose quantities have fallen below preset minimum stock levels. The details of those data items which are to be included in the stock report will be decided at the design stage. The content and presentation of the report will depend on the requirements of those who are to make use of it. If, for instance, the report is to go to the Purchasing Department for the manual preparation of stock orders, then the report need not necessarily contain details of suppliers as this information will already be held by the purchasing department. If, on the other hand, orders are to be generated automatically and printed by the computer, the supplier's names and addresses will need to be accessible 'on-line' at the time the orders are produced.

Volume. The volume of output obviously has significance in terms of selecting appropriate output devices.

Sequence. The sequence in which output is required, for example whether it should be random or sequential will be one of the factors considered in choosing the file organization method and storage media.

Frequency. How frequently the information will be required has to be considered in conjunction with the volume of demand. If, for example, a large volume of printed output has to be produced daily, this will occupy a printer for lengthy periods when it may be required for other output. The solution may involve the timing of the output, perhaps at the end of the day when the main tasks are finished. On the other hand the purchase of an additional fast laser printer may solve the problem.

If a job which produces printed output cannot proceed because a printer is temporarily unavailable, the technique of SPOOLing (Simultaneous Peripheral Operation On Line) can be used. This allows spooling or queuing of output to a storage device such as disk or tape until the printer is available, when it is despooled. Peripherals can operate autonomously after the initial data transfer command has been given by the processor and so computer processing can continue during the printing process.

File Design

File design is a process which must consider the contents of individual records, the sequence in which records are held on the storage medium and the order in which they may be accessed. In determining the most appropriate file organization and access methods for any particular application, a number of factors may be taken into account:

The 'Hit Rate'. This defines the proportion of a master file's records which need to be accessed in one run and is expressed as a percentage.

Example

During an invoicing 'run', a customer master file containing, say 1000 records, may be processed with customer order transactions affecting 850 of the customer records. The 'hit rate' for that run would be 850/1000 x 100 or 85%.

Access Requirements. Although the decision as to which file organization method to use can be complex, as a general, if rather simplistic rule, a 'high' hit rate of, say 80% would indicate the need for sequential access to a file, perhaps as part of a batch processing system. There may, of course, also be a need for random access to individual records in the same file and this would suggest that both sequential and random access should be provided. An example of such a situation is given below.

Example

In the above example of an invoicing application, the most efficient method of processing the file would be in sequence, so the master file would probably be sequenced according to the Customer Number key field and the transactions sorted into the same sequence. In addition, however, the users would wish to access customer records directly to check on customer balances, so random access is necessary.

Indexed sequentially organized files (Chapter 4) provide both these access facilities. Where the hit rate is 'low', say 15%, this would indicate that only random access is needed. Random organization (Chapter 4) fulfils this need, without the use of the large file indexes required with the indexed sequential method.

The file organization method clearly has consequences for the choice of storage media, either serial or direct. As is explained in Chapter 5 on Peripherals, magnetic tape only allows serial or sequential access, so where there is a need for any direct access, magnetic disk is the only real option. However, decisions still need to be made on the capacity and speed of access which is needed; there are wide variations in the performance characteristics of storage devices, even in a single category such as magnetic disk (Chapter 5 Peripherals).

Integrated Processing Requirements. Sometimes, a single input may update more than one master file. For example, the value of a payment received by a retailing firm from a customer, in settlement of their account, may be input once and used by the applications program to update both the customer's account and the firm's cash or bank account.

Input Specification

The systems analyst must consider:

The content of input records. The data requirements of a system will comprise information held on master files which, together with current transaction data, produces the required output.

Example

Data from customer orders for quantities of items specified by Item Code may be input to an Invoicing system to produce the necessary customer invoices. To obtain the output, the input data will need to be used to extract prices of items from the stock master file and calculate the value of goods ordered.

Source document design. Source data is usually recorded on pre-printed documents in order to standardize the format of input data according to computer requirements. Properly designed source documents also assist accuracy and checking procedures. The design of the form should take account of the order in which data items are to be keyed in. It will often detail the maximum size (number of characters) and the mode of characters permitted, for example, alphabetic or numeric. Simple explanatory notes to help in its completion may appear on the form, but procedure manuals and staff training will generally be necessary for efficient and speedy form completion.

Dialogue design. This concerns the structuring of the 'conversation' between the user and the computer. The dialogue makes use of the screen for the display of system prompts, user responses and system responses. User input is usually via a conventional keyboard, although other devices, such as the mouse or touch screen (Chapter 5 Peripherals), may also be used.

Volume and frequency of input. This will have consequences for the choice of input device. Large volumes of input data will normally be encoded onto tape or disk for faster data input, such as that which occurs in large batch processing systems. Smaller volumes on the other hand, may be input via a VDU, validated and processed immediately.

Timing of input. If the input needs to be carried out at the same time as other applications then a system priority has to be established or a larger number of input devices may have to be used.

The input must be scheduled so that the master files are kept as up-to-date as is necessary for users. In a real-time airline booking system, for example, the input needs to be immediate if customers are to be dealt with promptly and flight records kept up-to-date.

Processing Tasks

The clerical, machine-assisted and computerized procedures have to be finalized, based on the information gathered during the investigation stage. Specifications will be produced which fully detail the clerical tasks to carried out by staff at all stages of human involvement. For example, in a batch processing system, descriptions will be provided for the Data Control staff of the procedures for batching input documents and for calculating batch control totals. Program specifications are produced, which describe in detail the processing tasks to be carried out by computer. These specifications will be used, either by programmers to write the necessary applications software, or as a basis for deciding on which 'off-the-shelf' package(s) to buy.

e. System Implementation

User Involvement

Although a new system often aims to reduce the workload of users in the long run, during the implementation period, it is usual to continue with the work of the existing system, in parallel, until the new system is fully tested. Additionally staff will be occupied with activities needed to introduce the system, such as converting files to computer storage media, reading user documentation and following training programmes.

There are several clearly identifiable areas of activity in the implementation of a new system:

> (i) Development and testing of programs.
>
> (ii) Conversion of files.
>
> (iii) Education and training of staff.
>
> (iv) Introduction of new clerical procedures.
>
> (v) The changeover plan - 'going live'.

Development and Testing of Programs

At the end of the design stage, the programming teams are presented with a 'Program Specification' which sets out the system requirements in terms of what the computer is required to do, in other words the computer processing tasks. The programmers, using a programming language, code the programs according to the requirements in the program specification. The program specification also includes a testing plan which, through the use of properly selected input data, tests the working of the programs for the reliability and accuracy of the output. The procedures involved in program development are described in detail in Chapter 13.

Conversion of Files

Existing manual files need to be encoded onto the chosen storage media and this can be a formidable task. The encoding of large files will be a time-consuming process and coupled with the fact that 'live' transaction data will change the values in the master files, they may need to be phased into the computer system in stages. In a stock control system, for example, records for certain categories of stock item may be encoded and computer processed, leaving the remainder to be processed by existing methods and encoded at a later stage.

In favourable circumstances, a large scale encoding exercise may be undertaken to initially create the file and then, through an application program, transactions which have occurred since the encoding began can be used to update the file to reflect the correct values. Users will have to be made aware of which records have already been encoded into the system so that they can properly update them as transactions occur.

Where new files which did not previously exist are to be created, then the task is even more extensive in that the data has to be collected and organized before encoding. The validation of data before it is used in a computer system is vital so that users can rely on the accuracy of the output from the system. Validation is one of the system controls described in Chapter 7.

If a business has inadequate staffing to cope with the encoding exercise, a computer bureau (see Computer Services at the end of this chapter) may be used. Where possible, the bureau's staff should carry out the work on site, because the records will be needed for the continued operation of the business.

An additional problem is that records in their existing state may not conform with the file layouts designed for the new system and the data may have to be copied onto special-purpose input forms to assist with accurate encoding.

Education and Training of Staff

The education and training of the users of the system is vital if it is to be operated correctly and the full benefits are to be obtained.

Management need to be educated so that they can recognise how the system can provide the information they need. Generally, managerial staff will not carry out routine data entry, but some basic skill in using a VDU may be necessary to allow them for example to make immediate enquiries from a database. In a decentralized system, the need for such training will be greater than in a centralized system where **only spec**ialist computer staff are involved with computer processing. The role of different staff and the effects of computerization in terms of their training needs are discussed in Chapter 15.

The main categories of staff who will require education and/or training include:

> Management;
>
> Clerical Staff;
>
> Data Control and Data Preparation Staff;
>
> Computer Operations Staff.

By the time the system is ready to 'go live', all staff involved with the system should be competent to operate it efficiently. They should also have sufficient knowledge to assess its effectiveness. In other words, "does it do what is supposed to do reliably and at the right time?".

Deciding when to carry out the training can be difficult. If too early, some staff will have forgotten what they have been taught by the time the system is introduced. If too late, staff may feel panicked because they have not been properly prepared. Training programmes should, as far as possible, be designed to suit the working conditions of staff and the time-scale for implementation. It may be that residential courses will be needed for supervisory staff, who will then carry out the 'on the job' training of subordinate staff. This latter task may involve staff working extra hours because the existing system may still have to be operated prior to the implementation and for sometime afterwards during a period of 'parallel running'.

Introduction of New Clerical Procedures

The computer programs that have been developed or purchased form only part of the whole information processing system. To function correctly they have to be supported by the clerical procedures designed to interface with them. Testing of the system should also cover the operation of manual procedures such as the preparation and handling of source documents, the batching of input and preparation of control totals prior to input and dealing with error and other reports produced as output.

The Changeover Plan - 'Going Live'

'Going live', as the term suggests, involves using real data and using the system in the day-to-day operation of the organization. Prior to this the system should have been tested in simulated conditions and at that stage no reliance should have been placed on it.

Even if careful preparations for its introduction have been made, a system will rarely function properly at first. For this reason, a system's initiation should not be on an 'all or nothing' basis and should be supported by the existing system until it can be relied upon. Comparisons with the output of the existing system will help spot any inaccuracies and inconsistencies in the new system's output. There is no set period for parallel running as this will depend on the particular system and the circumstances surrounding it.

Pilot Running involves using a new system on only a limited area of the organization. An example could be the selection of a particular department to be involved in a new Personnel Recording system before the system's full implementation for all departments. This is a reasonably safe strategy, but Murphy's Law may dictate that the transactions which cause errors will be amongst those which do not pass through the pilot system.

f. Maintenance and Review

Maintenance

After its initial introduction, a system will not remain static. Dealing with necessary changes to a system is termed 'System Maintenance'. Problems will probably become apparent as the system is operated but even if they do not the information needs of the users will no doubt change. Some changes will come from within the organization as new possibilities for the system are identified. Others may be enforced on the organization because of changes in the external environment. Such changes may be in customer demand, the introduction of new or stronger competition in the market, mergers with other organizations and so on.

The most important catalyst for change is probably the desire for better and more timely information by management to assist their decision-making and planning.

At the design stage, the systems analyst should have allowed for the possibility of change. The analyst should have made it possible for changes to be made in the contents of files, output reports and processing routines without having to embark on complete program rewrites. The modification of software as needs change is part of every programmer's job and is called 'Software Maintenance'.

The hardware selected should be expandable perhaps in terms of memory, backing storage or in numbers and types of peripherals. Generally such expandibility can be assured by not purchasing a system at the top of a range.

Review

The systems analyst should regularly review each system with the relevant managers at least once a year. The system's performance needs to be evaluated in terms of the current user requirements. If differences are found then the cause has to be identified. It may be that the system has to be changed from its original specification, or it may be that the inadequacies are caused by improper implementation. There are a number of signs which can indicate inadequacies in a system, including:

  (i) output which is continually behind schedule;

  (ii) a regular backlog of input documents awaiting attention;

  (iii) a significant increase in errors;

  (iv) negative comments from staff operating the system regarding problems or positive suggestions for improvement;

  (v) related information systems being kept waiting for data from the offending system;

  (vi) customer complaints or loss of business as a result of poor service;

  (vii) the necessity for regular, excessive overtime by staff to clear backlogs of work.

Thus a regular review of the operation of the system is necessary if the need for system maintenance is to be identified quickly and remedial action taken.

Computer Services

There are companies who offer a range of hardware and software services; some have spare capacity over and above that which is required for their normal business operations, which they offer on a rental basis, whilst others exist solely for the purpose of computer service provision. The services include the provision of:

- standard, off-the-shelf packaged software;

- tailor-made software;

- consultancy;

- complete hardware and software packages;

- hardware and software rental;

- aid in data preparation and transcription.

Such companies are known variously as computer bureaux, software consultancies, software houses and systems houses. The rental of computer services is expensive but may be appropriate for an organization which only has a temporary need for a computer, or where an increased facility is needed during an unusually busy period. Where access is given to a central mainframe computer operating under a time-sharing operating system, clients are charged for the time which they are 'logged on' to the computer. Thus, with the use of a VDU and telephone link, a user can be linked to a powerful mainframe computer and have the impression of sole use. The computer is, in fact, sharing its processor time amongst many users. Such use assumes that the software required by the user is available on the central computer.

Assignment   **Look Before You Leap**

Wayfield Sports Centre is situated just outside the town of Borchester and provides a variety of sports and leisure facilities for the local population of ten thousand people. These include, squash, badminton, gymnastics, martial arts, weight training, sauna, solarium, dance and aerobics. The centre also caters for children's parties, when a soft play area is available. All the booking facilities are manually maintained. The sports centre staff also have to operate league tables for various sports, such as squash and badminton. Some of the large sports and leisure centres, located in larger towns and cities, have computerized all their main administrative tasks and their operation is similar to those of the Wayfield Centre. Of course, compared with the larger city centre complexes, Wayfield Sports Centre caters for far fewer people and has a smaller range and number of facilities. Despite its small size, the Wayfield Centre is proving extremely popular and the manual accounting and administrative systems are beginning to falter under the strain. Some activities such as aerobics require a class teacher who may, on occasion, be unavailable. Replacement teachers have to be found or clients need to be told of class cancellation. Backlogs of work are building up and extra staff may need to be employed. It is not unknown for facilities to be double booked, which is a source of irritation to people who have, for example, travelled a few miles for a game of squash. There is another squash club a few miles away, which provides an alternative venue for one category of user. There are also a couple of private leisure clubs which provide massage, sauna, solarium and weight training facilities. Although the Wayfield Centre has more facilities under one roof, in modern comfortable surroundings, these alternative facilities do present some competition.

The management of the Wayfield Centre (it has been recently privatized and is no longer under the control of the Local Authority) have commissioned for a feasibility study to be carried out by a software consultancy firm, Micro Systems. In your role as trainee systems analyst for Micro Systems, you have been requested by the senior systems analyst to make a preliminary investigation of the facility booking systems in operation at the Wayfield Centre and to produce a feasibility report.

Task

Produce a feasibility report on the facility booking systems at the Wayfield Centre and include the following sections:

1. An outline description of the application. Identify the overall business and individual system objectives which are to be satisfied;

2 A more detailed description of the system's existing operation, its good and bad points and the means by which a new system could improve upon it;

3. A description of how a new system would operate and its expected costs and benefits;

4. Possible alternatives and recommendations;

5. Costs of development and timescale for development and implementation (if the recommended system is adopted).

The study should concentrate on the application and the scenario outlined in the assignment.

Assignment   A Sauna, Please

The management of the Wayfield Sports Centre (see Assignment - Look Before You Leap) has received a feasibility report from Micro Systems, a software consultancy, indicating that computerization of the facility booking and monitoring system is worthwhile, both in terms of cost savings over a period of time and in improved services to the public. The assignment entitled "Look Before You Leap", required you to prepare the feasibility report, based on the information given in the scenario. In your role as trainee systems analyst, you are to further investigate the facility booking and monitoring systems and then design appropriate compu-terized versions. You will have to refer to the scenario described in the assignment "Look Before You Leap", but some further information is provided here.

Staffing

The Wayfield Centre employs twelve staff, including a centre administrator, an assistant administrator, two receptionists and eight sports specialists. The centre operates on a two shift system, so only six are on duty at any one time (one administrator, one receptionist and four sports specialists). Job descriptions are not rigid and, for example, the sports specialists carry out cleaning and general maintenance tasks, as well as taking an occasional turn on reception. Indeed, the centre administrators and receptionists are also keen on involving themselves in sporting activities in the centre.

Task

Produce a System Specification, including the following sections:

1. **Nature of the System;**

2. **Output Specification;**

3. **File Design;**

4. **Input Specification;**

5. **Processing Tasks;**

6. **Staffing and Jobs.**

Assignment   Revamping the System

A Systems Analysis Project

Revamp Limited is an electrical contracting company based in Blackpool in Lancashire. There are two directors, one of whom is responsible for management of jobs on site and estimating for possible contracts, the other being occupied with pricing, cost control and general maintenance of the company's accounts. The company employs a workforce of fifty, although there are periods, usually in winter, when fewer are employed.

All systems are manual at present, but it is in the particular area of cost control where the manual system fails to provide management with information vital to the profitability of the company. In addition, pricing of jobs is a time-consuming process and savings could be made with the use of a microcomputer system. Micro Systems Limited is a computer bureau based in Blackpool and the directors of Revamp Limited have requested the bureau to carry out an investigation of the job and cost control systems, with a view to their computerization.

You are employed by the bureau as a trainee systems analyst and you have been given nominal control of this project. The following information is provided by the directors of Revamp Limited.

General description of the Job Costing and Cost Control System, currently operating at Revamp Limited.

The system provides an estimate of costs, including profit, relating to individually identifiable jobs or contracts. The estimate or price quoted to the main contractor or customer is generally maintained when the job is completed, so it is vital that the original estimate does not fall short of the actual costs incurred.

The job costing does not present any great problems to the firm (except that it is time consuming), but during the progress of a job there is insufficient time to maintain close monitoring of costs. This can result in situations whereby the original cost has been exceeded before the job is complete. Although the original price is usually agreed to be the final price, if the situation mentioned should occur, it may be possible to take some remedial action with the customer or contractor before the job has progressed too far.

Procedures

Pricing or Job Costing

1. Having received a request from a customer or contractor to give a quotation for a job, one of the directors visits the site and estimates the quantities of materials and labour needed to complete the job.

2. The estimated quantities are used to calculate a job cost, by reference to price catalogues.

3. The job is given a unique number and a record of the job is kept in the job file.

Cost Control

4. Once the job is accepted, invoices for materials purchased are charged to the relevant job. A supply is 'tied' to a job by recording the job number on the invoice.

5. In addition to charging materials to a job, labour (including overheads) is also charged, labour being treated as just another supplier.

6. *When the job is complete, an invoice for the quoted price is sent to the customer and provided that the amount is greater than the actual cost, a profit is made.*

Task

1. Identify any other information you may need to make a proper analysis of the system.

2. Having identified the kinds of information you need, build a more detailed picture of the system, by suggesting the kinds of values you may expect to find. For example, you may feel that the maximum number of jobs likely to be in progress at any one time is about thirty five.

3. Produce a Feasibility Report concerning the job costing and control systems and include the following sections:

(a) An outline description of the application. Identify the overall business and individual system objectives which are to be satisfied;

(b) A more detailed description of the system's existing operation, its good and bad points and the means by which a new system could improve upon it;

(c) A description of how a new system would operate and its expected costs and benefits;

(d) Possible alternatives and recommendations;

(e) Costs of development and timescale for development and implementation (if the recommended system is adopted).

The study should concentrate on the application and the scenario outlined in the assignment.

4. Produce a System Specification, including the following sections:

(a) Nature of the System;

(b) Output Specification;

(c) File Design;

(d) Input Specification;

(e) Processing Tasks.

5. Identify the information gathering methods available to you and suggest, with reasons, which are most appropriate to this situation.

Chapter 15

☐ SOCIAL AND ORGANIZATIONAL EFFECTS OF COMPUTERIZATION

This chapter is divided into four main sections. The first looks at the applications of computer technology and considers the main benefits of computerization for an organization. The second section looks at the current effects of computer technologies on organizations and the third on employment patterns, working conditions, and career prospects. The final section considers some of the major effects computer technology has had and is having on society. Some possible developments for the future are also put forward for discussion.

Benefits of Computerization

Business applications such as payroll and stock control were among the earliest to be computerized. Although increasing use is being made of computers in manufacturing industry, science and medicine, business applications still constitute the greatest usage. A number of categories of computer application can be identified:

    (a)   Accounting Systems

    (b)   Management Information Systems (MIS)

    (c)   Decision Support Systems (DSS)

    (d)   Electronic Office Systems

    (e)   Computer-aided Design and Manufacture (CAD-CAM)

    (f)   Computers in science and medicine

    (g)   Artificial Intelligence

a. Accounting Systems

Accounting systems include:

Payroll

Payroll systems are concerned with the production of payslips for employees and the maintenance of records required for taxation and other deductions. In a manual system, the preparation of payroll figures and the maintenance of payroll records is a labour intensive task. Although tedious and repetitive, it is a vitally important task. Most employees naturally regard pay as being the main reason for work and resent delays in payment or incorrect payments, unless of course it is in their favour! The weekly or monthly payroll run affects almost all employee records in the payroll master file, so batch processing is normally used. This processing method allows numerous opportunities to maintain the accuracy of the information. The repetitive nature of the task makes it a popular candidate for computerization, especially with organizations which employ large numbers of people. The automatic production of reports for taxation purposes also provides a valuable benefit. Smaller organizations with only several employees probably do not regard payroll as a high priority application for computerization. The benefits are not as great if the payroll can be carried out by one or two employees who also carry out a number of other tasks.

Stock Control

Any organization which keeps stocks of raw materials or finished goods needs to operate a stock control system. Although stock constitutes an asset, it ties up cash resources which could be invested in other aspects of the business. Equally, a company must keep sufficient quantities of items to satisfy customer demand or manufacturing requirements. To maintain this balance a stock control system should provide up-to-date information on quantities, prices, minimum stock levels, and re-order quantities. It should also give warning of excessively high, or dangerously low levels of stock. In the latter case, orders may be produced automatically. A stock control system can also generate valuable management reports on, for example, sales patterns, slow-moving items, and overdue orders.

Sales Accounting

When credit sales are made to customers, a record needs to be kept of amounts owing and paid. Payment is normally requested with an invoice, which gives details of goods supplied, quantities, prices and VAT. Credit sales are usually made on for example, a 14, 21 or 28 day basis, which means that the customer has to pay within the specified period to obtain any discounts offered. Overdue payments need to be chased, so sales accounting systems normally produce reports analysing the indebtedness of different customers. Debt control is vital to business profitability and computerized systems can produce prompt and up-to-date reports as a by-product of the main application.

Purchase Accounting

These systems control the amounts owed and payments made to suppliers of services, goods or materials used in the main business of the company. For example, a car manufacturer will need to keep records of amounts owing to suppliers of car components and sheet steel manufacturers. Delayed payments to suppliers may help cash flow, but can harm an organization's image, or even cut off a source of supply when a supplier refuses to deliver any more goods until payment is made. A computerized system will not ensure payment, but it can provide the information that payment is due.

General Ledger

The general ledger keeps control of financial summaries, including those originating from payroll, sales and purchase accounting and acts as a balance in a double entry system. Reports are generally produced at the end of financial periods, including a balance sheet.

For many organizations, the systems described above can be computerized using packaged software. The main features of some financial accounting software packages are described in Chapter 12 Financial Systems and Packages.

b. Management Information Systems (MIS)

Although computers can perform routine processing tasks very efficiently, it is generally recognized that, for a business to make use of a computer solely for the processing of operational information, constitutes a waste of computer power. A MIS is designed to make use of the computer's power of selection and analysis to produce useful MANAGEMENT information.

A MIS has a number of key features:

(i) it produces information beyond that required for routine data processing;

(ii) timing of information production is critical;

(iii) the information it produces is an aid to decision-making;

(iv) it is usually based on the database concept (explained in Chapter 6).

The information provided tends to be related to the different levels of management and this is explained in Chapter 2.

The claims for MIS are sometimes excessive. It is rarely the complete answer to all a company's information needs, but when successfully implemented, it provides a valuable information advantage over competitors.

c. Decision Support Systems (DSS)

A DSS aims to provide a more flexible decision tool than that supplied by a MIS. MIS tend to produce information in an anticipated, predefined form and as such, do not allow managers to make ad hoc requests for information. DSS tend to be narrower in scope than MIS, often making use of microcomputer systems and software packages. Examples of DSS are, electronic spreadsheets, for example, Lotus 123, file managers and relational database management systems such as Dbase IV. The main features of these and other packages are described in some detail in Chapter 11. In addition, financial modelling and statistical packages are considered to be DSS tools. A major benefit is the independence they allow for information control by individual managers and executives. When, for example, a sales manager requires a report on sales figures for the last three months, a microcomputer with database package may provide the report more quickly than the centralized Management Information Services (Chapter 8).

d. Electronic Office Systems

The automation of office procedures tends at present to be rather fragmented, some staff making extensive use of computers, whilst others rely almost completely on manual methods. The Electronic Office is a concept which views the office as an integrated whole, where many procedures are automated and much of the communication is by electronic means. The main components of the Electronic Office are described in Chapter 9, but briefly, may include the following:

(i) Word processing;

(ii) Decision Support Systems (DSS) - discussed above;

(iii) Electronic messaging and electronic mail;

(iv) Electronic diaries and calendars;

(v) Electronic notice boards;

(vi) Telecommuting.

The last component, TELECOMMUTING has the potential to revolutionize working habits. Basically, it means the use of a terminal or microcomputer workstation linked to a company's computer at another location. In many cases, this removes the need for attendance at the office for workers such as programmers and typists or even executive staff. The main disadvantage is the loss of personal contact between staff, which can require considerable cultural readjustment. Such a system also has consequences for employee supervision and security of information.

e. Computer-Aided Design and Manufacture (CAD-CAM)

Computer-Aided Design (CAD)

With the use of a graphics terminal and cross-hair cursor (described in Chapter 5), or similar device, a designer can produce and modify designs more rapidly than is possible with a conventional drawing board. Ideas can be sketched on the screen, stored, recalled and modified. The computer can also be instructed to analyse a design for comparison with some specified criteria. Drawings can be rotated and tilted on the screen to reveal different three-dimensional views. CAD is used in the design of ships, cars, buildings, microprocessor circuits, clothing and many other products. With the use of CAD a manufacturer has a distinct advantage over non-computerized competitors, in terms of speed and flexibility of design.

Computer-Aided Manufacture (CAM)

A number of areas of computer use can be identified in the manufacturing process.

  (i) Industrial robots;

  (ii) Computer numerical control (CNC) of machine tools;

  (iii) Integrated CAD-CAM;

  (iv) Automated materials handling;

  (v) Flexible manufacturing systems (FMS);

Industrial Robots. Basically, a robot replaces the actions of a human arm and consists of 3 main elements, a mechanical arm with 'wrist' joint, power unit and microprocessor or central controlling computer. To be called a robot, it must be able to react, albeit in a limited way, to external events and alter its course of action according to a stored program. Such sensitivity to the environment is provided by sensors, for example, to recognize stylized characters and differentiate between shapes. The main areas of use are in spot welding, paint spraying, die casting and to a lesser extent, assembly.

Computer Numerical Control (CNC). CNC operation of machine tools has been widespread for some years because the repetitive nature of machining tasks lends itself to simple programming. However, as is the case with robots, the use of microprocessors allows the machine tool to vary its actions according to external information. The actions of the machine can be compared with a design pattern held by the computer. Any significant variations from the pattern are signalled to the machine tool which, through the microprocessor, reacts appropriately (known as Computer Aided Quality Assessment - CAQ). Other information regarding tool wear or damage can be picked up by sensors and communicated to the human supervisor who takes remedial action.

Integrated CAD-CAM. In fully integrated CAD-CAM systems, the designs produced using CAD are fed straight through to the software which controls the CNC machine tools, which can then produce the design piece. The CAD software checks the compatibility of the design with a component specification already stored in the computer.

Automated Materials Handling. There are around 80 fully automated warehouses in Britain. A fully automated materials handling system consists of a number of sub-systems:

  - stock control;

  - part or pallet co-ordination;

  - storage and retrieval;

  - conveyor control.

Installation generally proceeds one sub-system at a time, each being fully tested before proceeding with the next sub-system. A materials handling system, controlled by a central computer, allocates storage locations in the warehouse, automatically re-orders when a predetermined minimum level is reached, retrieves parts as required by the factory and delivers them by conveyor belt to the waiting robots or CNC machines.

Flexible Manufacturing Systems (FMS). Such systems are beneficial where production batches are small and necessitate frequent changes in the sequence and types of processes. The aim of FMS is to remove, as far as possible, the need for human intervention (other than a supervisor or 'machine minder') in the production process. The main elements of FMS are, CNC machine tools (with diagnostic facilities), robots, conveyor belt and central computer and controlling software. In simple terms, the computer has information on parts, machine tools and operations required. The robots serve the CNC machines by presenting them with parts to be machined and loading the correct machine tools from racks. In Crewkerne, Somerset, a factory uses FMS to produce bomb release mechanisms for military aircraft but the system is flexible enough to produce thousands of other components with the minimum of human intervention.

f. Computers in Science and Medicine

Science

To predict weather conditions accurately requires vast amounts of data regarding past conditions. Large supercomputers allow such volumes of data to be stored, recalled, updated, and analysed on a national and sometimes international basis. Computer graphics and computer enhanced satellite pictures are also used to provide interesting and informative weather forecasts for television viewers. Computer simulations can allow testing of product designs without, at least in the initial stages, the expense of building the actual product. Airline pilots are trained in computerized flight simulators which can simulate almost any event a pilot is likely to encounter.

Medicine

Computer-controlled life support systems can monitor a patient's condition via a number of sensor devices checking on, for example, pulse rate, body temperature and blood pressure. This frees nursing staff for other duties and has the benefit of providing a continuous monitoring facility. Computer-assisted diagnosis systems make use of artificial intelligence to assist a physician in diagnosing a patient's condition. This raises the question of how much reliance should be placed on computers with artificial intelligence. It seems reasonable that a doctor should use an expert system as an aid to diagnosis, but less reasonable that a treatment decision should be made on the basis of computer diagnosis alone. A particularly exciting development involves the use of computers to assist the plastic surgeon in the repair of facial injuries or deformities. The patient's face is scanned by a camera and the image digitized for display on a computer screen in three-dimensional form. This image can be rotated or tilted on screen by the surgeon and experimental 'cuts' made, the results of which can then be viewed on screen from any angle. In this way, a plastic surgeon can study the results of a variety of strategies before making a single mark on the patient.

g. Artificial Intelligence (AI)

Artificial intelligence is an attempt to model human thought processes and systems are evolving in the following areas:

(i) Expert or Knowledge-Based Systems (which are examined in Chapter 11);

(ii) Robotics (described earlier in this Chapter);

(iii) Natural Language (which is considered in Chapter 11).

Expert systems may, in the future, pose a threat to the autonomy at present held by doctors, lawyers and other professionals. It is not inconceivable that medical diagnosis and legal advice may be provided by machine. Such systems exist already but only provide limited support. The restraint, if any, on such developments may stem from ethical and moral forces, as well as the professions wish to protect their interests. It may be, of course, that humans will prefer to retain personal contact with their doctor or solicitor, even if a machine is making most of the decisions.

Organizational Consequences of Computerization

The introduction of a computer to an organization cannot be effective if computerization simply means the transfer of manual files to computer storage and the automation of some of the existing clerical procedures. To achieve the full potential of computerization, an organization needs to implement certain changes which will affect its environment, its staff and its form of management.

Changes in the Organisation's Environment

Computer hardware has to be kept in a suitable environment if it is to operate correctly. Although physical protection of hardware has improved considerably over recent years, large mainframe and mini computer systems need to be maintained in a relatively dust-free atmosphere within controlled moderate temperature ranges. Microcomputers tend to be more tolerant of their surroundings and can be accommodated in the relatively basic surroundings one would expect to find in any small office.

If computers have to operate in tough physical environments, for example, on warships or in battle tanks then the hardware can be designed accordingly. Fortunately, most organizations have less harsh surrounding in which to work. Nevertheless, there are generally some changes which need to be made in the PHYSICAL REQUIREMENTS of the environment.

The Physical Requirements Necessary to Accommodate Computers

Controlled Moderate Temperature Range

Most office environments will be suitable in this respect but the precise requirements will depend on the hardware to be used and the manufacturer's specification. More often than not, problems are caused by the overheating of equipment. Thus hardware should not be sited next to a radiator or in direct sunlight.

Clean Surroundings

As previously indicated, the cleanliness required of the environment will depend on the type of hardware in use. In general however, dust will cause problems, particularly with storage media such as tapes and disks. For the larger organization this may mean the installation of air conditioning within a separate room for the mainframe or mini computer system.

Electrical Installation

Although computers operate from the standard electricity supply, it is essential that a separate power supply is installed to prevent problems of cut-out and possible loss of information if the circuits are overloaded. In some cases where reliability is vital, a backup power supply may be needed to cut in if the main supply fails. Magnetic storage media such as disk or tape should not be stored next to power supplies as the surrounding magnetic field may corrupt the data.

Lighting

Where natural light is at times inadequate then suitable artificial lighting will be necessary. In most office situations where manual clerical operations are already carried out, then normal electric lighting is probably sufficient. Lighting also has to be considered in terms of its possible effect on the reflective surfaces which may surround computer equipment. For this reason the casings on hardware are usually of a matt finish. Some computer screens may not have non-reflective qualities so the positioning of equipment in relation to both natural and artificial lighting will have to be taken into account to avoid reflective glare. Although most computer monitors have brightness and contrast control, direct sunlight can make the characters on a screen practically invisible. Artificial lighting which is too intense or badly positioned can also cause screen glare.

Noise Control

Sources of noise from computer equipment are in the main:

> (i) Impact printers;
>
> (ii) Cooling fans built into the computer itself.

Printer noise varies with the type of printer. Impact printers, such as the daisy wheel or dot matrix type, obviously make more noise than laser printers which do not use an impact mechanism. Noise can be controlled through the use of insulating containers. Where printers are part of a mini or mainframe system, noise will need to be controlled for the benefit of the computer operations staff but it is likely that a separate room will contain all the main computer resources so other parts of the organization will be unaffected. In smaller organizations the use of microcomputers and dot matrix printers can lead to a noisy environment but insulating containers, sound absorbent screens and carpeted floors can help.

Cooling fans within computer equipment tend to cause a background noise to which people soon become used. It is not as loud as printer noise but it can be at a level which may result in unnecessary stress for office staff. Again sound absorbent screens around the computer can help protect staff from such noise but properly serviced equipment helps avoid worn and noisy fans.

Effects on Staff

The effects on staff within an organization will be extremely varied and the degree of effect will depend on the extent of involvement individual staff have with a computerized system.

Computerization within an organization tends not to be an instantaneous event affecting all functional areas at the same time. It tends to be progressive, sometimes planned and sometimes piecemeal.

Consider the following situation in a commercial trading organisation:

> (i) Assume that Sales Order Processing (SOP) is computerized and that the output includes Picking Lists (these are lists of products and quantities of each that need to be retrieved from the warehouse to satisfy customer orders).
>
> (ii) Assume further that Stock Control in the warehouse is not computerized but that the staff will receive computer printed picking lists.
>
> (iii) Assume finally that the Accounting function is not computerized. Staff in Accounting will receive sales details on computer printout from SOP from which they will produce invoices to send to customers.

a. Effects on Clerical Staff

The staff in these three departments, SOP, Stock Control and Accounting are all affected by computerization but to varying degrees.

Least effected are staff in Stock Control and Accounting who only receive computer output. They have to become familiar with the reading and interpretation of computer printouts. This is not a difficult task, but one which requires some adjustment on the part of staff.

At a more complex level, the staff in SOP are more significantly effected. The effects will require education and training for staff in the various parts of the computerized process as follow:

Preparation of Input Data

Computerization imposes a discipline on clerical and management procedures. To deal with data correctly it needs to be presented accurately and in a form suitable for input to the computer. Usually, prior to data entry, all source data, (in this case customer orders) have to be recorded on standard, specially designed Source Documents which match the order of data requested by the computer software. For example, if the first item of data required by the computer is an order number, then this should be the first data item on the source document. The second data item required should be next and so on.

Therefore, however the orders are received, by telephone, by word of mouth at the sales desk or by post, the first job is to transcribe the details onto the Source Document. Such tasks need to be documented in office procedure manuals and staff need to be instructed in their proper execution.

Data Entry

Staff involved in this task will need to develop keyboard skills. Even if the data entry operators are already skilled typists, some training or period of familiarization is required to use a computer terminal correctly.

Training will be needed in the day-to-day operation of the software. These include 'signing on' with codes and passwords, familiarity with computer screen prompts and the correct responses to make, dealing with simple error conditions when an incorrect key is pressed and correcting or editing keying errors during data entry.

Where the volume of data entry is such that a member of staff can be fully occupied with this task there are health and safety considerations to be examined. There are for example recommended guidelines concerning time limits for personnel operating VDU's. Headaches and eye strain can result from prolonged viewing of a computer screen.

Where the volume of data entry is limited, the specialist staff may not be justified and a number of clerical staff with a variety of duties may have to 'take their turn' at the keyboard. Thus more staff will need some basic training in the use of the system.

b. Effects on Managerial Staff

The day-to-day clerical routines will not usually directly involve managerial staff although this will depend on the size of the organization and the hierarchical staffing structure. However, their necessary involvement in the development, introduction and implementation of a computerized system and their responsibilities for the efficient running of their departments mean that the effects of computerization on the working lives of managers can be even more emphatic than the effects on clerical staff.

To continue the Sales Order Processing example, the manager of that department may:

    (i)   be closely involved in a consultative role with systems analysts in the analysis of the old manual system and the design of the new computerized system;

    (ii)   have to maintain communication with the staff in the SOP department to ensure that:

            - their views are taken into account;

            - envisaged changes are reported to them.

       This communication is vital if the staff are to feel 'involved'.

    (iii) require some computer education and training. A prerequisite of communication between staff is that the manager has developed some computer 'awareness' and computer 'literacy' sufficiently to understand the role of the computer and the changes in procedures within his department which are necessary.

This educational or training need has to be satisfied if the manager is to be effective in the role of ensuring that the operational procedures are being followed and that efficiency is being maintained. Without knowledge of the powers and limitations of a computerized system a manager cannot assess its effectiveness or suggest improvements.

At the managerial level of involvement, it may seem that the more mundane skills of operating a

VDU are not needed. Often this is not so. A manager may wish to access files from a terminal in the office, so a minimal level of skill is required.

Other Computer Applications Involving Management

There are a number of computer applications which make use of 'content free' software. This refers to software which is not fixed to one application or type of data. Such software packages are available for Spreadsheet work, and Database or File Management.

There is an increasing awareness that microcomputers or terminals linked to a central computer can be used by managers and executive staff (although not exclusively) to aid their decision-making, with the provision of more and higher quality information.

An example may illustrate this point. Spreadsheet packages can be used for the preparation of cash budgets and sales forecasting with the added facility of generating 'what if' projections. So a cash budget based on current and anticipated figures of cash due in and out of the organization over the next few months, can be quickly modified to present the results of an alternative strategy of say, an injection of cash from a bank loan.

Database packages can be used by managers for their own local information store on which they can make enquiry. In addition, where a database is held centrally, a manager could access files through the use of a Query Language (This is discussed in Chapter 6). To use such a language requires training, similar to that required by a programmer albeit at a simpler level.

The efficient and effective use of such packages demands a high level of knowledge and skill which will probably require some sort of training programme, perhaps with the software supplier.

Effects on Managers Not Yet Involved

The use of such facilities by one departmental manager or the issue of a general directive from top management within an organization will place pressure on other managers to follow suit. Of course the pressure may be in the other direction where departmental managers wish to get involved and pressurize top management for training and the introduction of new computerized systems

Changes in Job Descriptions

It can be seen from the previous section that where computerized systems are used within an organization and new staff are to be recruited, the job descriptions in advertisements should include a request for computer knowledge or skill, in the area which the job demands. Existing staff will have to have their job descriptions modified. In some circumstances this can mean an upgrading of the skill or professional level which may attract a higher salary. It can lead to delay in the introduction of computer systems. In local government, for example, some secretarial staff were prevented from using word processors because their union demanded an increase in their job grading. In some jobs it can lead to what is considered to be de-skilling. For example, in the newspaper industry the traditional skill of metal typesetting is now obsolete.

Effects on Functional Relationships

Earlier in this chapter, it is explained that computerization effects the ways in which different functions such as Sales and Accounts relate to each other, in terms of how information flows between them and the activities in which each is engaged.

Without computers, the Sales and Accounting departments would maintain their own files. Transaction data such as a customer order would be used to update each of the department's files separately. Each department would be responsible for maintaining its own files thus creating separate autonomous areas within an organization, each led by a Head of Department or similar executive staff member. Each department would tend to have its own working practices and provided information was presented to other departments in a form they could use, there would perhaps be little need for change.

Computerization imposes discipline and standardization. Information flows between departments may have to pass through a computer process and although the user requirements should take priority over what is convenient for the computer, some modifications will need to be made to the ways in which data is presented to the computer for processing. Earlier in this chapter, the example was used of customer order details being transcribed onto Source Documents designed to be compatible with the order of input to the computer.

A feature of manual systems is the separateness of related operations. For example a customer order will be used to update the customer file, the stock file and to produce a customer invoice in separate operations carried out in each separate functional area. A computerized system could allow these tasks to be carried out with a single input of the data.

Inter-departmental Conflict

Organizations are formed to allow a rational and coordinated approach to the achievement of certain aims which may be the provision of a service or product for which there is a profitable market. The problem is that organizations are made up of individuals who may not always be rational. Each individual has his or her own ambitions, fears and emotions. Management styles may well stem from such personal characteristics. This may lead to competition between department heads rather than cooperation in achieving the common aims of the organization as a whole.

Personal Fears

To many people, computerization is a venture into the unknown and many individuals feel threatened because they have insufficient knowledge or experience to give them adequate control over their own futures. Being made to look a fool, or worse, the possibility of being made redundant by computerization can be the main obstacle to the acceptance of change.

Resistance to Change

Sometimes because of inter-departmental rivalry or simply incompetence, a manager may keep secret certain facts which computerization may make available. This is another reason for resistance to the introduction of computerized systems.

Managers are forced to change their style of management because of the introduction of computers and may attempt to resist the threat to their power, by doing less than they might to make the innovation work and by constantly finding fault, without making constructive suggestions.

'The Enthusiast'

An alternative reaction, which is usually irrational, is the whole-hearted, eager acceptance of computerization as being the ideal solution to every problem. There are many circumstances where computerization is inappropriate or where the immediately available standard package is far from ideal.

Because organizations are made up of individuals, computer systems should be designed with the full cooperation of management and staff, enlisting their help wherever possible so as to take proper account of their individual or at least departmental information needs.

Effects on Management Style

Many managers work intuitively and have confidence in their own methods which have served them well. Such 'flying by the seat of the pants' often leads to a natural derision for any system designed by 'experts' and 'theorists'. Of course such confidence is usually based on previous success and the specialist in computer systems will often be young and, as far as the experienced manager is concerned, 'wet behind the ears'. Thus the computer specialist may have a difficult job in convincing existing management that a new computerized system will be an improvement on the old. The systems analyst will need to have the interpersonal skills to deal with such resistance.

One feature of computerized systems is the increase in the volume of information available to a manager and the speed with which it can be obtained. A resulting danger is that the manager may become too concerned with the low level decisions within his department, thus interfering with the responsibilities of lower levels of management or supervisory staff. The problem can be more serious if it extends upwards from departmental to corporate management. Information which should have been seen by the department manager may have been seen by the chief general manager first. Too much information and the wrong type of information can be worse than insufficient information.

c. Effects of Decentralization of Computing Power

Centralized and distributed systems are discussed in Chapter 6. Broadly, the development of systems using the combined technologies of computing and telecommunications have decentralized computer usage. A wide variety of systems is available to support decentralization, including Wide Area and Local Area Networks and stand-alone microcomputer systems. The main benefits for an organization may be as follow:

(i) The delegation of control of some information processing to branch level management, hopefully resulting in systems which respond to local requirements. The control of information processing is thereby the responsibility of those who use them;

(ii) More rapid, up-to-date information at the local level, because it is processed locally;

(iii) The rapid distribution of centrally produced information via network systems;

(iv) Provided that the local systems are linked to a central facility, then information which is locally produced can be transmitted and stored so as to be available at a corporate level. Overall control is not lost, but enhanced.

The above benefits are not automatic and may have certain implications for an organization. The main implications are:

(i) New hardware and software needs to be purchased, which is compatible with any existing centralized facility;

(ii) Local management and workers need to be trained in the operation of any new system introduced, if the maximum benefit is to be obtained. The use of microcomputers with, for example, database and spreadsheet packages requires extensive training of users. This can be expensive;

(iii) A complete re-appraisal of specialist staffing may be needed as a result of decentralization. For example, systems analysts already familiar with the design of distributed and implementation of distributed systems may need to be recruited;

(iv) Specialist personnel, including programmers and operators, may be needed at the local level;

(v) Decentralized systems present new problems in terms of controlling the security of information (Chapter 7). The added risks must be considered and covered.

Computers and Employment

The rapid advances in computer and micro-electronic technologies have occurred in a period of erratic change in the Western economies and it is difficult to quantify the extent to which computerization has affected the levels of employment. Although computerization is far from being wholly responsible for increased unemployment, it has undoubtedly been a contributory factor. No attempt is made in this text to relate numbers of employed or unemployed to computerization. Instead, discussion will centre on the identifiable effects of computerization on employment patterns and prospects. The following effects may result from computerization:

(i) Retraining

(ii) Redeployment

(iii) De-skilling

(iv) Changes in working practices

       (v) Regrading and changes in career prospects

      (vi) Redundancy

     (vii) Changes in working conditions (Health and safety).

Each of the above effects can be identified in different types of job.

a. Office Work

Computerization is common in most areas of office work, for example, word processing, electronic messaging, and accounting systems. Additionally in some specialized areas such as banking, automatic tellers are replacing humans for routine banking transactions.

Re-training

Generally, an organization will choose to make full use of their existing staff, rather than search for new staff who already have the skills required. Depending on the nature of the job, the retraining needed may be radical or quite minor. For example, a typist has keyboard skills which are quite readily transferrable to the task of word processing. The retraining needed centres on the concept of text editing, mailing lists, the use of floppy disks and printers. The aim is to give the operator the knowledge, skill and understanding to make maximum use of the facilities provided by a word processor. Word processing is a general skill which can be applied in different ways in different organizations. Similarly, the use of a software package for sales accounting or stock control needs knowledge and skills, some of which are transferrable to other packages. Familiarity with computers in general and expertise in the use of some packages, provides an individual with the confidence to quickly pick up skills for new applications as they arise.

Redeployment

Computerization generally reduces manpower requirements but increases the opportunities for business expansion. Redeployment means moving staff from one area of work or responsibility to another, generally with retraining. Redeployment is a common result of computerization in any area of work.

De-skilling

The judgement as to whether or not a job is de-skilled by computerization is a rather subjective one. For example, does a wages clerk using manual methods require a higher level of skill than a data entry operator? The answer is probably yes, although a trade union may argue otherwise in the interests of improved job regrading. On the other hand it is generally accepted that higher level skills are required to use a word processor than a typewriter.

Changes in Working Practices

Staff may be required to carry out a wider range of tasks as a result of computerisation. For example, in smaller offices a clerk may be required to answer customer enquiries and carry out data entry at a terminal. Flexibility rather than specialization is often the key to the introduction of new technology. The lines of demarcation in the newspaper industry had to disappear before computerization could take place.

Regrading and Career Prospects

Sometimes, improvements in job gradings are introduced in order to encourage staff to accept computerization. At the same time, career prospects in office work are generally diminished. In the banking industry, the prospects for managerial jobs have diminished drastically in the last two decades. Currently, few clerical staff who did not enter the job with a degree have prospects for managerial posts.

Redundancy

Computerization of office work inevitably reduces the manpower requirements for the existing level of work, but redundancy does not always result. This is usually because computers are introduced in response to an expansion in the business of an organization.

Health and Safety

Anxiety and stress could cause problems. Many staff, particularly older members, may feel anxious about the security of their job or possible redeployment. They may become unhappy about personal contact being replaced by a computer screen.

Most people, as they get older, prefer continuity rather than constant change and computerization usually means radical and frequent change. Anxiety can also result from a fear of 'falling behind'. This applies to many people working with computers, because the changes and advances are so rapid.

Ergonomics

Ergonomic design recognizes certain health and safety problems which can result from computer usage and attempts to design equipment and working environments which minimize the hazards. A number of health and safety concerns are recognized in relation to VDU screens:

- exposure to radiation;

- induction of epileptic fits;

- mental and physical fatigue;

- eyestrain, eye damage and visual fatigue;

- muscular strain.

Suitable working practices and well-designed equipment can largely avoid such dangers, for example, gentle lighting, lack of screen flicker and hourly breaks for VDU operators. Other concerns relate to the design of office furniture and the general office environment, including temperature and noise levels.

b. Manufacturing Industry

Most of the factors described in relation to office work apply equally in factory work, but the following additional points are worth mentioning.

Job Satisfaction. Shop floor workers who supervise and service the machines have a cleaner, less dangerous job than traditional skilled machinists. It may be surmised that young people, without the experience of the old skills, will look more favourably on such supervisory jobs than the older workers.

New Job Opportunities. If automated systems such as Flexible Manufacturing Systems (FMS) are to be successful, then the number of jobs in factories using FMS must inevitably decrease. Opportunities lie in the creation of a new range of jobs. Many such jobs are in software engineering and in the design of automated systems. The Japanese experience is that new, highly-skilled jobs are created in the development and design fields in companies which manufacture automated equipment and commercial machinery, whereas both skilled and unskilled jobs are lost in the companies using this equipment. The Japanese experience is being mirrored in the UK.

Increased Unemployment. Many older, skilled workers have been made redundant because of the loss or de-skilling of their jobs through automation. On the other hand, the redundancies may have occurred without automation because of loss of competitiveness.

Computers and Society

There is general agreement that computers and related technologies will bring great social changes, but there are wide differences of opinion about what they will be, the rate at which they will occur and the extent to which they are beneficial. It must be emphasized that many of the following points are highly subjective and open to debate.

Benefits
The benefits include:

- Increased productivity;

- Higher standard of living;

- Cleaner and safer working conditions;

- Shorter working hours;

- More leisure time.

Costs
The costs include:

- Polarization of people into two groups - the technologically advantaged and disadvantaged;

- Increasing crime and delinquency rates;

- The threat of a totalitarian state;

- Invasion of privacy.

The remainder of this section looks at two important areas of concern regarding the future impact of computers on society, namely TELECOMMUTING and PERSONAL PRIVACY. Some of the effects are already apparent.

Telecommuting - The Office at Home

At present, millions of office workers travel by car or public transport to their respective places of work. Nearly all organizations carry out their business from centralized offices because information needs to be exchanged, usually on paper documents and decisions need to be made, which requires consultation between individuals. Through the use of telecommunications, and centrally available computer databases, office staff of the future may work from home via a computer terminal.

There are a number of advantages to be gained from home-based work:

- Savings in travel costs;

- No necessity to live within travelling distance;

- Flexible hours of work;

- Equality between men and women. Bringing up children can be a shared activity;

- Savings for the organization in terms of expensive city-centre offices.

There are also several potential drawbacks:

- Loss of social contact;

- Need for quiet workroom at home. This can be difficult in a small flat;

- The difficulty of 'office' accommodation is compounded when two or three members of a family all work from home;

- Loss of visible status for senior staff in terms of a 'plush' office and other staff to command.

Computers and Personal Privacy

Since the 1960s, there has been growing public concern about the threat that computers pose to personal privacy. Most countries, including the UK, have introduced legislation to safeguard the privacy of the individual. The Data Protection Act of 1984 was passed after a number of government commissioned reports on the subject. The Younger Report of 1972 identified ten principles which were intended as guidelines to computer users in the private sector. A government White Paper was published in 1975 in response to the Younger Report, but no legislation followed. The Lindop Report of 1978 was followed by a White Paper in 1982 and this resulted in the 1984 Data Protection Act. The principles detailed in the Younger Report formed the foundation for future reports and the Data Protection Act. They are listed below.

(i) Information should be regarded as being held for a specific purpose and should not be used, without appropriate authorization, for other purposes.

(ii) Access to information should be confined to those authorized to have it for the purpose for which it was supplied.

(iii) The amount of information collected and held should be the minimum necessary for the achievement of a specified purpose.

(iv) In computerized systems handling information for statistical purposes, adequate provision should be made in their design and programs for separating identities from the rest of the data.

(v) There should be arrangements whereby a subject could be told about the information held concerning him or her.

(vi) The level of security to be achieved by a system should be specified in advance by the user and should include precautions against the deliberate abuse or misuse of information.

(vii) A monitoring system should be provided to facilitate the detection of any violation of the security system.

(viii) In the design of information systems, periods should be specified beyond which information should not be retained.

(ix) Data held should be accurate. There should be machinery for the correction of inaccuracy and updating of information.

(x) Care should be taken in coding value judgements.

The White Paper which followed the Younger Report identified certain features of computerized information systems which could be a threat to personal privacy:

(i) The facility for storing vast quantities of data;

(ii) The speed and power of computers make it possible for data to be retrieved quickly and easily from many access points;

(iii) Data can be rapidly transferred between interconnected systems;

(iv) Computers make it possible for data to be combined in ways which might otherwise not be practicable;

(v) Data is often transferred in a form not directly intelligible.

The 1984 Data Protection Act sets boundaries for the gathering and use of personal data. It requires all holders of computerized personal files to register with a Registrar appointed by the Home Secretary. The holder of personal data is required to keep to both the general terms of the Act, and to the specific purposes declared in the application for registration.

From the individual's point of view, the Act can be said to have a number of weaknesses:

(i)   Penalties for infringement of the rules are thought to be weak and ineffective;

(ii)   There are a number of exemptions from the Act. Some holders do not need to register and there are exceptions to the right of access to one's own file. There are also limits to confidentiality;

(iii)   The Registrar is appointed by the Home Secretary and cannot therefore, be wholly independent.

Assignment   The Legal Network

Barnes, Nesbit and Walker is a firm of solicitors based in Durham City, County Durham. Mr. Barnes is a senior partner and rather old-fashioned in his ideas on running the practice. He would rather dictate letters to his secretary than use a dictaphone. The two junior partners, Alun Nesbit and Rachel Walker, are keen to improve the efficiency of the practice. It is the intention to install a Local Area Network (LAN), using microcomputer systems as workstations and to computerize many of the office procedures. For example, legal documents will be prepared using a word processing package and high quality output obtained with a laser printer. The practice employs three personal secretaries, four copy typists and five general clerical staff. The management of clients' accounts will be made easier, in that each partner will have a workstation in their office to enter client charges as and when they occur.

Task

You are employed as a trainee office manager/ess by the practice. Mrs. Walker calls you into her office and asks you to prepare an informal report covering the following matters:

1. How the introduction of computers may effect the office and clerical staff;

2. The problems which may be encountered in trying to persuade Mr. Barnes to use the new system and suggestions as to how they may be overcome;

3. Training implications and possible strategies;

4. Physical preparations which need to made for the installation of the computer network.

Developmental Task

Contact your local government offices and ask for a copy of their health and safety guidelines for VDU operators. Use the guidelines to draw up a staff notice for those using VDUs in the firm of Barnes, Nesbit and Walker.

Assignment The Great Computer Debate

The Students' Union at Bedlington College of Further Education is running a debate on the following motion.

"The tangible effects of computer technology on the patterns and conditions of employment to date, provide cause for pessimism with regard to the future of Western Society."

Task

You have been offered the choice of speaking FOR or AGAINST the motion. Make your choice and prepare notes for a speech to last about ten minutes.

Glossary

Absolute address. The actual machine address of a memory location.

Access. The process of seeking, reading or writing on a storage device.

Access mechanism. A mechanism for moving the read-write heads to a position at which data can be read or written, for example, the moveable head mechanism in a magnetic disk unit.

Access method. The method used to retrieve data from a storage system, for example, serial, sequential or random access.

Access time. The time taken to retrieve data from a storage device, that is, from the moment the instruction is executed to the moment when the data is placed in memory.

Accumulator. A storage location, sometimes a special register in the arithmetic-logic unit of the processor, in which arithmetic operations are performed on numbers and where results are temporarily stored.

Acoustic coupler. A type of modem which allows computer data to be received or transmitted as audio tones using a telephone handset.

ADA. A high level programming language used for programming real-time applications.

Address. An identifier for a memory location in which data is stored. It may also be that part of an instruction which specifies the location of an operand.

ALGOL. ALGOrithmic Language; a high level programming language suited to mathematical and scientific applications.

Algorithm. A computational procedure or series of instructions for the solution of a particular problem.

ALU. An acronym for arithmetic-logic unit, a component part of the CPU or processor; used for arithmetic operations and logical comparisons of, stored data.

Analogue signal. A signal, such as that produced by the human voice, which is transmitted along a channel of, for example, the telephone network.

Analogue/digital converter (ADC). A device for converting analogue signals to the digital form useable by a digital computer. For example, the temperature measurements taken from a furnace can be digitized by an ADC and monitored by computer.

AND operation. A Boolean logical operation applied to two operands. If both are equal to 1 (TRUE) then the result or output is 1 (TRUE).

Applications software (programs). Programs to deal with user applications, for example, stock control or word processing. They may be packaged or specially written.

Artificial intelligence (AI). The ability of a computer to take on some attributes of intelligence, for example, learning and improving its performance through the use of repeated experience.

ASCII code. A set of character codes standardized under the American Standard Code for Information Interchange.

Assembler. Translator program to convert assembly language instructions into their machine code equivalents.

Assembly language. A machine-orientated programming language which uses mnemonic codes (memory aids) to identify instructions. Programs written in assembly language must be translated into machine code by an assembler program before execution.

Asynchronous transmission. The transmission of characters along a channel at irregular intervals, for example, those produced by keyboard operation.

Audit trail. A mechanism, usually built into the applications software, to allow the tracing of a transaction's history from input through to output. Auditing is an essential part of any accounting application as a guard against accidental or deliberate misuse of data.

Auxiliary storage. Synonymous with backing store, for example, magnetic tape or disk.

BASIC. A high level programming language suitable for on-line program development and popularly used to introduce beginners to programming techniques. Acronym for Beginner's All-purpose Symbolic Instruction Code.

Batch. A collection of transactions awaiting processing as a single unit.

Batch file. A facility available with the MS-DOS operating system for the automatic execution of regularly used sequences of commands.

Batch processing. A method of processing transactions which allows accuracy control totals to be associated with each batch. Each batch is dealt with as an entity, so that one error causes the rejection of the whole batch for correction and re-submission. Used where delay in updating is acceptable to users. Contrast with real-time.

Batch total. A total produced from selected values in a batch. for example, invoice quantities. Used to control the progress of a batch of transactions through each stage of processing. Totals are checked at each stage.

Binary number system. A number system with the base or radix of 2 and in which only two digits are used, one and zero.

Bit. Contraction of binary digit (0 or 1). A bit is the smallest element of data or instruction representation in a computer. Bits are usually handled in groups of, say, 8, 16 or 32, depending on the architecture of the computer.

Block. A group of logical records transferred between memory and peripherals as a unit. Also known as a 'physical' record.

Blockingfactor. The maximum number of logical records which can be fitted into a block.

Block marking. A function in word processing packages, for marking sections of text for special attention, such as moving, deleting or copying.

Blow. The process of writing onto a 'chip' memory such as EPROM (Erasable Programmable Read Only Memory.

Board. A rectangular circuit board which can be slotted inside the casing of a computer to give added memory or program facilities.

Branch instruction. An instruction which specifies the address of the next instruction, normally out of program sequence. A branch may be conditional or unconditional. Also known as a jump instruction.

Bubble memory. A non-volatile memory device which uses magnetized 'bubbles' to represent binary data.

Bucket. An area of direct access storage such as disk which may consist of a number of blocks of data and can be addressed as a unit.

Buffer. A temporary storage area for data being transmitted between devices and components of a computer system. Buffers are used in terminals, storage and other peripherals and in the CPU. They can compensate for speed differences between relatively slow peripheral devices and the CPU.

Bug. A defect or malfunction in a computer program or system.

Bus. An electrical connection within a computer system and along which data is passed.

Byte. A group of bits handled as a unit by a computer system. Generally, a byte is formed from eight bits.

CAD. An acronym for Computer-Aided Design. A designer makes use of a computer, screen and lightpen or similar device as aids to design.

Cambridge ring. A network configuration developed at Cambridge University and used in local area networks.

Ceefax. A broadcast system transmitting text information from central computer databases. Text is transmitted in 'frames' with television pictures for display on a television set with special adapter. One-way transmission only.

Cell. In relation to spreadsheets, a single location identifiable by co-ordinate references.

Central processing unit (CPU). The components of a computer system with the functions for control and processing, namely the control unit and the arithmetic-logic unit. Often known as the 'processor'.

Centralized processing. All computer processing is carried out centrally. Contrast with distributed processing.

CGA. Acronym for Colour Graphics Adaptor.

Chain printer. A line printer where characters are linked into a chain which rotates at high speed and characters are printed at the appropriate positions as they traverse the paper.

Character codes. A code use to represent characters, for example, ASCII.

Character printer. Prints a single character at a time, as do, for example, the dot matrix and daisy wheel printer.

Check digit. An additional digit appended to a number to provide a self-checking device for transcription errors, for example, the modulus 11 check digit.

Chip. A slang term for a small piece of silicon with etched integrated circuits. They may have different functions, for example, memory or processor chips.

Closed User Group (CUG). Reserved pages in a viewdata system such as Prestel, which are only accessible by a restricted group of users.

Cluster. In relation to the MS-DOS operating system, a cluster is a group of disk sectors which can be identified in the File Allocation Table (FAT) as relating to a particular file. Thus, a file may occupy a number of non-contiguous clusters.

COBOL. A high level programming language used for programming business and file processing applications. Acronym for COmmon Business Orientated Language.

CODASYL. An acronym for COnference on DAta SYstems Languages. Responsible for standards in Codasyl database management systems.

Coding sheet. A pre-printed sheet of paper used by programmers to record their program source code. The sheets are tabulated for a particular programming language.

COM. An acronym for Computer Output on Microforms. Data is recorded in a physically condensed form and can be viewed with a special projector.

Compiler. A program which translates high level source code into the object or machine code of the target machine.

Concentrator. A device for concentrating transmission from a number of low speed lines into a high speed line.

Conditional branch instruction. Program control is 'branched' out of its normal sequence when specified conditions occur.

Constant or literal. A value which is set at compilation time and does not change during program execution.

Control characters. Perform special functions, for example, carriage return on a printer.

Control total. A total accumulated on a batch of data to be processed. The computer accumulates the same total during data entry and checks its consistency. Used in batch processing.

Control unit. The functional component within the Central Processing Unit (CPU) of a computer which fetches instructions one by one, interprets them and 'triggers' the appropriate action.

Controlled redundancy. Used in connection with relational databases and refers to the duplication of certain key data items which allow connections to be made between different relations or files in a database.

Conversational mode. The user is in direct communication with the computer via a series of prompts and responses, usually via a visual display unit. Also known as interactive mode.

CP/M (Control Program Microcomputers). An operating system for microcomputers.

cps. Acronym for characters per second.

CPU. Acronym for Central Processing Unit. It is the 'brain' of the computer, incorporating the control unit and the arithmetic-logic unit (ALU).

Credit note. A document which signifies that a customer's account is to be credited by a given amount, thus reducing the customer's indebtedness to the supplier.

Creditor. A person or organization which owes money to a business for goods or services supplied on credit.

CSMA/CD. Acronym for Carrier Sense Multiple Access with Collision Detector. A method of access control used on broadcast computer networks such as the 'bus' network.

Cylinder. A grouping of tracks in the same vertical plane, as for example, in a disk pack. Synonymous with seek area - all the tracks available whilst the read-write heads are in one position. The concept of the cylinder is used in addressing indexed sequential files.

Daisy wheel printer. A rather slow, high quality output character printer which uses a print wheel with each character font on a 'petal' on its periphery.

Database. A collection of inter-related data stored together on a direct access storage medium to serve one or more applications.

Database Management System (DBMS). The programs required to control the use of a database. For example, Relational DBMS and Codasyl DBMS.

Data capture. The collection of data at the source point by automated means, for example, optical mark reading, point-of-sale (POS) terminals.

Data collection. The process of gathering raw data for preparation and computer processing, for example, the collection of timesheets for a payroll run.

Data control. The process of controlling the accuracy and completeness of data during the data processing cycle. In batch processing, for example, this includes verification and validation (batch totals etc.). The responsibility for day-to-day control lies with the data control staff in the Data Processing Department or Management Information Services.

Data description language (DDL). A language for describing data, generally the logical data, during database construction.

Data format. A description of the length and form of data values.

Data independence. The property of a database which allows the alteration of its overall logical or physical structure without changing the applications' views of the data.

Data item. The smallest unit of data that has meaning as information, for example, name, date of birth in a personnel record. Synonymous with 'field'.

Data manipulation language (DML). The language used by the programmer to process and manipulate data in a database.

Data transmission. The electronic transmission of data via a telecommunications link.

Debug. To remove errors from a computer system, for example, syntax or logic errors in a computer program. The process is usually supported by software utilities such as a trace or debugger.

Desktop publishing (DTP). A computer system with facilities for combined text and graphics presentation, 'cut and paste' and font selection, which are necessary for publishing.

Digitizer. A device to convert analogue signals into a sequence of digital values. For example, maps or pictures can be digitized for computer storage and processing.

Direct access storage. A facility which allows data to be retrieved directly from a storage device without reference to the rest of the file, for example, magnetic disk.

Directory. Used by the operating system to record the names of files, their size and the date they were created or last updated.

Disk pack. A set of disks mounted on a central spindle and accessible as a unit by read-write arms.

Diskette. A small, flexible disk or 'floppy' disk, particularly popular with microcomputer systems.

Distributed processing. A system where computer power is not centralized, but is distributed to geographically separate branches of an organization, or amongst user systems within the same branch. This can be facilitated through the use of networked computers.

Documentation. The written description necessary for the testing, implementation and maintenance of a system. The documentation broadly falls into three categories, program, user and operator documentation.

DOS. Acronym for Disk Operating System - MS(Microsoft)-DOS.

Double buffering. Where the input-output buffers are used in tandem to speed data throughput.

Double density disks. Floppy disks with track density of 48 tracks per inch (tpi). The actual number of tracks used is 40.

Drivers. Files which enable a package to make use of the particular capabilities of different peripherals, for example, screen and printer drivers.

Dry running. A process of checking the logic of a computer program by hand and off-line.

Dumb terminal. A terminal without any processing power of its own, that is, with no 'intelligence'.

Duplex or full duplex. Simultaneous transmissions of data in both directions with the use of two channels.

EGA. Acronym for Enhanced Graphics Adaptor. Used as a standard for the resolution of colour graphics screens.

Electronic Mail. The transmission of mail by electronic means via a computer network. There is usually a 'mailbox' facility for the storage of messages awaiting collection.

Electrostatic printer. A printer which uses electrostatic charges to 'fix' characters to the paper.

Encryption. The transformation of data passing through a communications link into an encoded form which prevents its interpretation by unauthorized persons 'tapping' the line.

Exchangeable disk. Hard disk storage which is removable.

Expert system. A computer system programmed using artificial intelligence techniques to provide information or decisions relating to some narrow area of human expertise, for example, house conveyancing, house plant care, medical diagnosis. Also known as 'knowledge-based' systems.

Facsimile Transmission (FAX). The transmission of a copy of a document via a telecommunications link. Usually, it is transmitted in digital form.

Feasibility study. A study carried out by systems analysts and interested parties to ascertain possible solutions to an information processing problem.

Fetch-execute cycle. The activity of the CPU in fetching, decoding and executing program instruction one by one in a cycle.

Fibre optics. A means of transmitting data in light form.

Field. A subdivision of a record containing an item of information. Synonymous with data item.

Fifth generation computers. A combination of advanced hardware and software; characteristics include, faster processors, the use of multiple processors for 'parallel' processing, natural language processing and more human-orientated input-output devices, such as speech synthesizers, voice recognition devices and 'mice'.

File. A collection of logically related records, for example, a stock file or a personnel file.

File allocation table (FAT). A table used by the MS-DOS operating system and stored on disk to record the allocation of disk clusters to individual files.

File organization. Methods of organization records in a file, for example, serially, sequentially or randomly.

File server. A local area network node which handles workstation access to shared storage and controls the exchange of files between network users.

Fixed head disk. A disk unit with one read-write head per track. No head movement is necessary.

Fixed length record. A record with a fixed physical length in terms of the number of bit positions it occupies.

Flowchart. A diagrammatic representation showing the flow of control in a computer system.

Footer. In relation to word processing, a standard line of print, defined to appear at the bottom of each page in a multi-page document.

Footprint. The physical desk or floor space needed by a computer system or peripheral.

Format - disk. A process which establishes the sector size on a disk for a particular operating system and establishes a file allocation table (FAT) and root directory.

Format - text. A word processing function to arrange text in a particular way, for example, with a straight or ragged right hand margin.

FORTRAN (FORmula TRANslator). A high level programming language particularly useful for programming scientific and mathematical applications.

Fourth generation languages (4GLs). Higher level languages which allow applications to be generated with the minimum of procedural programming; includes Applications Generators.

Frequency division multiplexing (FDM). The separation of different data streams with the use of different frequency bands for each.

Front-end processor (FEP). Usually a minicomputer handling incoming and outgoing communications traffic for a mainframe computer, which is left free to carry out the main processing tasks.

Functional area. A section or department within an organization with a particular function, for example, sales or accounts.

Function key. A programmable key on a keyboard. There are usually ten or twelve and they are used by different software packages for different functions.

Gateway software. Software to allow access from a network to external computers and their databases.

Generation. May relate to the version of a file. In file security, historical copies can be kept, which are identified by generation according to relative age - 'grandfather, father, son'. Generally associated with tape file processing.

Gigabyte. One thousand million bytes.

Golf ball. Spherical print head with character fonts in relief on the surface.

Graph plotter. A computer output device which produces graphical material under computer control. There are two main types, the flat bed and the drum plotter.

Half-duplex. Data transmission in both directions, but not simultaneously.

Hard sectoring. Small index holes determine the beginning of sectors on a disk. The sector size cannot be altered.

Hashing. A technique using an algorithm to generate disk addresses for records within a random file. The technique aims to achieve an even distribution of records and to minimize overflow.

Hash total. A control total used in batch processing. Totals are derived from values such as account numbers and are thus meaningless apart from their control function. Also known as nonsense totals.

Head crash. A collision between the read-write head and the surface of the disk, which usually results in severe disk damage. May be caused by dust or other impurities on the disk surface.

Header. In relation to word processing, a defined heading which is to appear at the top of every page in a multi-page document.

Hexadecimal ('Hex'). Number system with the base 16. Uses digits 0 to 9 and then A, B, C, D, E and F. Often used as shorthand for binary codes in technical manuals for computer systems and by programmers who make use of assembly language.

High level language. A language remote from any particular machine code. Each instruction in a high level language usually equates with a number of machine code instructions.

Hit rate. A percentage figure expressing the proportion of records in a file 'hit' during a processing run.

Hit rate = number of records 'hit'/number of records in file x 100

Host computer. A computer providing a central service to a number of other computers in a network.

Icon. A symbol on a screen menu representing a program option.

Impact printer. A printer which uses an impact mechanism, usually against an ink ribbon to produce characters on paper.

Indexed sequential. A method of organizing a file on a direct access storage device such as disk, where records are organized in sequence according to a primary record key and indexes provide a means of referring to records directly.

Information flow diagram. A diagram which identifies the flows of information between different functional areas of a business.

Initialize. To set variables to an initial value at the beginning of program execution.

Input device. Any peripheral device which transfers data from an external source into the memory of the computer.

Intelligent terminal. A computer terminal with some processing power and storage capacity.

Integrated package. A package which provides several general-purpose packages in one, for example, spreadsheet, word processor, database and communications.

Inter-block gap (IBG). The physical gap between blocks of data on magnetic tape to allow the starting and stopping of the tape between block transfers.

Interpreter. A translator program which interprets and directly executes program statements. Contrast with compiler.

Iterate. Commonly, to undertake a series of steps repeatedly, usually until a certain condition or result is achieved. More correctly, a process of calculating a result through a repeated series of steps, in which successive approximations are made until the desired result is achieved.

Key-to-disk. A method of encoding source data onto magnetic disk prior to input and processing.

Kilobyte (kb). A unit of computer storage - 1024 bytes.

Latency. The rotational delay which occurs as the read-write head waits for a revolving magnetic disk to bring the required block of data into the read-write position.

Light pen. A 'pen-like' input device which uses a photo-electric cell to indicate positions on a screen, for example, to select items from a menu on screen.

Line printer. A printer which effectively prints a line of text at a time. Contrast with character printer.

Linker. A program which incorporates any necessary machine code routines, from a library of standard routines, into an object program after compilation.

LISP (LISt Processing). A programming language where data elements are used in 'lists'. Its main application is in the field of artificial intelligence.

Local area network (LAN). A network of connected computers confined to a small area, say to a group of buildings on one site.

Logo. A high level language designed by Seymour Papert to encourage an 'active' approach to computer-aided learning through the use of 'turtle' graphics. Shares many of the features of LISP.

Low-level language. A machine-orientated programming language as opposed to a problem-orientated high level language. Generally, each low level language instruction has a single machine code equivalent.

Machine code or language. The pattern of bits directly executable by a computer.

Macro-instruction. An instruction in a source language (high level or low level) which, when compiled, produces a number of machine code instructions.

Magnetic disk. A disk-shaped backing storage medium which provides direct access. Each magnetizable surface is divided into tracks and sectors addressable by the computer. Each addressable location may contain one or more logical records.

Magnetic tape. A serial access backing storage medium. It consists of a reel of plastic tape with a magnetizable coating to allow the representation of data. Generally, records are stored and accessed sequentially because the medium is non-addressable.

Magnetic ink character recognition (MICR). An input method whereby a reading device 'recognizes' stylized characters printed in magnetizable ink. Used almost exclusively by the banking industry to read coded data from cheques.

Main memory. The primary memory of a computer system which stores programs and data currently being processed by the CPU. Contents are lost when the power is switched off and so is supplemented by backing storage.

Master file. A file which contains permanent or semi-permanent information on a subject. Usually affected by transactions during the updating process.

Megabyte (mb). Roughly one million bytes - a measurement of computer storage.

Message switching. A technique of switching messages between nodes in a network. Usually carried out by a mainframe or minicomputer at the 'hub' of the network.

Micro Channel Architecture (MCA). A computer system architecture pioneered and patented by IBM. Forms the basis of IBM's PS-2 range of microcomputers.

Microprocessor. A central processor (control unit and arithmetic-logic unit) on a single chip.

Millisecond (ms). One thousandth of a second.

Mnemonic. A memory aid generally used for representing machine code operations in assembly language, for example, LDA for LoaD Accumulator.

Modem (MOdulator-DEModulator). A device for converting the digital signal produced by a computer into an analogue form suitable for transmission along a telephone line. Also capable of carrying out the reverse process for incoming data.

Mouse. A hand-held cursor-control device.

Multiplexer (MUX). A device which transmits data arriving from several sources along a single transmission medium, by modulating the carrier wave for each data stream. Two major methods of producing separately identifiable signals are time division and frequency division multiplexing.

Multi-processing. The use of multiple processors for executing programs.

Multi-programming. The processing of several jobs apparently at the same time. Programs and data relating to jobs are partitioned in memory and the CPU makes use of its high speed to switch control between them. This is possible because when a job is occupied with input or output, the CPU is free to carry out other tasks.

Multi-tasking. The concurrent processing of several tasks, relating to a single user, in memory at the same time.

Multi-user. A facility to allow more than one user to use a computer at the same time. Requires that the operating system can share the computer's resources and protect users' files from other users.

Nanosecond. One thousand millionth of a second.

Natural language processing. Allows a user to use 'free-form' English as a means of communicating with a computer. May be typed or spoken.

Network. A number of computers connected together for the purposes of communication and processing.

NLQ. Near Letter Quality. A standard of printing by some dot matrix printers, which attempts to approach that of daisy wheel printers.

Node. A component in a computer network, for example, one microcomputer station in a local area network.

Non-volatile memory. A storage medium which continues to hold data after the power is removed, for example, ROM, EPROM and PROM. Contrast with RAM which is volatile.

Object program. The machine code or object program produced after compilation of the source program. The object program is executable on the target machine.

Off-line. Not under the control of the CPU or processor.

On-line. Under the control of the CPU or processor.

Operating system. The basic suite of programs which supervise and control the general running of a computer system.

Optical character recognition (OCR). The recognition by an OCR device of characters (usually stylized) by measuring their optical reflectance.

Optical disk. A high capacity storage device (measured in gigabytes) which makes use of laser technology to record and read data on the disk.

Optical mark reading (OMR). Process whereby an OMR device identifies values on a pre-printed document by the position of pencil marks. Usually, boxes on the document are indicated as representing particular values and each can be indicated by a pencil mark in the relevant box.

OS/2. Acronym for IBM's multi-tasking, multi-user Operating System 2.

OSI model. Open Systems Interconnection model. Developed by the International Standards Organization, it lays down standards for network systems.

Output device. Any peripheral which transfers data from the internal memory of the computer to the outside world.

Parallel processing. The technique of executing a number of computer instructions in parallel. A number of inter-connected processors called transputers are needed to do this. Most computers only have one processor and carry out instructions one after the other.

Parallel running. When a new system is implemented, the old system is continued until the users are satisfied that the new system is functioning correctly and reliably.

Parallel transmission. The transmission of bit groupings in parallel.

Parity. A minimal form of error checking in data transmission, whereby an extra bit is added to a group of bits to make the total number of bit 1s even (even parity) or odd (odd parity). The parity is checked after each transmission.

Partition. A division of memory, either disk or RAM.

Pascal. A high level, block-structured programming language named after Emile Pascal, a French mathematician.

Peripheral device. Any computer device under the control of the central processor, but external to it.

Picosecond. One million-millionth of a second.

Pilot testing. A method of system implementation which only applies a new system to a portion of the live data. The remainder is processed by the old method until the users of the pilot data are satisfied concerning the system's accuracy and reliability.

Plotter. Flat bed or drum graph plotter.

Pointer. An arrow or 'finger' in the cursor position which allows the selection of menu options on screen, possibly with a 'mouse'.

Port. A place of entry to or exit from a central processor, dedicated to a single channel, for example, a printer port.

Prestel. A public viewdata system accessible by telephone line and Prestel adapter. It provides pages of information on a wide variety of general and specialist information.

Primary key. A data item which ensures unique identification of an individual record.

Print server. A local area network node which shares its printer facility amongst all users on the network. Print jobs are queued and may be executed in turn or according to assigned priorities.

Processor. See central processing unit.

Program specification. A specification produced by a systems analyst as part of a system specification and detailing all the requirements of the related applications software.

Program testing. The process of running a program with test data to check the correctness and completeness of output.

Prolog. A programming language based on mathematical logic. It is used extensively in artificial intelligence (AI) applications and is particularly suitable for database applications. Adapted by the Japanese for programming their 'fifth generation' computers.

PROM (Programmable Read Only Memory). A chip which can be 'blown' or programmed by the user to produce non-volatile memory store (ROM).

Protocol. A set of rules governing the format of messages transmitted in computer networks. Compatibility needs to be established between communicating devices so that they can 'talk' to each other.

Pull-down menu. A facility commonly available in integrated software such as Framework, whereby the user can 'pull' a menu onto the screen by selecting an icon or symbol on screen, or a word from a range at the top of the screen.

Quad-density disks. Floppy disks with a track density of 96 tracks per inch (tpi) and double the number of sectors used on double-density disks.

Query language. A language designed for users to make ad hoc enquiries of a database.

RAM. Random access memory - the main memory of the computer.

Random access. A facility for accessing a storage medium for any record or data item, without reference to the rest of the file. Also known as direct access. Main memory and disk storage provide this facility.

Read only memory (ROM). Storage medium which allows only 'reading' and not 'writing'.

Record. A group of related data items forming an entity. A subdivision of a file.

Relation. A two-dimensional array or table forming a 'flat' file. Terminology associated with relational databases.

Relational algebra. A language providing a set of logical operators for manipulating 'relations' (files) in a relational database.

Relational database. A database made up of relations or two-dimensional tables.

Remote job entry (RJE). The transmission of a batch job via a telecommunications link to a central computer for processing.

Repeater. A signal amplifier, which passes packets of data onto the next node in a network.

Response time. Generally refers to interactive systems (via VDUs or other terminals) and indicates the time which elapses from the entry of a query or command at the keyboard and the receipt of the computer's response on screen.

Reverse video. A reversing of background and foreground colours on a VDU screen to highlight selected characters.

Rewrite. To overwrite an existing record with an updated version of it. This is only possible with direct access storage.

Ring network. A network topology where computers are connected in a ring structure. Evolved in Cambridge and known as the Cambridge ring.

RISC. An acronym for Reduced Instruction Set Computer in which the decoding circuitry is limited to the most frequently used instructions, thus producing smaller, faster processors.

RPG (Report Program Generator). A high level programming language designed to allow trained users (as opposed to specialist programmers) to generate reports from computer files.

Schema. The overall logical definition of a database.

Search. The scanning of data items for those in accord with specified criteria, for example, salaries in excess of £10,000 in a Personnel file.

Sector. A subdivision of a track on a magnetic disk. Constitutes the smallest addressable unit on a disk.

Seek time. The time taken for moveable read-write heads to move to the selected track or cylinder on a magnetic disk.

Sequential access. The retrieval of records according to the sequence of their organization, for example, a customer file stored in Customer Account number order.

Sequential organization. A method of storing a file so that records are sequenced according to a primary record key, for example, a Stock Code.

Serial access. Retrieving records in the order that they are physically stored, in other words, as they come.

Serial organization. Simply, records stored one after the other, not necessarily in sequence, for example, an unsorted tape file.

Serial transmission. Transmission of data, usually via a telecommunications link, whereby the 'bits' follow one another in a serial fashion. Contrast with parallel transmission.

Set (Codasyl definition) A set is a named collection of record types. Each set specified in a scheme (logical database definition) must have one record type declared as its OWNER and one or more record types declared as MEMBER records. For example, a Customer record may 'own' a number of Order records.

Simplex. Transmission of data in one direction only.

Soft sectored. Sectors are marked on magnetic disk by means of software rather than physical markers.

Source program. A program written in a programming language (high or low level). It must be translated into machine code before execution.

Spooling (Simultaneous Peripheral Operation On Line). Making more efficient use of hardware during input-output operations by using faster peripheral devices in parallel with normal job processing, as a temporary substitute for slower devices. For example, output destined for printing may be spooled to an area of disk and dumped from there to the printer while the processor is left to carry on with other tasks.

SQL. Structured query language. A non-procedural 4th generation programming language.

Star network. A network topology, whereby a main 'host' computer at the 'hub' services a number of peripheral systems.

Stop bit. A bit used to indicate the end of a character in asynchronous transmission.

Structured programming. A programming design technique which makes use of control structures such as 'IF ... THEN ... ELSE' and 'DO ... WHILE ...' to combine and control separate functions within a program. Only three basic control structures are used; sequence of operations, selection of alternative operations and repetition or iteration.

Subroutine. A self-contained routine, coded once within a program, which may be 'called' at any point during the main program. After execution of the subroutine, control is returned to the instruction immediately following the call.

Subschema. A limited logical view of a database derived from the schema (overall logical database view) to be used by an applications program.

Synchronous transmission. The transmission of data in 'streams'. The sender and the receiver devices are synchronized so that individual characters are identified within the stream. No start or stop bits are needed. Special 'SYN' characters are transmitted periodically to maintain the synchronization. Contrast with asynchronous transmission.

Syntax. The formal rules of grammar and structure governing the use of a programming language.

Syntax error. Where the syntax rules are broken in program coding. Generally, such errors are indicated by a compiler or interpreter.

Systems analysis. The study of an activity with a view to its computerization.

Systems analyst. A person specializing in systems analysis.

Systems software. Program purchased as part of a computer system and which are concerned with the general running of the hardware and not with specific applications. Examples include, operating systems, utilities and compilers.

Tape deck/drive/transport. An operational device for the processing of magnetic tape files.

Teleconferencing. The conducting of a conference through the use of computers and telecommunications links.

Telecommuting. Working from home with the use of a computer link to the actual office.

Teletext. Systems such as Oracle and Ceefax which use spare bandwidth on television transmissions to send 'pages' of information from a computer database to television sets fitted with special adapters. The database provides information on a variety of subjects of general and specialist interest.

Test data. Data specially prepared for the testing of program output for accuracy and consistency with the requirements of the program specification.

Timesharing. The technique, often used with interactive systems, whereby the CPU shares out its time amongst a number of users, with the aim of giving good response times to each. The allocation of time is known as 'time slicing'.

Token ring network. A local area network industry standard. Its main proponent is IBM.

Top-down design. Designing a program according to its overall logic, in terms of its identifiable components and then defining those components in further detail and so on, until the required level of detail is obtained.

Trace. A software facility which traces the path of a program's execution. Useful in the detection of logic errors.

Transaction file. A file containing transactions to be used in the updating of a master file.

Transaction logging. The recording of transactions on a separate serial file at the same time as they update the relevant master files.

Translator. A program for the translation of source code into object or machine code, for example, a compiler, an interpreter or an assembler.

Transputer. A processor with serial links to allow communication with other transputers. The basis of parallel processing computers.

Update. A process whereby a master record is amended by a transaction to reflect the current position.

Utility. A program which performs a common task such as sorting a file or copying a disk.

Validation. A process, usually carried out by a validation or 'data vet' program, to check that data falls within specified valid criteria, for example, that hours of overtime worked fall within a range from 0 to 20.

Verification. The process of checking the accuracy of data transcription, usually in a data encoding operation such as key-to-disk, prior to batch data input. Commonly, verification involves the re-keying of the data by another operator and the verifier machine compares keys depressed with data already stored.

Viewdata. Generic term for database systems which provide two-way communication with users via telecommunications links and terminals. The database may be public (e.g. Prestel) or private. Information is provided in 'pages' which can be accessed either by page number or through hierarchical indexes.

VDU. Acronym for visual display unit and comprising screen and keyboard.

VGA. Video graphics array. A resolution standard for colour graphics displays.

Voice output. The technique of simulating the human voice by computer means.

Voice recognition. A technique to allow computer input to be supplied directly by a human voice.

Volatile. A property associated with computer memory, whereby it loses its data when power is removed.

Wide area network (WAN). A network which makes use of the telecommunications network to link computer systems over a wide geographical area.

WIMP. Acronym for Windows, Icons, Mice and Pull-down menus, all of which are commonly used in user-friendly, menu driven packages.

Winchester disk. A high density, hermetically sealed disk originally developed by IBM in the early 1970s. The technology is now extensively used for hard disk microcomputer systems.

Window. An area of screen dedicated to a particular function. The user may have several 'windows' on screen at one time.

Word processor. A computer system used for generating documentary material. May be dedicated to the task or may be a computer system with word processing package. The essential components are screen, keyboard, disk store and printer.

Word wrap. A feature of word processing. As text is typed, words move automatically to the start of a new line if there is insufficient room for them at the right hand margin.

Write protect. A mechanism to prevent accidental or deliberate overwriting of a disk's contents.

WYSIWYG. Acronym for What You See Is What You Get. Used to describe word processors which allow the screen to show text exactly as it is printed.

Index

The following books are also published by Business Education Publishers Limited and can be obtained either from your local bookshop or direct from the Publisher by photocopying the order on the next page or by telephoning 091 567 4963.

THE BTEC SERIES FOR STUDENTS

Core Studies for BTEC (2nd Edition)
Aug 1989   £16.50
Paperback 680pp A4 format

The first edition of this text was published in 1986 to cover the first and second year core areas of BTEC National Courses in Business, Finance and Public Administration. With its substantial coverage of the core areas, Organisation in its Environment, Finance and People in Organisations and its case study based assignments, it has proved to be the most popular book used on BTEC courses nationally. The new edition is an updated version of the first book retaining a large number of its most popular features.

Business Law for BTEC
Nov 1987   £14.95
Paperback 368pp A4 format

This book provides a comprehensive coverage of Business Law taught on BTEC courses at National and Higher levels. It incorporates a range of assignments for which a lecturer's manual is available to Educational Institutions free of charge from the publishers.

Marketing for BTEC
July 1989   £ 16.50
Paperback 340pp A4 format

This is a new text suitable for students studying marketing as an option module on BTEC National level courses or marketing as a full or part unit on BTEC Higher National level courses.

Information Processing for BTEC (2nd Edition)
March 1990   £13.50
Paperback 300pp A4 format

A new edition of a popular text which covers the BTEC Information Processing Option Modules One and Two. It incorporates a range of assignments for which a lecturer's manual is available free of charge from the publishers.

Transferable Personal Skills for BTEC
Feb 1989 £12.50
Paperback 311pp A4 format

A new text which covers the range of personal skills identified by BTEC in its statement of common skills. It is written in an easy to read style which students will find stimulating and informative. The text facilitates the development of a transferable personal skills training programme.

Computer Studies for BTEC
Oct 1987   £14.95
Paperback 432pp A4 format

The book was written specially for the first year core areas of the BTEC National Computing course. A lecturer's manual is available free of charge from the publishers to cover the range of assignments included in this book.

Small Business Computer Systems for BTEC
Aug 1989   £12.50
Paperback 256pp A4 format

A new book designed to cover the SBCS module on the second year of BTEC National Computing courses. The book contains a range of practical skills based assignments which can be used to form the basis of an assignment programme.

Travel and Tourism
Sept 1989   £16.50
Paperback 320pp A4 format

A major new textbook designed to cover the course content of Travel and Tourism modules at BTEC National and Higher National levels and to be used as an introductory text for undergraduates.

Getting Started with Information Technology
Oct 1988   £11.50
Paperback 302pp A4 format

Aimed at students who are new to information technology, this practical book takes a step by step approach to introducing word processing, data bases, spreadsheets, accounting and integrated packages.

THE BTEC SERIES FOR LECTURERS/TUTORS

Core Studies: A Tutor's Guide
Aug 1989 £18.50
690pp A4 format

Marketing : A Tutor's Guide
Sept 1989 £17.95
400pp A4 format

Transferable Personal Skills : A Tutor's Guide
Feb 1989 £16.95
500pp A4 format

Small Business Computer Systems : A Tutor's Guide
Sept 1989 £15.50
320pp A4 format

OTHER PUBLICATIONS

Transferable Personal Skills : A Student Guide
Jan 1989 £12.50
311pp A4 format

Law for Housing Managers £14.95
468pp A5 format

Community Health Services
March 1990 £16.95
500pp A5 format

BUSINESS EDUCATION PUBLISHERS LIMITED

Leighton House 10 Grange Crescent Stockton Road Sunderland SR2 7BN **Tel 091 567 4963**

ORDER FORM

THE BTEC SERIES FOR STUDENTS	Retail Price	Quantity Required
Core Studies for BTEC (2nd Edition) 1989	£16.50	
Business Law for BTEC 1987	£14.95	
Marketing for BTEC 1989	£16.50	
Information Processing for BTEC (2nd Edition) 1990	£13.50	
Transferable Personal Skills for BTEC 1989	£12.50	
Computer Studies for BTEC 1987	£14.95	
Small Business Computer Systems for BTEC 1989	£12.50	
Travel and Tourism 1989	£16.50	
Getting Started with Information Technology 1988	£11.50	

THE BTEC SERIES FOR LECTURERS/TEACHERS/TUTORS		
Core Studies for BTEC - A Tutor's Guide 1989	£18.50	
Transferable Personal Skills - A Tutor's Guide 1989	£16.95	
Marketing for BTEC - A Tutor's Guide 1989	£17.95	
The Abbotsfield File - A Business in Action 1984	£39.95	
Small Business Computer Systems - A Tutor's Guide 1989	£15.95	
Teaching Business Education 1990	£12.50	

OTHER PUBLICATIONS		
Community Health Services 1990	£16.95	
Law for Housing Managers (2nd Edition) 1986	£14.95	
An Introduction to Marketing 1989	£16.50	
Transferable Personal Skills - A Student's Guide 1989	£12.50	

Surname

Initials   Mr /Mrs / Miss / Ms

Address/Organisation

Post Code   Tel:

Tick Box as appropriate

Please Invoice :

☐ Individual

☐ Organisation (Please quote order number or reference)

* *All books are available by placing an order directly with the publisher (B.E.P.) or through any bookshop.*
* *For orders received from any Educational Establishment for books in the BTEC series an additional book will be supplied free of charge for every ten books ordered.*
* *For all books supplied postage is paid by the publisher (B.E.P.) .*
* *All invoices are payable within 30 days.*